Wisdom of the Dead

Wisdom of the Dead

Churches Beware

Emmanuel

To order additional copies of this book, contact:
Xlibris Corporation
1-888-795-4274
www.Xlibris.com
Orders@Xlibris.com
40019

CONTENTS

Introduction...9

chapter 1

Who then can be saved? 13
Who created Evil and Darkness?..19
Why do we live if were going to die? 28

chapter 2

A New World Order!...41
The falsified smile!...69

chapter 3

Bound forever! 79

chapter 4

Your Day of Judgment!...109

chapter 5

Day of the Angel! 147
The Shrewd Manager! 152

chapter 6

Words to the Wise!..209
No one Sin is Greater than Another! 214
Notes of Wisdom! 217
Wisdom of the Dead! 251

A Prophet is not accepted

in his own hometown.

A

Doctor does not heal
those
who know the Doctor.

If you know me you must know Him who sent me.

Introduction

The purpose of this book is to teach those who are members of the New Church that has entered the world, to live the life that they represent; that is if they are representing the life spoken of in the doctrine of the new church. To be the person at home that they are seen to be out in public every day, and in church on Sunday if they are involved in the organized churches of the world. There are other issues and truths covered in this book that should be of much interest to all Christians around the world, even if they are not yet ready to become a member of the New Church. We will be speaking of things such as the everyday lives of angels in the heavens as well as the devils in the hells. I will cover the importance of every man learning the Word for himself, being guided only by the Lord; while at the same time stressing how important it is as well for each human being to receive basic teachings from the Word through the churches in the world. The problem is, these Churches do not know when to let go of a person, so as to permit God to take over in their lives. For the worldly Church was only intended to provide basic teachings of the Word to the ignorant and the babes of the Church. And because Christians remain stuck in the falsified teachings of the Churches, because their religions are taught according to their opinions, and not necessarily the Word, Churches become larger and larger, and the Christians become more and more ignorant in their knowledge of the Word. For there comes a time for every man or woman to break away from the Church so as to learn the advanced teachings from God. But God has not provided these teachings to the Churches of the world because they teach doctrines based on their own personal beliefs instead of what the Word actually teaches. They wish to tickle the ears of the congregation, rather than worry about always teaching the truth. This is okay for babes, but it does harm when we later truly search out the truths to the Word. And for this reason the Lord must send the New Church into the world at the end of every Church, so as to reinstate truths in the Church, and to bring about a Last Judgment. You will read of the consummation of the Church as it applies to every human being separately. You will hear things you could not even imagine to be true as far as God, the Church, heaven, hell, angels and spirits. You will come to realize whom the real God and Father you worship is, and what

He expects from each of us. If you read these words according to the understanding
from your physical bodily senses, you will be reading them for naught. For all that
is written within these pages is written in faith and from a life grounded in faith. All
that I put in this book is what I receive each day directly from God through spirits
and angels. None of these words are my own and therefore I take no credit for the
wisdom bound up in these pages. Therefore I learn these things as I write them
down, as you can learn them simply from reading them; only you must read them
and receive them in faith. Do not trust your own senses when reading these words
and do not confirm anything, believing the truth to be final within the perimeters
of any one single statement. For if you have read my other books in order you will
come to realize that each book written is an addition to the truths within the ones
written by my hand earlier. Some things will be for babes, and some will be for the
learned; it all depends on the level of love you have for God, for this love is directly
proportionate to what truths you will receive from the Lord. So sit back and draw
it all in, adding line upon line; precept upon precept.

CHAPTER 1

Who then can be saved?

It is a belief that has left many in the world today without hope. Church people one on one never, for the most part ever give a non-Churchgoer any hope of being saved. They even teach that if you are not of their religion that there is much doubt as to whether you will ever be saved. This however, is not true in the least, and is as far from the truth as you can get. They are not to be blamed however, for "THEY KNOW NOT WHAT THEY DO." Yes, that's right, when Jesus made this statement on the cross; He was speaking of those of the present Church, and its teachings. These are the Jews that representatively Crucified Jesus Christ. For the Word does not ever speak of actual Jews, but it speaks of the Jewish nation in a representative sense. In the story of "The Rich man and Lazarus," the rich man represented the Jewish Nation, which in turn represented the present Church. For it is the Church which keeps the truths of the Word from the Gentiles (who are represented by Lazarus). They also teach according to their beliefs and customs, teaching nothing that does not prove their doctrine, or belief. You must be seeing in the world today how true this is, for man still feeds his flesh, even more so within the Church. Now the Church will of course be the last one to admit to these claims; nonetheless, they are true. So before we can learn that all men, including non-churchgoers will eventually be saved, we must first teach the world, through the Church, that God interprets the Word in a much different way than what man has presented it to the world today. The Church that we will be using to bring this about is called the "NEW CHURCH." And this Church does not reside within a man made building, but within the Temple that God built. But I do not wish to mislead those of you who are of the opinion that the building that God build is your fleshly body, for it is not. The Temple of God, or the building that God built is the inner man, or spiritual man. And when we turn our lives completely over to God, our inner man becomes a person who is known as Christ. For every man must become one with Christ, so as to become regenerated, and be prepared for heaven. Every man must mortify the deeds of the flesh, or die to his flesh, before he can come to as well as be one with, the Lord. Now you may say to yourself, "This is madness," but you will soon see, that for all those of you who from now on come to live by faith, these things will all be seen as truth, so as to be completely understood in faith alone. If however, you do not live by faith, grounded in works of charity, none of this will make any sense to you. The works of charity that every man in faith must do, are not a product of his thoughts however, and must be given by the Lord. For no man can do good from self. So works of charity, spoken of in the Word are the offspring, or the living actions that come from a man who is truly in faith in the Lord. This does not mean you are to go out and knock on doors, or preach in the streets, or bring your friends and neighbors to church, as a guilt trip to them. But God will bring those who will be saved, according to His schedule, to each of us, when it is our time to play a part in someone's salvation. But man does not save man; God saves men when their time comes to pass. And every man has a set time as to when he will come to the Lord. This set time will later be explained in detail, as it is the Lords will to do so. But for now, you must know that if a man does not yet appear to be saved, that it is not yet his time, and you can do absolutely nothing to bring that time about one second before it is to be. You can live your life as an example to all, but you cannot force your beliefs on anyone. Because you are a Church from within, if you live for the Lord, you need not seek for someone to preach to or teach, for the Lord, like clockwork, will send them your way. But no one can be coerced, and all must be according to a mans will. God gives us this free will, and he teaches that none of his children are to take it from another. So to force religion, or a doctrine, or belief on someone, separates you from the Lord; and removes you from His perfect will. Do you really think a perfect, all loving God would have entrusted the salvation of his children into the hands of those children. So as long as we are children, we cannot rule with the Lord, as it speaks of in Revelation. The ones spoken of who will rule with the Lord, are those who become one with the Lord. And who do you think becomes one with the Lord? Those who become members of the New Church become one with the Lord. And every one of you will become members of the New Church, in your own time. But those of you who believe you are saved, according to the world's standards, or according to what your physical senses tell you, are very wrong. For it is a truth that man lives in a reverse order, as apposed to the order of the Lord. What we see and hear with our physical senses is misleading, and does not agree with Gods teachings. For according to mans beliefs, the world is about to one day run out of oil, and we will all be left to fend for ourselves for a new means to heat our houses, to fuel our automobiles, and many other things that oil provides for. And all along, it has been a truth that God is the same yesterday, today, and forever. So what he provides for one generation he will surely provide for another. But because man does not see, nor understand that we have a perfect, Omnipotent God, he does not understand what will become of tomorrow. And so he makes up theories of his own, and presents them to the world as truth, or scientific evidence. And of course because the world does not know their God, or they do not have faith in his Divine Providence, they believe the lie. These things as well will be removed as each of us becomes regenerated, as well as becoming members of the New Church.

And when each of us enters the New Church belief, and doctrine, we will begin to see things from a faith point of view. We will see things, which have been for ages kept from the unlearned man. For now we know and see in part, but then we shall see as things truly are. God is not a God of confusion, which is why as long as we choose to confuse His Word; we must remain in a deep sleep. Man thinks that every story told in the bible is real, and that they were written from actual facts taken out of mans history. Little does man know that history did not unfold, or take place as man has written, or read it. For as ignorance is given life in the world, it is followed by a type of forgetfulness, or sleep. And as man sleeps he dreams up issues, and instances from the past. And once told over a certain period of time, man makes it into fact, and eventually teaches it to the world. It is easy to make the world believe his false testimonies because man has no way of disproving them. Man has many times become famous from the false testimonies and scientific theories he has provided to the world as truth. But many things man teaches are offshoots of the teachings of the bible, which are only made up stories that are representations of the things that truly happened in the spiritual world, and that never even remotely took place in the material world. But man could not use the stories of the bible for certain theories and tall tales which he has applied to our history, because man believes, according to his understanding of the literal Word in the bible, that the world has only existed for six thousand years. Those of course who do not follow the teachings of the bible have other stories, based on facts that the world is much older than the bible speaks of. Such stories as to when the Dinosaurs roamed the earth. But as time goes on the stories change, and man provides his theories, as well as supposed foolproof evidence that the Dinosaurs lived not quite as long ago as they had originally thought. Now I believe I have heard stories which speak of them being on earth as recently as ten thousand years ago. And whether they know it or not, they are much closer to the truth than ever before. But still man has not figured out why Dinosaurs were put here in the first place. This is partly because man is so use to everything being created for self, instead of for the good of others. For the truth of the matter is that Dinosaurs were put on earth for the service of mankind, so as to provide certain services to him. And they were not just here eight thousand years ago, but they have been on the earth many times in the past, according to their need they provided to mankind. This need may be explained at a later time, for it is not important at this point in time. Needless to say, God provides everything to every man equally, according to His Divine Providence. When I say to every man however, you must realize this does not mean every fleshly man that lives within the material world. But when the Word speaks of God not being a respecter of persons, he is speaking of our spirits, who are as much a man as we now think we are, and actually a better, or more perfect man. So within mans life, which is forever, he will experience every experience that has, is, or ever will be in existence. And this goes for every man until forever. But what you don't experience now, or tomorrow, you will experience in a hundred, a thousand, or even a million years, or ages from now. But no man experiences an affection, situation, or reality that every human being does not also experience in all of creation. Because of this, "There is nothing new under the sun," and what does not take place for a million years will soon return in the next million years, just like clock work. But we must all remember; "With God one day is as a thousand years, and a thousand years as a day." So as you can see, the world has been here a long time, which is one thing man has gotten right, at least recently that is. But he has very few details to add to this discovery, and so he makes them up. We have been buying into this system for ages, and when man finally reaches the regeneration state, God finally gives him the truths to remove himself from this system. For man is hopelessly corrupt, even though he cannot change of his own power, but must eventually seek God, and then he is on his way to salvation. We cannot help who we are, and believe me, God knows that. If we could we would not have to seek God, and so we would not. Do you really think man has not ever before harnessed the technology that he has today? Do you really believe that God has only allowed us to reach this point, and that nothing of importance even existed prior to the past six thousand years? If God has no beginning, and He has no end, where do you think He, and everything He ever created was, one hundred million years ago? Two hundred? A BILLION? OR HOW ABOUT TEN AGES AGO? If God was there, here, and everywhere ten ages ago, where was man? Well, first we have to realize that God needs man for his final end in creation, which is to act out love. For without our created forms, God would have no form to love another, nor for another to love Him. And we are of course able to love Him through His created form. For just as we were all created in His image, so too is God a Man. But in order to understand how He is a Man, this would require many pages, of which this is not the place to write them. But for those of you who are interested, I have already written on this subject in my book titled "Wisdom of Man-Secrets from Heaven." So to continue, where do you think man was ages ago, when God was everywhere, and yet could not be seen by human eyes anywhere? And if He could not be seen by human eyes, how did anyone love, or even worship Him. And if man was not around to love or worship Him, what was the purpose of God? If you say to rule, who did he rule, and why? If it was not to rule, but to teach others to love as He loves, as well as to love others and allow them to love Him back, how was this accomplished without a human being, or some creature? Did animals love Him, or even understand who or what He was? Of course it goes without saying, that this could not be the case. So if evidence shows that no being was ever created by God that could be rational, and have free will to choose for self, but a human being, then it would stand to reason that human beings have always existed. For everything exists for the good of man, and the perfection of the heaven of Angels. And though I cannot beyond a doubt prove to you that Angels are men as well, you will have to believe this out of faith, and rationality. And with these two things you should be able to put the pieces to the puzzle together, and come up with the truth. But you will never find all truth, you will only continue to seek, and find it till forever, and can keep adding each truth to your "Book of Life," which is your long term memory, that you will never lose till forever. As far as myself, God has given me enough truth, and continues to add to that truth, so as to provide to those of the world who approach me in my lifetime, as many truths as they are willing to receive in their lives, as well as pass on to others in turn. For if we are not prepared to share our revelations with others in the world, what sense is it for God to give them to us. For we are not created so as to provide for self, but to serve, and provide for others. If we are not willing to do these things, we are not ready for these truths. But be it known, each of us is on equal ground, and no one man has the edge over another person. When you receive whatever you wish to receive, is all up to you, for each of us is the navigator to his own destination. For man to understand all of this however, he must first want to understand, and then his spiritual journey will begin. So who will be saved? Everyone will be saved, as this is the way it should be. To see this, just put yourself in place of God, and give all His strengths to yourself. Then look at it all through loving eyes, for if not through loving eyes, we cannot understand God. Do these things and you will see that it is a must that every human being eventually be saved, and go on to be an Angel in heaven. And by the way, do not think that spirits and Angels ever existed before mankind came into creation, for spirits and Angels were all created from man, and in turn are men. But Angels are more perfect men because they are the cause, whereas man is the end effect of that cause. As well the material world is the means. So life began with a Man, who in turn created spirits and Angels from His affections, who in turn were created spirits, and went on to become more perfect Angels. And the circle of life took off, so as to grow in size and number till forever. We cannot receive the given truths as to the fact that all men are saved until we learn what it is like to truly love, as well as learn to allow ourselves to be loved. For if you are looking through the eyes of the world, you cannot see love in it actual form, nor can you live it. We must separate ourselves from the love of the world, and the love of self, and then things will begin to make sense to us. For as we remove one thing that belongs to the world, God replaces it with something from Heaven. We are all angels temporarily trapped inside this fleshly house, learning the lessons of life and love. Until each of us learns the needed lessons, which prepare us for heaven, we will continue to live for the flesh, as well as the ways of the world. The real reason we are all here is to learn that we are not here for ourselves, but to do for others, and not ourselves. For God is every mans provider in life, and every time a man does for self, when he has been put in place to do for another, he steals from God and robs himself of a blessing. He also becomes more connected to the material world, and less connected to heaven and God. So the way it goes is—the more the world is a part of your life, the more your life is material and made up of fantasy. The less the world, and its ways are a part of your life the more you are spiritual, and your life begins to take on more reality. Do not live your life any longer for the flesh, or the ways of the world, for these take you farther and farther from God, and heaven. You must humble yourself; learn to be a servant, and always practice mercy, and forgiveness. There is no human being who should not receive mercy and forgiveness, for there is no human being who deserves mercy and forgiveness. So if none deserve it, and we are to ever give it to one, we are to give it to all. For God is not a respecter of persons, and so sends His rain on the unjust as well as the just, in its due season. And what this means is that no matter whether you are a Christian or a sinner, God protects you when you are in good, as well as provides for you. When you are not good He cannot protect and provide for you because you must reap that which you sow, and if you are in sin or evil, you separate yourself from God, and can have no part in or from Him. For you cannot ever receive good until the evil is first removed. And this goes for all men, not just supposed sinners, but also supposed Christians. It is a God given fact that there is no man, who has or ever will exist who is a better person, or less of a sinner, that any other. You can raise yourself above others as often as you wish, but you are the one who will lose out, and no one else. And as much as you might wish that you are a more loving, or less sinning person than another, it will never happen; for God loves us all the same, and will not give to anyone while it is not their season, or time for receiving what ever they are to receive. If you wish to win Gods favor, go out and give yourself to another, and become a servant. Do not attempt to rule over, or put another down, in the attempt to show that you are superior in any way. For no servant is greater than his master, and no master is greater than his servant.

Who created Evil and Darkness?

There are very many details to this age-old question, and we will cover this subject as completely as the Lord allows me to do so. For even with all the details I have been given on this subject, I still learn new ones every day of my life. This is because there is no actual truth to any subject, and every subject can be explained from now till eternity, and still never be completely covered, or explained. Therefore when man attempts to confirm truth as far as any subject is concerned, he makes it into a lie, or falsity. For we can only add details to truth, and make its subject broader and broader each time, but we cannot ever confirm the actual truth to any subject; for there is no actual truth as long as there is a God. This is because God is truth, but He is infinite, which makes all truths infinite. It is also a fact that every thought that is created in the spiritual world is created from many thoughts, and these thoughts provide a single thought to a man in this material world. And so no single thought is ever a single thought, but only appears to be in our world. If you wish to state a truth therefore, you should realize that it is never the truth by itself, but is only a part of the actual truth, and every truth is always a part of the actual truth. So when I state a truth to you, or state a fact that is a part, or percentage of the actual truth, you should never confirm my statements to anyone as the whole truth, but only as a partial truth, which lacks many other details that would make it more understandable as those missing details were provided, which they will be to certain people at certain times. For as we grow and mature as spirits or Angels, we receive more and more details to all truths that are a part of our life's love. We all know many truths at this day in time, but what we don't know is like an ocean compared to a drop of water, when compared to what we do know. We look at the idea of God, and we see but a human figure, which is all-powerful, all knowing, and all present, and yet we cannot fathom the idea of His omnipresence. We are right to see God as a man, but we do not understand from our elementary thoughts, that God does not, and cannot exist within time and space. He does however fill all space, as well as manages the intervals of time, within His existence. So because we are creatures who need to measure time in order to always keep track of our past deeds and happenings, God has created objects which work with our senses that will measure, and keep track of this time. But what we do not truly understand is that time, and the objects that measure time have still been created, and owe their existence to someone, or something else. Because of this, they are created, and are not real, but illusions. The appear to be very real, but this is because they are supposed to, and God manages all things in this material world so as to appear exactly in this manner. Everything in our world owes its appearance of reality to our physical senses, and they are created, and not real as well. Not only that but we think our senses exist within the material realm, when in actuality they exist in the spiritual realm. We see, hear, feel, smell, taste, touch, and rationalize all from the spiritual world, where each of us are living spiritual beings. And so what is the purpose of this material world? To act as a shell, or covering for our spiritual bodies. For without these forms of flesh, we could not act out our thoughts of affections, for we would have no actual form. But remember, these actual forms are only real according to our physical senses in this material world, which are the senses of our spirits living in fantasy. We as spiritual creatures do not need these fleshly bodies once we leave this material world until we wish to return to our fantasies, what ever they may be. For we are mind beings, as the Lord God is, and we only require bodies so as to love. We don't think with our bodies, we don't rationalize with our bodies; we don't calculate equations with our bodies; and in the spiritual world you don't even go from one place to another with your body. But whenever a body is required in the spiritual world, one is gladly, and immediately provided by God. However, because we as human beings only know of the things of this material, and sensual world, we only understand those things, which can be proven by our senses. We do not for one second trust anything according to our faith. But as God puts it in His Word, to enter the Kingdom of heaven we must be as a little child. What this means is that we must come to have childlike faith. What childlike faith is can be explained as follows: If a little child were standing at the top of a sliding board, and they were afraid to slide down this sliding board because of its height; they would still jump from that height into their father, or mothers arms, because they would trust either one to catch them before they hit the ground. From all the different scenarios a child goes through with its parents throughout life, he builds this trust that he can have with no one else for as long as he lives. Well, this is the faith we must build with God, before we will ever be permitted to enter the Kingdom of heaven. For we must come to understand that the things of this world are in a reverse order, and need to be reverted back to their original order, as they were before we were born. And the only way this can be done, because of mans ignorance, or lack of intelligence, is to live by faith in God. To trust the things He is telling us because they lead toward the actual truth. To believe what man tells us does not lead to truth, but to hell. So I hope you can see up to this point that God is not a material being, and He does not even exist within the material realm. Because He is not of this material world, you cannot find truth from the things of this material world. All truth exists within the spiritual realm, which is where eventually every man goes on to live out his finite life in an infinite world. Is there anything beyond this infinite world, or is that where it all ends? You will have to remain with me to find out, for the journey is just beginning. So! Do you understand yet, who and what God is? Do you know the difference between the Lord God and man, as we understand man that is? God is a man; a perfect man; and we were created in His image. We do not fully understand this, but we soon will. To be created is to not be real, or alive, for life cannot be created. God is life, and God is the all in all. He cannot be separated, or divided; and He cannot be created, or re-created. God is one, and He is the original one, of whom no equal can be found. He is much more than any man can comprehend, and so man had to decrease His essence, or being in order to just be able to comprehend a small portion of who and what He is. Even today, very few men in either world can fathom the immense idea of God, and his Essence, or Substance. We will get to that subject in its own time, but first I wish to speak of other things pertaining to this subject. There are a few things that are noticeable in our material world, that do not exist in our material world. And no matter how many brilliant scientists have lived throughout time, none have explained these things so as to be understood by the average man, because they cannot be understood by the average man. Even the scientists cannot explain the spiritual world, because they cannot see it, touch it, measure it, feel it, hear it, taste it, or smell it. And if it cannot be explained from our senses, they do not see it as real. When the truth is, you cannot see what is real, touch what is real, hear, taste, smell, feel, nor understand what is real, as long as you are living according to the ways of this material world. If you were to bake a cake, and present it as evidence that it is real, because you can see, taste, touch, and smell it, you would be wrong. Because until that cake is eaten, and becomes a part of the human body, which eventually becomes a part of the blood, which eventually becomes a part of the life of that person, which eventually enters the spiritual world through that life, and is joined to the Lord through the spiritual world, it is not yet real. Nothing we see is actually real, but only apparently, through the senses of our spirits, and their fantasies. Everything is thought of in the spiritual world from different affections, and in turn these thoughts travel down through the heavens, into the world of spirits, and on into mans thoughts, where they are given the appearance of life. But the real life is when the objects created from these thoughts are given form, and they serve their use, or purpose in this material world, which serves mankind, who is the image of life, and is connected to life through the spiritual world from within, which is connected to the Lord, who is life. Everything is actually joined to this life, and all things work toward becoming a part of this life. Such as when we eat different foods, or drink different liquids; they become a part of the body, then the blood, then the mind, then the spiritual world that lives within each of us. Even rocks have the yearning to become a part of life, and they do so through things like erosion, where minute particles of them very gradually, over long periods of time, erode into the water system, and are consumed often by men, in which case even they become a part of life. And if you think about it long enough, you will see how all things in the spiritual world are connected with all things of the material world, and all make up the circle of life, which is life forever. When we consume food and drink, our bodies do not accept everything we take in, and so we must all have body waste. This body waste is discharged from each human body, because it is rejected by the body, and once again becomes a part of the earth, or ground. The waste that is rejected from each human being is a part of the things, which make up the hells. For anything that a human body, which is in good, rejects, it rejects it because it can have no part with the heavens. At the same time, if a person is in evil, their body will not reject certain minerals and elements, and these can at a later time harm that human body. Hence the term, "You reap that which you sow." For every mans ruling love, or spirit actually creates, and continues to create every moment, that human body. So if that person's spirit is joined with the hells because he wishes to be in evil, or sin, his spirit at that moment will be creating bodily fibers that are from the hells, and are detrimental to the health of that human body. When that person's inner man, or spirit is drawing from affections from the heavens, he is every moment during that time, creating fibers that are good for that human body. But sometimes they are good for that body, when they could actually be harmful to another human, and this matters not, because others are protected by that person's atmosphere that surrounds them. The only time a harmful mineral or element, or bacteria you might say, from you or someone else, could come into contact with another human being would be if the other human being were in evil or sin, and their atmosphere were permitted to join with the former persons atmosphere, and allowed harmful things in because of their state at that time. An example would be that you can catch a harmful virus from someone, but only if both persons atmospheres allow it. This of course is not caused by time and chance, but by a persons state at any given point in time. For you must be in evil, before evil, or sickness is allowed into your body. You may not appear to be in evil on the exterior, but you are. You could be harboring a grudge, seeking vengeance on someone, thinking of killing or harming someone, jealous of someone, or any variety of things, and these thoughts could cause harm, or sickness to come into your body. Man does not know of these things however, and many even see them as childish thought, but they are true nonetheless. Our human bodies are more complicated than we will probably ever imagine, but they are as well oiled machines, as far as being obedient to our thoughts of affections. We can either create our world through the Lord, and the heavens, or we can create it through Satan, and the hells. This is called free will, and every man receives it in his life. Everything that is seen in this world is a correspondence, or representation of the actual thing in the spiritual world. Whatever sickness, or disease, or handicap a man falls under in this world is in direct proportion to his state in the spiritual world. We all already know this basically, but we never really wanted to accept it as reality. But whatever you bound on earth will be bound in heaven, and whatever you loose on earth will be loosed in heaven. In other words, whatever affections your spirit draws from in this material life, it will draw from as well, in the spiritual world. And even though it appears that the sin or deed began in your thoughts in this world, they actually began in the spiritual world, where you drew your thoughts from in the first place. It's like this: There are two wells in existence; one is good and truth, and the other is evils and falsities; one is from the heavens and the Lord, the other is from the hells and Satan. If you draw your thoughts from the hells, and put them into act in this material world, as your own acts, then you are in hell. If however you draw your thoughts from the heavens, and put them into act in the material world, you are in heaven. But what you make your own remains your own, until you remove that affection through the repeated shunning of that evil affection. If you continuously shun evils, even though you commit them, they will eventually be removed from your life, but only gradually, according to how often you shun them, and how sincere you are. For the Lord knows everyone's heart, and so we cannot fool Him. Now at the same time, if you draw on good affections, and in turn call these affections your own, you are still in sin because you are saying that you are good from yourself, and are not giving the Lord the credit for the good affections in your life. For it is a fact that no man is good, but you need not confirm this fact, for it will confirm itself as we go on to continuously attempt to live for the Lord. So if no one is good, we cannot ever boast as to our good deeds, for they are not our own, but are only acted out in us, through the Lord, and from the Lord. I say through because we are in the Lord and He is in us as well. So now we have some idea of how good and evil work in a material world, such as our own. If you think evil thoughts, and do not shun them rather than make them your own, they create evil and sickness in your physical bodies. If you think good and loving thoughts, yet knowing they are from the Lord alone, you will be a healthy person, mentally and physically. If you were to speak to an anatomist, he would tell you that the blood flow actually begins in the human brain, for this is the beginning of life in the material world. It is also the gateway between the spiritual and material worlds. Therefore this world is created from the thoughts of affections from spiritual world. These thoughts of affections began in the beginning as all good thoughts from the Lord, but once man received them as his own thoughts, he began to boast that good originated from himself, and not God, and therefore sin was born into man. Therefore, evil originated, and was created by man, and not actually God. For if no man is good of himself, nor can he be good of himself, it would be going against God, and would therefore be evil, to think that we are good of our self, not giving the credit to God. This crediting good to our own account is what was called eating of the "Tree of Knowledge of good and evil." For every man begins his life with a knowledge of good from God, and as he begins to rely on his own understanding, he begins to receive a knowledge of evil; therefore eating of the "Tree of knowledge of good and evil." So now you know who truly created evil, and where evil is created till forever. For God can have nothing to do with evil, and neither does He choose to do so. So where does the darkness come in? Well, it is not a part of God, and cannot exist with God. For no darkness can exist within light, and God is pure light. As I have stated from the beginning, God is the all in all, and He is omnipresent. What this tells us is that He is not only present in the created realm, which is space, but He is present everywhere, including the spiritual world. But what is the difference between the spiritual world and the material world, and how can God be in both worlds at the same time? Because He fills all space, but does not exist within space. But how can He not exist in space, and yet fill all space nonetheless? Well, how can light fill the noonday sky, and yet it does not exist in our world? If you say it does exist in our material world, where everything is animal, vegetable, or mineral, or gas, then you are saying we can enclose light within a glass jar, and entrap it with a lid. So, does light really exist within our material world, or is it just an appearance? How about fire, does this exist within our world? For pure love, which is what God is, is pure fire; but is fire in our world also an appearance alone? For it is a truth that fire cannot be enclosed within a jar either, but must always have an opening to the atmosphere of some kind. Why does fire need this opening? Why does it go out when there is no outlet to the atmosphere? Because fire is connected to God through the atmosphere, so that God can provide what appears to be real fire to our world. When all along the fire of this world is dead, as is the fire on the suns surface. They give the illusion of real fire, with the light and heat actually coming from God in the spiritual realm. The same goes for thought, for we think it is of our material world, when all along it comes from our spirit living in the spiritual world. For you cannot touch thought, you cannot hear it, see it, feel it, smell it, nor harness it. And now we come to darkness, and where it comes from. We read in our bibles these words:

> First in the Old Testament: In the beginning God created the heaven and the earth. And the earth was without form, and void; and DARKNESS was upon the face of the deep. And the Spirit of God moved upon the face of the waters. And God said Let there be light: and there was light. And God saw the light, that it was good: and God divided the light from the DARKNESS. And God called the light day, and the DARKNESS He called night. And the evening and the morning were the first day. And God said, Let there be a firmament in the midst of the waters, and let it divide the waters from the waters. And God made the firmament, and divided the waters, which were under the firmament from the waters, which were above the firmament, and it was so. And God called the firmament heaven. And the evening and the morning were the second day. And God said, Let the waters under the heaven be gathered together unto one place, and let the dry land appear; and it was so. And God called the dry land Earth; and the gathering together of the water called He Seas: and God saw that it was good (Genesis 1:1-10).

Then in the Old Testament: In the beginning was the Word, and the Word was with God, and the Word was God. The same was in the beginning with God. All things were made by him; and without him was not anything made that was made. In him was life; and the life was the light of men. And the light shineth in DARKNESS; and the DARKNESS comprehended it not. There was a man sent from God, whose name was John. The same came for a witness, to bear witness of the light, that all men through him might believe. He was not that light, but was sent to bear witness of that light. That was the true light, that lighteth every man that cometh into the world. He was in the world, and the world was made by him, and the world knew him not. He came unto his own, and his own received him not. But as many as received him, to them gave he power to become the sons of God, even to them that believe on his name. Which were born not of blood, nor of the will of the flesh, nor of the will of man, but of God. And the Word was made flesh, and dwelt among us, (and we beheld his glory, the glory as the only begotten of the Father), full of grace and truth (John 1:1-14). End of quotes:

In both of these scenarios we read of darkness, and each time the darkness applies to man, and not God. Such as the darkness was over the face of the deep, or the light shineth in the darkness, and the darkness comprehended it not. God is the light, and when man is not living for God he is in darkness. Darkness over the face of the deep means that mans mind is empty of the truths of God; and that all men live in fantasy. The light shineth in the darkness means that God lives within every man, including the bad, and that we do not see it, nor have any actual knowledge of it. Throughout the whole Word when we see the words darkness, or night, we are not to understand actual darkness, or actual night. For the darkness represents a lack of the knowledge's of the Kingdom of heaven, and God. And night is the state every man enters just before the morning state, or the state where the old church in him is about to end, and just before the beginning of a New Church in man. We think the Word speaks of this material terraqueous globe we all dwell on, but this is not the case. For the whole of the Word speaks of the Lord, and the different states he went through in the world. And at the same time, the world we read of here is not, as I have said, this terraqueous globe, but every man is a world. For it is a truth that the Ancients called man a Microcosm, which is a little world. And for that matter, man is also a little universe. So for those who have the idea that darkness is mentioned in the Word, as the darkness we all see in this world, they have been miss-led. As a matter of fact, the darkness of this world is not real, but has also been created. For if God is pure light, a light ten thousand times brighter than any light we have ever seen, and he exists everywhere, that would mean that the darkness had to be created within that light. For there is no outside of that light, nor can there be any separation. So if darkness exists (apparently), within the light, it has to be a created darkness, and therefore is not real. This darkness we see is also not bad, for it was created for the good of mankind. For it is very difficult for man to sleep in the day, because the day was set-aside for man to perform his uses in life. Night in this world is also a time when the evil are found doing their evil deeds, and therefore man is warned to stay inside at this time. Man actually receives the heat in his body from within, and this from the life within that is God. Therefore, one of the actual purposes of the sun in our world is not to provide heat or light to our world, though it is given that appearance, but to create darkness by the rotating of the earth. For the sun does not ever move from its place, and neither do the stars. And even the light from the sun that provides apparent light, opposite the darkness, the light still comes from God, who is within as well as without our sun. As I said, the sun is used to create night, or darkness by the earth rotating away from it, for a whole world of darkness has been provided by God to cause this all to take place. For if we existed in a universe of light, we would be in the presence of God always, and even the evil would be blessed when they were not meant to be. If we were in constant light, our night would have to be controlled by our eyes and body temperatures, separate from one another, which would mean that there would be no way of making plants, trees, and all vegetation grow. For even though it is only apparent that the sun provides light and heat to the vegetation of this world, it still gives man the fantasy that this is how things work, and God cannot ever change his plan. Can you imagine what could be accomplished, if man truly knew that all things of his person were actually controlled by his own atmosphere around himself, and not the world around him? But of course God did not give all, or most men this knowledge, because it would do more harm than good. So what we really have out there in our sky, or horizon, is a large planetary sphere called the sun, that has an atmosphere of fire within, and an atmosphere of fire and light without, and both of these are God. Another purpose of the material sun in our sky is to act as a mineral bed for our material world, or globe. For as the earth runs low on certain minerals, they are separated from the large furnace in the sky, and sent to earth as meteors and asteroids, as man calls them. But as far as what man really knows about our sun, he has been confused for ages, and will continue to be confused so for ages to come. Even his knowledge of the stars is in error, for it is a fact that each star is an apparent sun as well. But this would make no difference in our conversation at this time, so I will move on. So there you have it, there is a spiritual darkness, which is a lack of knowledge and understanding of God, and there is darkness in our world that simply put, is nothing more than a made up scene, or curtain, to provide the necessary scenes to man in this world, at any given point in time. We are creatures of light, and we were put inside of a world created within a sphere of darkness. And all references of light in our world are nothing more that holes in the curtain of our world, that let in light from God. But he creates the scenes, and he chooses the type of forms to use for everything. So who do you think created darkness? Was it God or was it man? Answer: God created darkness in both worlds, and man created evil and sin. Darkness is good, as can be evil, in the hands of God. But in the presence of man, darkness and evil are harmful to man, because he lives for self and the world. When we come to live for God however, we come to know the true purposes for darkness and evil, and therefore God can then provide us with real truths to the Kingdom of heaven. For as long as we are the evil generation, we are kept in sleep, but when we are regenerated, we are awakened from this sleep gradually. What God gives us in life has nothing to do with the material world, and so we do not usually recognize the things God does for us. For everything he does is seen in the spiritual world, and is only connected to the material world through correspondences. That means what we do in the material world is of no real concern to God, for it is only the end affect to the beginning cause from the spiritual world. He sends us all good affections, and we do with them as we please. To end the subject on darkness and evil, I would only say that with God all things are good, and with man they are turned into evil, when he is not living for God. If you make your own decisions in life, without consulting God every time, you are not truly living for God, and are in sin.

Why do we live if were going to die?

If you were to place one hundred million men in a single world, and none existed at the same time in this material world; but each of these hundred million were born, one after the other in this material world, these men would all experience the same exact experiences in their lifetimes, so that each walked in the others shoes or footsteps. For we must all endure the same experiences in life, if we are to be able to have compassion for others, eventually. But we must still mature as human beings before we can understand this compassion. We as human beings don't know we have gone through all the same situations as all other men however, and so many of us at first, in our lifetime, put ourselves above others. We as human beings do not know, nor do we understand how we mature as spirits, or how we all walk in another's shoes. So, because of this, we act as brute beasts when we are first born into this world. For we enter this world in a type of sleep, and we are awakened a little bit at a time, throughout the process of our lifetime, or regeneration. But where we think we live life in this material world only once, we do not truly understand the process, and I must lay it out to you, with the Lords blessings and guidance, of course. So as I go through the details of this lifelong mystery, please keep in mind that man lives his life according to his physical senses, and only believes what he can see, hear, touch, taste, smell, and feel. This is because the average human being has not truly learned what it really means to live for God in faith. He does not understand that what is real is actually what we cannot see, nor hear, taste, touch, feel, or smell. This world is made up, or created by mans past fantasies, and continues to be created by such. Something only feels hard to you because your mind tells you it is hard, and how you should receive the feeling within your brain. For it is a truth as well, that when we dream, we can easily feel things hard as well, which we take as not being real. This is because the human mind is set to register, so as to tell us that the things we see in the daylight, when we supposedly wake up, are actually real, and our senses tell us they are real. But man has not yet learned that the human mind is a powerful tool, and God uses it to make us believe anything he wishes for us to believe. But he wants the good of mankind, which is to teach mans spirit. However, man wishes only to serve his flesh, and to provide the things that please it in this world. So if you wish to know the real world, while you live in this world, you must get to know your dream state better, for that is the real world. So we as spirits live in that world, but we are asleep when we are at home in this world. Which is why when we eventually remove our ties to this world, the more we do so the more we come to live in the spiritual world. Man however, cannot learn or live this life because he is not willing to give up the things of the flesh. If you were able to do so, you would enter the spiritual world. But more will be said on this later, if it is the Lords will that I do so. But for now, lets continue with our subject, for it is an interesting subject. So when a man is born in the material world, it is because this material world is the seedbed of the angelic heavens. For no man can be born in the spiritual world, which is the real world. Do you know why no man can be born in that world, which is the real world? Because we are not truly born, and are only apparently born, and so we must be apparently born in the material, or make believe world. For all things that are real are in the spiritual world, and only that which is real can exist within that world. For thought is real, but what is thought of in our material world is not real. The spiritual world is thought, and is real; the material world is what is thought of, and is not real. Just as, to us, we think that our thoughts are real in this world, but we do not believe that what is thought of when we dream is real. So too, when spirits and angels think, they believe their thoughts to be real, but what they dream of in our material world, they see as not real. An example would be that I am a spirit, who is asleep in this material world, and therefore I see this material world as not real. But this is because I know I am a spirit. For if you do not know that you are a spirit, you have no knowledge that this material world is not real. So why are we not born in the spiritual realm? Because when we are in that realm, we have returned to God, who gave us the spirit in the first place. This means we are from God, and so we are god, but we are god in a lesser sense than that of the Lord. For though we are from God, and though we are god, we are submitted to God because we have been apparently separated from him by our own atmosphere. For if you are all thought, and you can separate or control each thought, and you can then put an imaginary bubble around each of these thoughts, which are separate affections; then you can create a separate being from yourself. And even though that apparent separate being is still you, it is submitted to the whole of you, and is bound by your rulership, if you so choose to rule over it, which you do because you love it, and want the best for it. And the Lord does choose to rule over each of us, until we mature, and can be cut loose on our own, so as to do his will, as though we were doing so from ourselves, but knowing that all is truly from the Lord alone. So we are truly god, but we are god living in a world of fantasy, or partial sleep. And because God is all powerful, he can do as he pleases, and he can divide, or separate parts of himself from himself, by the atmospheres of sleep or fantasy, that he created to always be around each being that he creates. And because of these atmospheres, he can provide or take away from anyone, as he so chooses, and according to what they sow in life. But as far as living in a material world, as a fleshly human being, this can only take place in a make believe world, as our own, for none of it is real. And when we apparently die in this world, and go on to wake up in the spiritual, or real world, we will put off the flesh, or baby sitter, and put on a substantial, or spiritual body. And this will continue to be our body till forever. But if there is no apparent human, fleshly body, there is no need for the spiritual body, for the spiritual serves the material, and lives within the material. It also lives outside the material, but not separate from the material. So as it is, this world provides the form that is thought of within the spiritual world, and so takes on the life and form of the spirit from within. This world is the beginning of the spirits life, at least what he knows as life, so as to teach each spirit, and then we go on to live as though we were in this world, but actually living within another. There is a term called transmigration, which applies to what happens to every man, and this is how each man lives forever, within another human being. This is not however what some may see as reincarnation; for the same human being is not born into another material body as a single entity, having a different consciousness, but still being the same person. The ruling consciousness of every material human being is the collected thoughts of all within his spiritual society, but is controlled, and changed by the constant changing states of that human being. This is how we are all taught in life. For no man is always good, and no man is always evil, otherwise he could not continue to learn in life. But a human can only be as good as his ruling love allows, and his ruling love is created by the collective thoughts of affections within the soul, or spiritual society of that person. For we are many people living within a single human body, sharing the same life. We are only born in the material flesh once, for this allows the mixture, and creation of loves, or different affections. We live out a life together within a single human body, and we all learn together as one; then we die or sleep, and we become just spirit from that point on. We do not come back as flesh, and for that matter, we are not flesh now, but who we are is a spiritual being, that is surrounded by a fleshly machine that submits to our every thought, or wish. We think we are that person, but we are not. Now as I was saying earlier, a man is born into this material world, he lives his life in this world as he pleases, and he supposedly dies. He of course has children before he dies (eventually), because God will provide him with a female to do so. If God has not provided him with a female, or if he has no children, with his female mate, it matters not. For he will return, and he will one day have offspring. But some do not have children because their life is to learn other things, and does not yet require offspring. But all human beings will eventually have children, for we all endure the same experiences in a lifetime, even though we are not aware of what a lifetime truly is. God has also given him the urges and lusts that are necessary in order for him to love his mate, for these things do not just appear. But because God can have nothing to do with evil, and the act of sex is actually dirty, the god of this world is the one who gives man the urge, or desire for sex, which he does so by turning mans love towards his mate. Yes, a mans love for his wife is supposed to be, but if it were not permitted by God for man to be tempted by woman, and Satan at the same time, there would be no physical human being. For as I said, we are the seedbed for the angelic heavens. So man lies with his mate, and they bring forth a child. It matters not whether the child is male or female in the material realm, for the Father always provides the spirit, while the mother provides the body, or flesh. So even if a female child is born, she will become male before she is saved, or regenerated. But she will become male as to her spirit, for the spirit is one, as the Father is one. Err go the saying, "And the two will become as one flesh." But they become as one flesh in the spirit, not in the material world. Now you may wonder, where does the first woman come from, and I would tell you she came from the spirit, when he was separated. For every spirit is androgynous, having two images, or sexes. But when a spirit enters the physical realm, it does so either as a male, or a female. Once he has been regenerated, and becomes a New Church, he reunites with his other half, and the two once again become one. But it matters not what human being they reside in at the time, for this world is only for appearances. And the two actually reunite because they share affections in the spiritual world. Now when the first man and the first woman were born, and they came of age to mate, they knew not that they were of the same soul, and this was owed to the fact that they were partially in a sleep state, of forgetfulness. And even though they came from the same spirit, or affection, they were only joined as one in the spiritual realm, and were two separate beings, Male and Female, in the material realm. You can call these two Adam and Eve, if you so wish. As this man and woman grew in size and maturity, they took on other affections from God, as well as the world, or Satan. These affections were actual spirits from God and the world, but mostly from God, since we begin life as innocent beings. As we grow we take on our own attributes, and affections, as we learn. The first man and woman were actually taught directly from God, from within themselves. But they actually thought they were talking directly to God. When he would show himself to them, he did so through angels. For no man can truly see God and live. And the way the first man and woman were taught is the way all men and women are taught. But before someone can be taught or regenerated by God, they must first return to this innocence. This innocence is called the New Church in them. So this first man and woman grew, and they eventually grew old and passed on, or died, as some may still believe at this point. But before they died, they left their seed in their offspring, and this is where mankind was given its beginning. But remember, the first man and woman had to have many children, so as to get the ball rolling, you might say. But because a spirit cannot actually impregnate a woman, unless the seed is provided through the material world, all women must be impregnated from within the material world, and no actual material Virgin can become pregnant, without the seed of the male from the material world. So did the first group of human beings become born through incest? No, they had no knowledge of where they were from, because of the sleep state man was still under. And as far as there being deformed children born from brothers and sisters mating, God provided at first, so that this never happened, but eventually taught them to not mate within families, by allowing the deformities, so as to keep them from doing so. But God did not actually allow these things, but man reaped that which he sowed, as it says in the Word. Now we today, for the most part see incest as terrible, and so we steer clear of it. But if you don't know of the harm it will cause, and it appears as normal to you, God will not allow you to be harmed, and neither will he allow the offspring to be harmed. We must understand one thing however folks; we are all blood brothers and sisters, and this is not why incest was prohibited by God. Incest is prohibited because God wishes for different to mate with different, so as to continue to create better, and more different affections in the future. If a brother and a sister, or first cousins mate, the similarities would be too much alike in their offspring, and people would all look too much alike, and have all the same habits. But as I said, God likes change, or differences in his children, and so he permits the deformities, and such, so as to steer us away from incest. Many of us are also taught to feel strongly that it is wrong, and so we do not attempt, or even consider it. If man were to always procreate within his own spiritual society, which is similar to incest, societies would take much longer to perfect themselves, or to better themselves. So incest is not permitted today, and all men for the most part, know that incest is wrong, and we do not commit it. However, when it was permitted, it was not wrong, it did not feel wrong, and all were protected by God. He could have easily caused things to happen in another way, but he chose the one he chose because he has the freedom and the power to do so. But if you begin to sort out families, and generations, and go all the way back to the beginning; we all have the same source, and creation had to begin with one male and one female. If it were not done in this manner, we would not all be connected in the spiritual world, as we are. For we are all connected by one single affection, from the first man, who is the Lord; and he cannot be separated. But we must understand that to be a male and a female within the same entity, which is what the Lord is, is not to be seen as any separation. For in the spiritual world, the two are as one. Moving on, all things in this world are truly controlled by the mind, and so right and wrong are formed from the mind, by God. Remember, what you do in this material world has no bearing on your salvation. So now, God provided all the affections which man drew from in the beginning, and when man drew from these affections, he gave them life, and they became his own. When he had offspring, he passed these affections, as well as his life or spirit, on to his offspring. And so his offspring became a more perfect him. But the more perfect him is not the material son he brought into the world, but the spiritual man who lives within that material man. And as it was with each man, so too is it with each woman. But the woman will always represent good, and man will represent truth, until they are regenerated; which is when things are put back in order. When the good once again joins with truth it will become man, or good and truth joined as one. So as I was saying, as each offspring is born, so too is that man more perfected in his offspring. The material man has passed on or died, but he, or his spirit continues to live in his offspring. And as we continue in life, within the material world, we are providing a place for life to other spirits, who are affections we take on as our own. And these also go on to learn, and mature from within material man. So every spirit and angel is given life by dwelling within material man till forever. We become better, or more perfect as each affection is added to our spiritual society, which is the consciousness of every spirit or Angel that lives within that society. Depending on which spiritual society we draw our thoughts from, at any given time, one society is more perfect and loving than another. If we keep drawing from the more perfect society, we will eventually become a member of that society, by God allowing us to change societies. Man, as a spirit will forever be more perfected, but each at his own pace in the spiritual world. But no man is ever truly alone, but shares his life and consciousness with many others. This is why we have so many thoughts every moment, even though each thought is actually a separate spirit or person. Each of us represents a single affection of love, which is truly found within the Lord, and makes up his affections in reality. We are the Lord because we are his separate thoughts of affections, even as the spiritual world is made up of all of our thoughts of affections. You can therefore draw your thoughts from one society in heaven, or hell; or you can draw from every one, at any given time; but never from all at the same time. For only the Lord can do this because he is the all in all. It is like a computer that can store all known information, all at the same time, and sort it all out at the same time, so as to provide each thought to its prospective destination within each subject, at any given time. So the Lord sends one thought to one man, another to another man, another to someone else, and so on; and so on. And all along the Lord sorts it all out, because he can do so, and we cannot. For it is true that we can take a certain amount of thoughts and sort them out, because we are created as little gods, or microcosms; but he is God, or the Grand Man, and he can take every thought at once, and sort everything out according to his own will, or purpose. We as human beings have been taught throughout the ages that the world is young, only about six thousand years old, going by the bible; and maybe a few hundred million years old according to the scientists of our day; but still the scientists do not described the earth as being inhabited by man throughout this period. As well those who teach the bible, only believe that man has existed for about the six thousand years I have mentioned. None of this makes sense, and man today cannot even explain things, using these timetables as evidence. This is because God did not just pop up a hundred million years ago, make some uninhabited planets, and sit back and wait before he created man or animal. But to understand it all, we must first understand God. First of all God does not exist in time, nor could he do so and still allow the Word to be seen as true. For if God were the all in all, being all things, everywhere, this would mean that space would have to be everywhere, and that God would have to be space; for he is everything, right? But! If God is space, what is thought, which we recognize within our minds? What is a dream, and where does it exist? What is light? What is darkness? What is heat? (For if God is everything, he is heat; so how does he generate the heat, which he is?) What is sound, and where does it originate? It must originate with God, if he is all. But many of these things cannot rationally, nor scientifically be explained, if God is space. What is the essence of space, or what is it all made of? For everything in this material world must owe its existence to something prior to itself, for this world is said to be finite, whereas God is said to be infinite. So going from these facts, how can God be infinite, and we be finite, if God is space? For all is God, and God is all; he cannot be separated, or divided, right? So if God is space, and we are space because we take up space, we must be God, right? For what is from God, is God. Also, Jesus said in the Word that we are in God, and God is in us. To put it another way, we are in space and space is in us. That makes sense to me, so this cannot be used to prove of Gods nature or essence, right? Well for now, lets continue and see what we come up with. If we are space, and are finite, that means we have an ending somewhere. But if we are in God, and God is in us, where is our ending, being that both God and man are both space, and are one and the same according to that space? For remember, God cannot be divided, since division would cause him not to be everywhere, right? We know division cannot exist without separation of some sort, and God cannot be separated, and still be everywhere. So if God cannot be divided, he cannot be space, and cannot exist within space. For God cannot be everywhere, if he is placed in a box called space. For whatever God is within space, he must also be outside of space, so that his essence, or nature remains constant or the same at all times. So if God is not space, and does not even exist within space, what is he, and what is space? Well, God is thought, according to how we understand thought. And because God is thought, and everything exists because of, and within thought; God fills all space without actually existing within space. For space is in God, but God is not in space. He actually fills space without existing within it. And to prove it he left us a clue as to what he really is. Thought fills your human body even though it does not actually exist within your human body. You think it is in your body because there is a atmospheric bubble around every human being, which gives them the appearance of life. This bubble causes and controls everything about each human being, separate from the rest of creation, even though it is not real. Look at it this way: God is this gigantic sphere, which consists of pure thought. And within this sphere of thought he has created other little spheres, but only apparently, and not really. And these apparent spheres are called sleep, or fantasy, and each of us lives within one of these spheres. The closer we get to God the more out sphere lets in the real world, or God. The farther away from God we get, or live, the more our sphere lets in sleep or fantasy, and we are more so in hell. And this sphere is always controlled by the amount of hellish, or heavenly affections, which we allow into our own separate sphere in life. For this sphere remains with each man, or spirit, or angel forever. So if you allow more evil affections in, you are in hell more often than not. If you allow good affections in, you are in heaven more often than not. So God is pure thought, and every man is less pure thought, on down to the level of pure fantasy in some cases. These are men who are seen in our world as mad, or insane. And all of creation, as well as this material world lives within God, and he fills all things with his presence. For even the evil dwell in his presence, and do not know it. For if God were not with the evil as well as the good, the evil could not exist, and would immediately die if God were not there within them. For if God is said to not be with someone, it is only because they are not receiving him in their life, and therefore do not know he is there; but he surely is. So everyone and everything owes its existence to God every moment in time. We are not created only once, and go on to live forever, but we are created every moment we live, and must be created accordingly until forever. In other words, if God were to stop thinking of us for a second, we would cease to exist for a second. For each of his thoughts is a person, or an affection, and is given life by performing a use in creation. For whatever thought is not being used in yours, or my life at this second, is being used somewhere else within, or throughout creation, and the spiritual world. So because every thought is constantly being used in the spiritual world, every man eventually experiences the same experiences in life, eventually, and will do so again, till forever. For if you fall off a horse once, you have to eventually get back on, so as to eventually learn how to ride a horse; and this is the case for every man. And some men, when they fall, are afraid to ever ride again in that lifetime, and must do so in the next, so as to eventually learn how to ride a horse. But this is only an example, and life is much more complicated than just learning how to ride a horse. Basically life is about love, and we all have many different affections of love to learn to eternity, and we will all continue to do so forever. So there you have it! God does not exist in space but fills all space. He has always been there as far as we are concerned, and anything more he does not feel we need to know at this point in life. Whether we learn beyond that point eventually is all up to him. But there is much too much about God that man cannot comprehend, and so he gives to us that which we can receive at any given point in our lives. For all men mature at different rates, and there are different men being born into the world every second of every day. Where it appears that you are not learning in this material world, you are doing so in the spiritual world. You and I are a thought from an affection, and we are being used every moment of every second of every day. Now in this material realm, where we believe that mankind has only been around for a short time, man has believed this fallacy for ages upon ages, and will continue to do so. But as man will always come to be given the most awesome truths to ever come from the heavens throughout time, at different times; so too will man experience times of stupor, and will be given very few truths from the Lord in the heavens. This alternates with mankind, as well as the spiritual world till forever, so that man will forever experience states, or changes, or seasons. For as the earth endures the four seasons of spring, summer, autumn, and winter, so too do the generations of mankind to come, and will do so till forever. Churches will be formed, and each will fall away, so as to forever continue to bring in a New Church within every man. When each man becomes a New Church in the material realm, the world will not know it, but it will only be seen in the heavens, where a New Christian heaven will be formed each time a New Church is begun. There are other heavens, which are only representative heavens, or churches, and they will remain in the spiritual world until their time comes to become a New Church, and a New Christian Heaven. These heavens, or representative churches are such as the Muslims, Islam, Buddha, and all other religions that are not Christian. But do not think that all Churches in our world who call themselves Christian are truly Christian either. For there are many false, or representative churches in our world, but all will eventually become true Christian Churches in the heavens, in their own time. But each man must eventually die to his flesh, not in the flesh. For nowhere in the Word is dieing in the flesh mentioned. This is another misconception man has had for ages. But as I was saying earlier, man has lived since forever, almost as long as God, but not quite. But Gods age, and mans age mean very little when learning of life and love, and what will become of man in the future. We need only know that we need God, and God prefers us till forever. Why he prefers us is for the same reason he created us; which is to give love life, and provide it a form so as to love others, as well as God. For separate from the forms God gave us, we are simply put, God! And God receives no pleasure in loving himself. Therefore he created forms from sleep or fantasy, whichever you wish to call it. This is the only possible way of anyone or anything to be separated from God. And yet we are not truly separated, but only appear to be. And as I have stated, such as God is, so too did he create us to be as he is. For as many lives live within him, and owe their existence to him, so too is that the case with mankind. And as we mature, we are given these knowledge's, or truths. So as far as why we live, if we are going to die, I can say this: We cannot ever die, because what is alive stays alive, and what is dead stays dead. Our spirit, or who we truly are is alive, but the body we inhabit is dead, and will always be dead, even though it will have the appearance of being alive. So when a man thinks he dies in this world, he is only going to sleep; so as to then wake up in the spiritual world, seeming as though he were still in the material world. Some endure more dissatisfying deaths than others, and some actually horrifying deaths, but this is only in appearance, and is not truly what has happened. When a person apparently dies in this world, only the evil within them senses the pain that goes with death, and never the good. And since flesh is evil, and the spirit is truly good, only the flesh suffers, and not the actual person. So no matter how horrible a persons death may seem, it is only an appearance, and can only be seen by someone who is in evil at the time. God does not allow good, loving beings to witness horrible, evil, deaths; which is why many times people cannot watch someone die, or be killed in an accident. This is why the good cannot even stomach death, or harm which happens to another. So let it be known that when a person dies in this world, of a dissatisfying death, the good have already left the body, and only the evil remain. But God does not even take pleasure, nor does he allow the evil to feel the pain associated with these horrible deaths, but they are in a fantasy at the time which corresponds to the opposite of what the evil person inside really was; and this causes them great grief, and mental pain. For God is by no means the terrible, vengeful, destroying, punishing God we have all made him out to be in the past. And what we see in this world with our eyes is by no means the truth, if you can believe this. No loving God, who claims to be God, could allow little children, or babies for that matter, to die horrible deaths, and allow them to feel the pain associated with such death. And anyone who believes he could do this is not ready to receive God in his or her life. For God is truly pure love, and can have nothing to do with death, physical pain, punishment, murder, or hatred. To believe he could do so means we do not yet know God, and must continue to pray that he show himself in our life. The fears that go with death in this word are there for the unlearned, as well as the evil. These fears were allowed by God so that man would attempt to do good, or the right things in his life, so as to live as long as possible. But also so that man would not wish to kill others, in fear of the laws of the land, and fears of him being put to death as well. For if man knew that death was not so bad, and that heaven eventually awaited him, he would not wish to please God, but would live to please his flesh instead; which is evil. Now God has given me these things to give to those who love him, and wish to do his bidding in the world, but those who are not included in this group will not even be able to understand, or receive these sayings. These words are put here to bless Gods church, or churches in the world; and they will do just that. They cannot be received by the babes, or the ignorant of the church, for they would only corrupt them, or use them for their own self-gain. Therefore if you are at all able to receive or understand these words, you should by all means continue to read them, and put them to work in your life. For you have been greatly blessed above many others. In closing this section, I would only say that those of you who think you are alive now have not truly seen life. For when you die of your flesh, your true life then begins, and the old one will be but a slowly fading memory, shortly to disappear.

CHAPTER 2

A New World Order!

Today we live in a world where everyone wishes to put his or her business on the street. There is a growing number of reality television shows out there that cater to this very need as well. Not that the world is getting worse mind you, but we are beginning to care less and less as to what people know about the inner workings of our personal lives. Then you have those shows where nannies are brought into people's homes, so as to fix the problems the parents have created for them selves over a period of time. Or they are swapping husbands or wives, each living the others life for a week or so; and each is to tell the other what is wrong with their family, and of course they get a big check in the end. But what is the real reason behind all of these new television shows we are airing today? The real reason is that man has run out of news to broadcast, and must find new stories to make public. Therefore the ones responsible for finding new news are offering money to those who have a story to tell to the world. There are not very many limits as to the content of the news, or story they provide, for as we can see, you can find just about any type of sin on television these days, for that is what makes news today. So sin has now entered the public arena more noticeable than it has been for a long time, and this is the way the world will represent change until forever. For what is now taking place has taken place before, and will do so for many ages to come, never ceasing to come back around like the circle of life we have all heard about. Now we look at those who buy into these sinful desires today and we place the blame on all those who accept the Sodom and Gomorrah type of actions, which are common place for most all men today. For even though we may sit back on our high horse and act as if we were "Holier than Thou," most of us deep back within our thoughts would like to join in on the action, if we were not recognized by others as being one of them, who will all one day go to hell. But let it be known that we will all go to hell in our own set time. We all have been guilty of all the same sins or crimes throughout time, and so we were all told in the Word that we should not, and cannot boast, for we have nothing to boast about. Yes we live in a sinful, evil world; full of men who would love to end your life as quick as they look at you, and the only reason they do not do so is because of the laws of the land, which God has caused man to forever keep in place. And even the law makers and keepers change the laws to go in their favor from time to time, but this is because man has been given free will, and God has chosen not to intervene as long as man does not ask for his help. We however, do not realize how easy it is for God to intervene in our lives, if we ask for his help, and so we do not, for the most part, do so. Therefore, even with the laws of the land in place, man still disobeys the commandments, and lashes out at his neighbor every chance he gets. As I said, yes we live in an evil world, but we are never required to accept the ways of the world, and can go beyond the ways of the world any time we please. We have even been told in the Word how to get away from the ways of the world, and that is by removing the cravings of our flesh. Do you like to smoke? Ask God to help you quit, continue to ask him to help you quit, and when he is ready, you will surely quit smoking. Do you want to quit drinking, or doing drugs? Ask God to help you quit, and keep asking him to help you quit; and when he is ready, you will certainly quit. Or how about this one? Do you lust for other women, and find you cannot stop looking at them when they walk by? Ask God to help you to stop looking and lusting, and really mean it by putting forth the effort to quit; then ask God to help you quit, then continue asking him, and when he is ready, you will surely quit lusting, and looking at other women. How sure am I that God will cause you to quit these things, or anything else that is not acceptable for Gods plan for you? I will bet my life on it, for I have lived it, and know of others that have done so as well. There are many things God will do for us, of which there is no end, but we must first understand God, and what he will and will not do in our lives. For remember, he has given us all free will, and will never go against it. The things I am speaking of are not just for those who believe themselves to be Christians, but also for anyone who is found in good, throughout their lifetime. But just as we receive good things for being good, we receive bad things for being bad. And we do not decide, nor should we ask for any certain thing in life from God, for he knows our needs, and he knows what he wishes for us to receive from this day, on down to the day we leave this life. So when we pray, we should pray for the good of others, not for anything that we may need or desire. Now, lets switch gears for a bit, and speak on some other matters pertaining to Gods plan. I ask you to stick with me, and really think about the things I am about to tell you. Again; do not confirm anything, but take in all things I tell you with a child like faith. Always build one truth upon another until you finally come to the realization that God really knows what he is doing, and we can learn many things from him if we never say to ourselves that we have all the truth. When you say you have all the truth, or you know the truth, you are creating a lie, or falsity. For it is a truth that all truth lies in the Lord, in which there is no end to any truth, ever. Now, to begin with, do you realize that God is the all in all, the first and the last, the beginning and the end. Well, he is also the same yesterday, today, and forever. We can confirm this about God because it is an absolute truth, which requires no further confirmation. So because God is the same yesterday, today, and forever; he is yesterday, today, and forever. What I mean is that time does not exist outside of God, and actually goes on inside of him, or his being. Man is not just created and boom, he remains alive, and in existence till forever. No, God must create each and every man every second in time, if time were real, until forever. But because time is not real, God must continually create it as well. And because God can create the present over and over again, he can create the past, as well as the future over and over again. Don't believe me, just stay with me and you will come to believe and understand all things, which I am saying. What if God were to never create the past again, and all that lived in the past, now live in the present, or even now in the future? If all men continue to grow in maturity, wisdom, and understanding until forever, as is Gods plan; where would we later, or even now attain the beast like, or primitive thoughts of affections which we all eventually need to draw on again and again in our lives? For every man continuously goes through changes in his moods or states, and must have the affections available so as to provide the thoughts that go with these changes in state. For we should know that those who reach peace in the Lord do not any longer feel pain, remorse, jealousy, revenge, anger, lust, hatred, and many other affections which are negative. For these affections disappear once we find the Kingdom of Heaven within ourselves. So if these eventually disappear within every man, where do these affections come from when man in this material world goes through changes in state, and must draw on affections such as were just mentioned? That is assuming you are aware that all mankind is eventually saved? And if you are at this time aware of this, then there are many questions that need answering, so as to put all the pieces of the puzzle together for you, as well as myself. Therefore the Lord has given me these truths, so as to pass on to those who are ready, or who hunger for them. So, if every man matures, and grows in wisdom, where do these beastlike affections now, as well as in the future come from? They come from men, who are now living in the past. But the past to us is the present to them. For the past within the Lord is the same as the present in the Lord. I know this is a hard saying to grasp, but hang in there, for I am not yet finished. God is by no means bound by time or space; and because he is not bound by such he can create either at his own pleasure, or will. For there is nothing God cannot do, for he can even make that which is, as if it were not; and he can make that which is not, as though it were. All because God is what you would understand as pure thought, and all thought. Therefore, everything, which resides within the created universe, resides within thought, and can easily be ruled, or controlled by thought; that is the Lord, who is all thought. So if he is now thinking about the past, it is present to him. If he is thinking about the present, or the future, it is still the present to him. And he can go on and on, creating Aeons upon Aeons of time in his thoughts; which will be the present to him, but past, present, and future to us. Now if you can fathom this, there are Aeons upon Aeons of time as well as space out there, and they are living live as we speak, in the same exact manner that we are living life. Some are providing the thoughts of affections for our past, some for our present, and some for our future. As well, we are providing the same to other Aeons of generations of people in existence, within the thoughts of God. And as we mature, and continue to learn truths in the Lord; he gives us the necessary truths in our lives, or minds, so as to continue to learn in him till forever. Every man will be saved in this manner, and every man will always have access to the hells in this manner, so as to forever provide free will to all of mankind. So where is God right now? He is everywhere, and yet he is nowhere, depending on where you are right now in him. For we must remember, God does not exist within time or space, but he creates, and fills time and space with his presence as thought, or Love, or Wisdom. Every man represents a single affection within the Lord, and the Lord provides this single affection, which is a man in a smaller form, with a life of its own; but this is only apparently, for we cannot really be separated from the Lord God, for we are the Lord God, in a smaller form you might say. We are kept under supervision, or in check, throughout time, or creation, because we have, according to our own fantasies, mixed with our opposites in creation, and are kept in a form of sleep. God, or the Lord can cause this with us, even though we are he, because he set it up this way in the beginning. For he created atmospheres of his opposite, and put a single affection from himself within these atmospheres, and so he created his material universe, as well as his children, which is what we are. So if we are the Lord, or gods, why can't we have absolute control over the created universe, as well as the cosmos or heavens? Because even though God cannot be separated, or divided, he found a way, within himself, so as to separate his affections, but not ever give complete rule of things to any of these single affections, and to give limited rule, which would continue to grow until forever, as each man, or affection learned to join with other affections as one in the Lord. For it is a truth that man of himself does not wish to share his things, himself, or his rule with any other, until a portion of God is allowed into his life. And because of mans free will, each man must choose to allow God into their life, and each will do so at many different levels throughout time till forever. And as we more and more allow, or ask him to come into our lives, and to provide our proper thoughts of good, which can only come from him, we all continue to get closer and closer to perfection, however never actually reaching perfection. For if man were to reach perfection, he would then be infinite, and would be God in the whole. But as long as there is a small portion of fantasy, or sleep in our life, we will continue to forever be under the guidance of the Lord. The Lord will also never trust any portion of his rule to a man who is not worthy of the responsibility, or a man who is not in love first. So if a man is in power, and he is not found to be in love while he is in power, he is not doing the Lords work, and is in hell, with the Satan's. So do you now see how man will forever continue to be saved, and all are predestined to heaven? Let me go a little further, and give more details as to how this is accomplished through God. When you go to sleep at night, and you dream, you are now residing within the spiritual world, as a spiritual being. But who ever dreams all night long, for the whole duration of their sleep period? Therefore, when each of us loses consciousness of where we are, as well as who we are, we will be given another persons consciousness before we wake up, and this person can be anyone who is within our spiritual society at the time. And of course God has complete control over who is in what spiritual society, at any given time. For instance: I can go to sleep tonight as myself, remembering all the things I said and did today, but when I awaken tomorrow morning I can awaken as someone else, having the memory and the consciousness that belongs to that person alone; knowing their complete lifelong history. And because I awaken as this person, I am responsible for this persons decisions for that whole day, until I once again enter sleep that night. Now even though I believe I am this fleshly person, I am not actually; for I am a spirit or Angel who was born long ago, or sometimes recently, but recent born spirits are usually not very wise, and are committed to the unlearned or babies most of the time. Even so, most of us are all spirits and Angels from long ago, who are still living and growing in wisdom within fleshly human beings. We are all separate affections, as well as separate men, because somewhere back in time we were all born as a single human being, and were given responsibility, at all times, for the actions of a single human being. But where we all think we are truly one, we are actually many. We were many even in our first lifetime in the material world. For there are many affections, which are men's lives that are living within us, or our spiritual society, providing our constant thoughts throughout our lifetime. Yes, we are considered as one in the flesh, but as many in the Lord, who is the spiritual world within us all. What we don't know is that we are all images of the Lord, we are little gods, and we act as little worlds. We are little gods because we are responsible for the lives of many while we live life in this human body within the material realm. We are little worlds because we have at different times as many lives living within us as there are on a single planet. As I think of it, I say to myself, hey! I know almost every detail of my life since I was a child, so how can someone wake up tomorrow as me, knowing everything I know now, and them believing for sure, that they are me. Well, every spirit or angel has access to the memory of another spirit or angel because we are all connected in the Lord, which is exactly where we are right now. The only reason I do not have the memory of every spirit or angel ever born, at this moment, is because only the Lord can store all the memory of everyone ever born. You could say he is the main computer, and we are just computer chips, who are loaded with different information, every day of our lives. But when we are loaded with this information, we believe that we have always had it, and that we have been this same person since this human body, which we possess, was born into the material world. Today I am Daniel Gross; tomorrow I could be Carol Gross, AND WALK IN HER SHOES; and the next day I could be a Chinese, African, Russian, or Spanish person, half way across the world, who doesn't even know who me or my wife are, so as to walk in their shoes as well. But as we continue in this life switch, as you may wish to call it, we do not retain our original memory, of yesterday, but we take on the memory of the person we are today. So whose life do we assume every day, and why? Every human being, spirit, or angel must continue to learn, and grow in wisdom until forever. Therefore we must trade lives with people every day in the material world, so as to experience, and eventually conquer every trial, or situation in life, or creation. In order to accomplish this we must enter the life of another, who is in that situation at any given time. We can go to sleep tonight, and wake up tomorrow on the planet Mars, and be a certain citizen of that world, or planet. We could sleep tonight, and wake up somewhere else in the world, where it is exactly the same time as when we went to sleep. For we all are aware of time differences in the world. Do you know why there are moods, or states in life? Because you can go to sleep as a happy woman and wake up as an unhappy man. Or you can go to sleep as a scared man, and wake up as a very brave, and proud woman. If I go to sleep tonight, depressed, and thinking of suicide, someone else will wake up as me tomorrow, still thinking of suicide; and this is controlled by the company we keep in the spiritual world. For if you draw from suicidal spirits today, they will return to that human body tomorrow, but as someone else. So if someone else enters your body tomorrow, your suicidal thoughts, and affections will enter into another human being tomorrow, and will harm that person's life, possibly. So be careful what you think, say, and do in life, for we affect many other lives, which we are not aware of. Where a tree falls, therein will it lay. So, when you go to sleep at night, whatever your thoughts are set on is what decides whom you enter tomorrow, and what trials you will endure. It is a fact, that in the Word, death, or to die means to sleep, which leads me to this statement. It is appointed to man to die once, and then the Judgment. Have you heard this statement before? You should have for it is in the bible, and it is so true. For every man lives for the day, sleeps, or dies to his flesh that night, and is reborn in his spirit, but within another human being. Each man also goes through the four seasons in his life, in which it ends in the winter, where he will once again sow his crop, and will reap in summer, which is when he is reborn, within another. The four seasons he endures during his lifetime of a day is morning, noon, evening, and night; so as to begin life anew at the next morning, or spring. But he cannot reap in spring, for he is a child, and is in innocence from the Lord. Noon is summer, or young adulthood, and this is when we begin to reap that in which we sowed in the past life, or yesterday night, which is winter. And as there are four seasons in creation, so too are there four stages in mans life. Starting with childhood, then young adulthood, adulthood, and old age. Spring, summer, autumn, and winter. Morning, noon, evening, and night. These are the times of our lives. But lets now speak of the fact that God recreates the past, so as to feed the present and the future with beastlike affections until forever, and gradually advancing on up to all levels of wise affections. If the past were not recreated, men would all be wise, and loving, because we all advance, or grow in love, wisdom, and knowledge until forever. Yes we are born less wise, and more beastlike than when we are older, but as man has advanced throughout the ages, he is by no means as beastlike as those in the past. The Lord cannot recreate these beastlike affections in man during the present because man must advance throughout time, and never remain the same. So the beastlike affections must come from our past, but the past is always in the Lords present. For even the past, and the future are the present within the Lord. So what do we have so far?

1] Man is first created with a beastlike nature, but he is by no means a beast.

2] Every affection that man draws from the Lord throughout his lifetime, stays with him, and makes up his love in life, till forever.

3] Once any man becomes wiser or more mature, he cannot go back to living in the beastlike manner in which he once lived, and he must continue to grow in wisdom and learn many different affections of love.

4] Affections are men, or people, and they will remain the same till forever. Whatever affection a man represents, he will represent till forever, and will provide that affection to all of creation till forever.

5] Because a man must provide beastlike affections to mankind till forever, and because even he must grow in wisdom and love till forever, it is his opposite, or counterpart who will provide the beastlike affection to all of mankind, and not his heavenly affection, which is what we all eventually represent. And because we all represent heavenly affections eventually, we must all remain as beasts in the past, for the past is the opposite of the future. Therefore what we will all become is the exact opposite of what we all once were. And because of this, even our opposite life, image, or counterpart will forever continue to provide a use for all of mankind.

6] Does this mean that all men will forever continue to be reborn, or reincarnated? Yes it does, however it will not be in the future, but in the past. For it is a truth that man is created to provide a use for the past, present, and the future.

7] It is not however; the fleshly body of ours that is being reborn in the past, but our inferior half of our spirit is born into this human being, and becomes a part of his consciousness, or life. We will never be the controlling spirit of that person, but will mix with his spirit, so as to create another spirit. Kind of like conception, or having a child from one man and one woman. And we cannot enter this person's life unless he first draws from the spiritual society in which we as a spirit live. But because he is born of a beastlike nature, he will at first draw from our beastlike affections, which are our opposite affections in hell.

8] Do not think that all hells are evil, or that one is as bad as another. For there are levels of degrees in the hells, as far as good and bad, as there are in the heavens. For the opposite of the lowest heavens is the best of the hells. And the opposite of the best heavens is the worst hells. For the opposite of not so good, is not so bad; and the opposite of very good, is very bad.

9] So in the past they draw from beastlike affections in the future, and the beastlike affections that are in the future are replenished by those of the past. And all are the present within the Lord alone. If those men in the future were not replenished with beastlike affections from the past, they would eventually run out of beastlike affections, and mankind would cease to exist. For every human being, spirit, and Angel lives within their own equilibrium, which is midway between heaven and hell; and they must remain there till forever, choosing either good thoughts from heaven, or evil thoughts, or not so good thoughts from hell. For man must always remain in free will to choose good and evil for himself. However, if man does not continue to provide the evil from the past, so as to storehouse it in the future, man could not continue to exist anymore, for the design of Gods original creation of mankind would be disrupted, or destroyed.

10] So basically, man will always begin his life as evil, because of him wanting to feed, and please his flesh. The past must continue to be recreated, and the future remains as the storehouse for the past. Man will always go through moods or states in life, and he needs these negative affections, as well as the positive, to provide his thoughts within each and every state he enters in his life until forever.

Now I wish to continue to speak on this subject, for there are many things that need explaining, if we are going to be able to grasp the idea I am attempting to share with you. And I know there will be many, who cannot accept these sayings, and for those of you who fit this category, I can only say, it is not yet your time, and I suggest you keep praying for guidance and enlightenment. Now you are probably wondering why there has to be a past, continuously recreated in time or the created realm by the Lord, when there are already good and evil affections in the spiritual world now, that provide all of mankind with his good and evil affections for his thoughts every day. Well, the good affections for thoughts are continuously being provided by the Lord in heaven, through influx that is constantly passing down through the different heavens, until it eventually reaches every man. And when these affections reach each man, he either uses them for good thoughts and acts, or he can turn them into evil thoughts and acts, depending on whether he is in a good state or a bad, or evil state at that particular point in time. And you may say well, isn't there enough evil men in the world today to provide all the evil affections needed for mankind's continued existence? The answer is no, there is not, because man draws his affections from the spiritual world, and not the other way around. And because God replenishes the good affections in time constantly, man must provide the evil affections in time constantly. For creation is not a thing that is accomplished, and then it stays till forever. God must continue to create all things every moment in time. And where God recreates the good, man recreates the evil, not knowing that he does so however. For mans affections create the material world, from the spiritual world, even though the original source is always God. And as long as there is a single affection in the material world for any material thing, that thing will continue to be recreated within the material realm by the thoughts of man. Man does not realize this because he never remains in one place long enough to notice it. We think we do, but sleep takes care of this situation every day. There are however things that God will not allow mans thoughts to recreate, and this is things of the past that are only meant for certain Ages in time. Such examples would be Dinosaurs, cavemen, or anything else that does not fit in our era, or things that would not be for the greater good of mankind. For Dinosaurs would be destroyed by man today, and would not serve as any use for man, as they did when they were created. Yes they will be created many more times, in our past, but to generations who use them for what they were meant for, and they will not wish to harm man. So because of this, man must also exist in the past, present, and the future just as God does. The difference is we are created, and he is not. We are finite, but he is infinite. We will forever owe our existence to the Lord continuously recreating us all, whereas the Lord will never owe his existence to anyone. So man does not provide, or supply evil affections in the present, but he draws on, or takes from the supply of evil affections that are constantly being supplied by those in the past; and by mans mixing his affections with those he draws from the storehouse, he creates new evil affections so that the hells can stay in stride with the heavens. For remember, for every affection that exists within the heavens, there must be an exact opposite affection of bad or evil to be found within the hells, at all times. As the past mixes with the future, in the Lord, new affections are born, which means new men are born. The good are stored in the Lord, and the evil stored opposite the Lord, in fantasy, or the hells. And not only does every man have to be supplied with his own evil, as well as good affections, until he leaves this material world, but every spirit and angel must be supplied with his own good and bad affections as well. But all of these can by no means be supplied with their affections of evil, simply by those men who live in the material world today. For not only do world populations continue to grow throughout time, but so do the number of worlds. And remember this, spirits and angels do not supply themselves with affections, but draw them from others. And each spirit is a single affection, and Angels are many, but they provide affections to the material world. Spirits and angels receive their affections from their own society, and not outside that society. But if an affection is a man, no matter what world he exists in, and we all continue to advance in wisdom, love, and maturity, what happens to the evil affection, that those in hell use to represent, but have moved on to a better society in the spiritual world? And what happens when man no longer acts or lives as beasts do, and he is a little, or a lot more godlike? In other words, is it not a fact that if man is to continue to become better, or greater in heavenly wisdom, and the lowest of these in the world are still above the beasts in good affections by far, and in wisdom; where do the beastlike affections continue to be provided for the spiritual realm? For if man is offered the greatest affections of wisdom and love, he must also continuously be offered the most worst of the affections of wisdom and love, which are beastlike to the most extreme. Where do these affections come from? Again, the past! And again, they cannot be offered by the present. So no matter how advanced mans wisdom becomes, he must always, according to Gods plan, be offered the lowest of affections until forever. If man did not exist within the thoughts of God this could never had been possible, but because of our Father and Gods love, he has made it possible. You may say to yourself, well what is so loving about a God that provides evil to his children? But he is not providing evil to his children; he is allowing the evil to become his children, eventually. For there is not a creature that has ever lived that can disregard Gods love till forever, without eventually becoming a loving being himself, no matter how long it may take for him to do so. For God did not directly create evil, but man did; and God will save all men in spite of themselves; good and evil. But because evil spirits are meant to reside in the hells forever, never leaving that place, the evil spirits must be constantly replaced as they are advancing in good, and entering the higher realms. One comes in and the other, which has earned his departure, goes on to a better society. This is accomplished by the past being constantly recreated. Now evil was permitted to exist so as to create lives that were separate (at least apparently separate) from God. For God cannot be happy just loving himself, and wanted to create children to love, and to be loved by him, and others. We are not really separate from God, and we do not even have a separate consciousness from him, but he allows us to live as though it were this way. By doing it this way, we see our selves as separate beings from God; at least at first, until we have matured, and have been regenerated by God, so as to eventually know whom we are. For who we truly are is God, but we are Gods affections bound by flesh, until our school of love and life is complete. As we grow worthy of his trust to rule certain people, things, and governments with the Lord, he will allow us to do so. But only he knows when each of us is ready, and only he can choose when to cut us loose. Yes, we are God, but we only represent one single affection of God. But what is of God is most certainly God, is it not? Yes it is! The fact that he chose to separate single affections from himself, and to house them permanently in a bubble called an atmosphere, and to allow them to believe they are separate beings from himself, and the rest of mankind, was Gods own will, and he has all the right to do as he pleases, for he is God. So even though we are all God, we will forever be required to submit to Gods rule and authority, for he alone knows what is best for us all. But do not forget we are all heirs to his throne, and we are truly his children, and therefore he sets no limits as to what each and every one of his children can achieve in their lifetime, and this is why he allows us all to continue to live forever. So if man has been around for ages upon ages, which should be understood by the simple fact that the past began with God, and in God. So if it began with, and in God; and God is the same yesterday, today, and forever, then man has been around since eternity. And who does not know that eternity has no beginning or end. Yes, man is finite, simply because he owes his existence to God alone, but to prove that man had a beginning can only be done by God, since he was truly the only one there at the time of mans beginning. Man was there, but only in a made up world, which does not really exist. So I will state once again, man has been around for ages upon ages, or since eternity, and everything God has created, or permitted to be created by man, has been for mans benefit alone. We find the bones or fossils of creatures in this world that have been buried for a hundred thousand, a million, or even ten million years, and we assume they lived for themselves in these time periods, and apply no connection to the fact that man was there in this same time period, living right along side these creatures. We have made no conclusions to the fact that these creatures may have been put there for mans benefit, and to actually aid in mans daily efforts or chores, somewhere along the line. These creatures are known as Pre-Historic animals, or Dinosaurs. And they not only lived during the building of the Pyramids in Egypt, but they have lived during many different Ages, and will return just the same, for many Ages to come, until forever. For the past does repeat itself as we understand it, but it repeats itself in the past, where the past still exists within the Lord. We as men have all seen Dinosaurs before in our lives, even though we do not remember, and we have seen many lives living within human beings since the beginning of time, even though we have no recollection of any beginning of time. For all men will live forever as Angels, always within a single human being. But the human being will be different for many days to come, many years to come, and even many Ages to come. For as I have explained, we enter a different human being every morning in which we awaken from the spiritual world, or our sleep. If you sit and think about it, even though God gives me these amazing revelations even as I am sitting here typing, we should all see, to some degree, that God has drawn a perfect plan for creation. And once we hear of the whole plan, if it is his will that I announce it all in full, or at least most of it, I am sure you too will agree, it is amazing. But let me first ask you a question: Do any of you really think God would create any creature that would harm a man, or even kill him, if he were a good man? So what kept Dinosaurs from killing good men? For I am sure we are all aware that they did not possess any exceptional reasoning power, to cause them to rationalize that it is wrong to kill a man, good or evil. Answer: Dinosaurs were created to serve man, and nothing more. Yes, they were used later for food, but this was not Gods predestined design, it was only a foreseen thing, in which God knew would eventually come about because of mans free will. And even though we were all once guilty of this crime, because we lived in the past, long ago, we will no longer see actual, material Dinosaurs again in the future. For they no longer have a place in this world we live in, where machines are used instead. They will however continue to exist throughout the past Ages, so as to still serve their intended purpose for mankind. If God were to never allow Dinosaurs to exist in the world ever again, why would he put them here in the first place, seeing that God is the same yesterday, today, and forever. Not only that, but God is not a respecter of persons, and he provides all things to all generations, so that all men experience the same situations throughout their lifetime. But even though we will all live forever, this does not mean that Dinosaurs will one day show up again in our future. For we have no need to learn to build pyramids any longer, for they are temporary, and are of this material world, which will one day fade away with time, if it is Gods will. We need only know that the wisdom behind the pyramids is found in God, and those he intends to show. For even though a generation may be ignorant in worldly knowledge, this does not mean they cannot be given Godly knowledge, no matter what the state of knowledge, or technology in the world. It is a truth that God will send his chosen back to the world within all different technological eras, and that the Kingdom of Heaven is forever presented to the innocent of the world, no matter what their maturity level in the world may be. For it is a truth that the Most Ancient Church, which is the Celestial, or Heavenly Church has existed throughout the past, no matter how wise or ignorant man may have been found to be. This is why God said his Wisdom will appear as foolishness to those who see themselves as wise in the world, and he will teach only those who see themselves as foolish, or unlearned in their own eyes. The pyramids have withstood the test of time to show those that were obedient to God, and were able to build wonderfully designed pyramids, as well as those who were disobedient to God, and these later built pyramids show the outcome. For when man later began to rely on his own knowledge, he not only lost the knowledge to build pyramids, but he killed off his Gigantic helpers in the Dinosaurs, as the evil began to once again grow throughout the world, as the church also declined in good and truth, and its consummation was eminent. Even today these pyramids stand as a testimony to these truths, and man chooses to use his own worldly explanations to explain Dinosaurs and pyramids. And as the future takes form, the pyramids are being created anew in the past, as a continued testimony to those to come. Do you ever look at the foundations of mankind's buildings, and then look at the foundation of Gods buildings, and wonder if we can ever achieve the wisdom of God? Well, my dear brothers, we cannot ever reach that height, but he allows us to go as far as our mind can ever take us. Do you however, believe that foundations, and signs of the times, are all that the pyramids were meant to teach us? They are also teaching us that man is the base, or foundation for the spiritual world, and that it is bigger because man wants it all, or at least as much as he can get out of this material world. On the other hand, the smaller in size we grow, or reach, the closer we come to the spiritual world, until we eventually vanish out of mans sight. We also gather from the point of the pyramid that the higher we go in the spiritual world, the higher we travel in the heavens, and the less we wish things for ourselves, but wish the good of our neighbor first. The Pyramids are a perfect material example of the Kingdom of Heaven. He who is greatest in this world will become least in the heavens, and he who is least in this world will become greatest in the Heavens. For to be higher up in the spiritual world is to be closer to God, and greatest in the heavens, but least in the material realm, where the peak of the pyramids are seen as their smallest point. God cannot build pyramids in the material world without using creatures from the material world to build them, and we know what creatures he used, don't we. For God is not a worker of magician's tricks, but causes all things in this world to be created from this world. There are no pyramids being built now, because there are no Dinosaurs around now; and there are no Dinosaurs around now because man has come to a point where he relies mostly on his wisdom to create and build in this world, and God has stepped back so as to show him what will become of mans creations and devices. Man has always wanted more, and he has for generations come up with ways to make more, and to make life easier on himself. For an example: could you imagine a man today cutting down a tree with a two-man hand saw? And can you imagine him cutting it into pieces with a saw, as well? Man believes that if he devises a way to save time, that he can cut more wood, sell more wood, and make more money. But who sends the buying customers to him in the first place? God does! Who allows it to get cold enough to need wood to burn in the first place? God does! And who allows a man to live each day, and to get out of bed, and gives him the strength to cut the wood in the first place? God does! So if a man uses a chainsaw to cut down a tree, or even two trees in a day, who will guarantee whether or not he even sells one stick of wood when he is done? God does! This not only applies to wood, but to every job a man, or woman goes to every day. God chooses if we get a raise, forty hours, or even if the boss sends us home early for three days, and we only get paid for two. God decides if we work all week, or even if a self employed, or some other type employed person, has any work at all each week. He decides if the weather is good, or if we get three feet of snow, get snowed in, and don't get paid for two or three weeks. And all these things are decided by God, even though all men have free will. How? Because you are not a single man in this world, but your human life is controlled by many, many human beings from the past, who live within you, and God chooses which ones to let live within you, so as to effect his will in you every day. Yes we have free will, but we don't know where we are drawing our thoughts of affections from each moment, and God does; and so he can decide who is where, within each man. Still don't understand? Lets try one more time:

You are a human being, or man, and you have free will. But you are not one human being, or man wrapped up in that fleshly person you call yourself. You are also a spirit, or spiritual being, and your spirit lives within the spiritual realm at all times. Your spirit lives within what is called a society, and it lives there with an unlimited number of other spirits and Angels. And every society, or man has at least two evil spirits, and two Angels living within him, at all times, but this number grows as man grows and matures. So since each spirit or angel represents a single affection, and your thoughts in a single day are made up of millions of different affections, you have millions of spirits or angels, or both, living within you in the period of a single day. And these spirits and angels are people just like you. The only difference is that you think you are that fleshly person that you look in the mirror at every day, but you are not. That flesh is nothing more than the base of a pyramid, and supports the spiritual world within. And just as there is a spiritual world living within man, so too is there one living within the pyramids of old. You don't see them because they actually exist within another world; but we will cover that at another time. So as I was saying, this fleshly human body we carry around every day is only the form, or shell for our spiritual society to live in and act out our thoughts and life, till it takes on another human form. But it could take on another human form tomorrow. This is because God cannot control a person's free will, but he can control what spirit enters your fleshly body tomorrow morning before you wake up. And this spirit can be of any nature he chooses, because he chooses what state you will be in when you wake up. But this spirit must represent the affection, or state in which you were in when you entered sleep that night. And God has control of these issues. Therefore, God is in control of every human being, till forever. Even if God wishes a certain thought or act from you in the middle of the day, he can cause this by the spirits he allows into your society that day, with each spirit being in the exact state he wishes them to be when they are called on by you and your thoughts. The changes in affection and state are always done within the spiritual realm, within your society, so as to never cause confusion within this material world. We will continue this subject in days to come, but for now I will end by saying, things in this world are by no means what they appear, and we should never put our complete trust in man.

We will now move on to some writings of the Swedish scientist and Christian author known as Emanuel Swedenborg. These writings I am about to quote were inspired in him by the spiritual world, directly from the Lord. But in order to receive these wonderful revelations from God, you must begin in faith, and remain in faith throughout these works. This work is a continuation of the four Doctrines in which the Lord presented to Swedenborg, of which I have already presented the "Doctrine of the Lord," to you in my last book. These doctrines were held back from man until their set time, and are to be included in the works of the "Little Scroll," mentioned in the book of Daniel, as well as the book of Revelation. They do not complete the scroll, but are only to be included in it. And now I begin with the second of the four doctrines written by Swedenborg, of which I am in full agreement.

"The Doctrine of Sacred Scripture" (All page numbers will coincide with original numbering; which was before printing.)

[1] The Sacred Scripture, or the Word, is the Divine Truth itself. It is generally agreed that the Word is from God, is divinely inspired, and therefore holy; but hitherto it has remained unknown wherin its divinity resides; for the Word in the letter appears like common writing in a strange style, lacking the sublimity and brilliance which are apparently features of the literature of the world. For this reason the man who worships nature instead of God, or in preference to God, and who consequently thinks from* himself and his proprium** and not from* heaven from* the Lord, may easily fall into error respecting the Word and into contempt for it, and say within himself as he reads it; What does this mean? What does that mean? Is this divine? Can God, to whom belongs infinite

wisdom, speak in this way? Where is its sanctity, or whence derived but from mans religious credulity? * The propositions ex and a, both translated "from", are here used in contrast, a indicating the responsible agent or originating source, and ex an instrumental agent, or intermediary, contributing to the performance of an action, but not itself the source. ** The Latin word Proprium means "what is ones own." Swedenborg uses it in a special sense involving "what is of the self."

[2] He however, who thinks in this way does not consider that Jehovah himself, who is the God of heaven and earth, spoke the Word by means of Moses and the Prophets, and consequently that it must be Divine Truth itself; for what Jehovah himself speaks is Divine Truth. Nor does he consider that the Lord, who is the same as Jehovah, spoke the Word written by the Evangelists, much of it from His own mouth, and the rest from the spirit of His mouth, which is the Holy Spirit. For this reason He Himself declares that in His words there is life, that He is the light, which enlightens, and that He is the truth.

2. That Jehovah Himself spoke the Word by the Prophets has been shown in "The Doctrine of the New Jerusalem Concerning the Lord," Nos. 52,53. That the words which the Lord Himself spoke in the Evangelists are life, is declared in John:
    The words that I speak unto you are spirit, and they are life (John 6:63).

In the same Evangelist:
    Jesus said to the woman at Jacobs well, If thou knewest the gift of God, and who it is that saith to thee, Give me to drink; thou wouldst have asked of Him, and He would have given thee living water. Whosoever drinketh of the water that I shall give him, shall never thirst; but the water that I shall give him shall be in him a well of water springing up into everlasting life (John 4:6,10,14).

By Jacobs well is signified the Word, as also in Deut. 33:28; and for this reason also the Lord sat there, and spoke with the woman; and by water is signified the truth of the Word. In the same Evangelist:
    If any man thirst, let him come unto me, and drink. He that believeth on me, as the scripture saith, out of his belly shall flow rivers of living water (John 7:37,38).

In the same:
    Peter said to Jesus, Thou hast the words of eternal life (John 6:68). For this reason the Lord says in Mark, "Heaven and earth shall pass away, but my words shall not pass away (Mark 13:31). The words of the Lord are life, because He Himself is the life and the truth, as He teaches in John:

I am the way, the truth, and the life (John 14:6); and in the same:

In the beginning was the Word, and the Word was with God, and the Word was God. In Him was life; and the life was the light of men (John 1:1,4). By the Word here is meant the Lord as to Divine Truth, in which alone there is life and light. For this reason the Word, which is from the Lord, is called a fountain of living waters (Jeremiah 2:13; 17:13; 31:9); a fountain of salvation (Isaiah 12:3); a fountain (Zechariah 13:1); and a river of water of life (Revelation 22:1); and it is said that:

The Lamb which is in the midst of the throne shall feed them, and shall lead them unto living fountains of water (Revelation 7:17); besides other passages, where the Word is also called the Sanctuary and the Tabernacle, in which the Lord dwells with man.

[3] From these considerations however, the natural man still cannot be persuaded that the Word is Divine Truth itself, in which is Divine Wisdom as well as Divine Life; for he regards it from its style, in which he does not see these things. Yet the style of the Word is the Divine style itself, with which no other style, however sublime and excellent it may seem, can be compared, for any other style is as thick darkness compared with light. The style of the Word is such that there is holiness in every sentence, and in every word; indeed, in some places, in the very letters; and consequently the Word conjoins man with the Lord, and opens heaven.

2. There are two things, which proceed from the Lord, Divine Love and Divine Wisdom, or what is the same, Divine Good and Divine Truth; for Divine Good is of His Divine Love, and Divine Truth is of His Divine Wisdom. The Word in its essence is both of these; and since it conjoins man with the Lord and opens heaven, as has just been said, therefore the Word fills the man who reads it from the Lord, and not from himself, alone, with the good of love, and the truths of wisdom. His will with the good of love, and His understanding with the truths of wisdom; thus man has life through the Word.

[4] Lest therefore, men should be in doubt that the Word is of this nature, the Lord has revealed to me its internal sense. This in its essence is spiritual, and resides in the external sense, which is natural, as the soul in the body. This internal sense is the spirit, which gives life to the letter, and it can therefore bear witness to the divinity and holiness of the Word, and it can convince even the natural man, if he is willing to be convinced.

[5] II

In the Word there is a spiritual sense, hitherto unknown.

The following points will be explained in this order:

1. What the spiritual sense is. 2. This sense is in the whole of the Word, and in every part of it. 3. Because of this sense the Word is Divinely inspired, and holy

in every word. 4. This sense has hitherto been unknown. 5. Henceforth it will be made known only to those who are in genuine truths from the Lord.

1. WHAT THE SPIRITUAL SENSE IS. The spiritual sense is not that which shines forth from the sense of the letter of the Word, when one searches the Word and explains it to confirm some dogma of the church: this sense is the literal sense of the Word. The spiritual sense however, does not appear in the sense of the letter: it is within it, as the soul is in the body, as the thought is in the eyes, and as affection is in the countenance; and these act together as cause and effect. It is this sense especially that makes the Word spiritual, not only for men but also for Angels; and therefore the Word by means of this sense communicates with the heavens.

[6] From the Lord proceed the Celestial, the Spiritual, and the Natural; one after another. What proceeds from Hid Divine Love is called the Celestial, and is Divine Good; what proceeds from His Divine Wisdom is called the Spiritual, and is Divine Truth. The Natural is from both and is their complex in the ultimate [or lowest] degree. The angels of the Lords Celestial kingdom, who constitute the third or highest heaven, are in that Divine proceeding from the Lord, which is called the Celestial, for they are in the good of love from the Lord. The angels of the Lords Spiritual kingdom, who constitute the second or middle heaven, are in that Divine proceeding from the Lord, which is called the Spiritual, for they are in the truths of wisdom from the Lord. * Men of the church in the world however, are in the Divine Natural, which also proceeds from the Lord. From this it follows that the Divine proceeding from the Lord to its ultimates, descends through three degrees, and is termed Celestial, Spiritual, and Natural. The Divine, which descends from the Lord to men, comes down through these three degrees; and when it has descended, it contains these three degrees in itself. Such is the nature of everything Divine; therefore when it is in its ultimate degree, it is in its fullness. This is the nature of the Word. In its ultimate sense it is natural, in its interior sense it is spiritual, and in its inmost sense it is celestial; and in each it is Divine. That the Word is of this nature is not apparent in the sense of its letter, as this is natural; because man when in the world has hitherto not known anything concerning the heavens; and consequently has not known what the spiritual is, and what the celestial; thus he has not known the difference between these and the natural.

[7] The difference between these degrees cannot be known unless by a knowledge of correspondence. For these three degrees are quite distinct from each other, like end, cause, and effect; or like what is prior, posterior, and postreme [or last], yet they make one by correspondences, for the natural corresponds to the spiritual, and also to the celestial. What correspondence is may be seen in the work on "Heaven and Hell," where it treats of the correspondence of all things in heaven with all things in man, Nos. 87-102; and the correspondence [of all

things] in heaven with all things on earth, Nos. 103-115. It will also be further seen from examples quoted below from the Word.

[8] Since the Word interiorly is spiritual and celestial, it is therefore written by means of pure correspondences; and what is thus written is in its ultimate sense, written in such a style as is seen in the Prophets and Evangelists which, although it appears ordinary, yet has stored up within it Divine Wisdom and all Angelic Wisdom.

[9] 2. THE SPIRITUAL SENSE IS IN THE WHOLE OF THE WORD, AND IN EVERY PART OF IT. This cannot be better seen than from examples, such as the following:

John says in Revelation, I saw heaven opened, and beheld a white horse; and He that sat upon him was called faithful and true; and in righteousness He doth judge and make war. His eyes were as a flame of fire, and on His head were many crowns; and He had a name written that no man knew but He Himself. And He was clothed with a vesture dipped in blood: and His name is called, "The Word of God." His armies, which were in heaven, followed Him upon white horses; clothed in fine linen, white and clean . . . He hath on His vesture and on His thigh a name written, King of kings and Lord of lords. And I saw an angel standing in the sun; and he cried with a loud voice . . . Come and gather yourselves together unto the great supper . . . That ye may eat the flesh of kings, and the flesh of captains, and the flesh of mighty men, and the flesh of horses and of them that sit on them, and the flesh of all men, both free and bond, both small and great (Revelation 19: 11-18). No one can see what these things signify except from the spiritual sense of the Word, and no one can see the spiritual sense except from a knowledge of correspondences; for all the words are correspondences and not one word is without

*   Authors Note: The heavens consist of two kingdoms, one of which is called the celestial kingdom, and the other the spiritual kingdom. This may be seen on the work "Heaven and Hell." Nos. 20-28. meaning. The science of correspondences teaches the signification of the white horse, of Him that sat upon it, of His eyes which were like a flame of fire, of the crowns which were on His head, of His vesture dipped in blood, of the white linen with which they who were of His army in heaven were clothed, of the angel standing in the sun, of the great supper to which they should come, and gather themselves, and also of the flesh of kings, captains and many others which they were to eat. What each of these particulars signifies in the spiritual sense may be seen in the little work on "The White Horse," where they are explained. It is therefore unnecessary to explain them further here. In that treatise it is shown that the Lord is here described as to the Word; by His eyes, which were as a flame of fire, by the crowns, which were upon His head, and by the name, which no one knoweth, but Himself, is meant the SPIRITUAL SENSE of the Word, which

no one knows but the Lord Himself and he to whom He wills to reveal it. Further, that by His vesture dipped in blood is meant the NATURAL SENSE of the Word, which is the sense of the letter, to which violence has been done. That it is the Word that is thus described is clearly manifest, for it is said, His name is called the Word of God; and that it is the Lord who is meant is also clearly manifest, for it is said the name of Him who sat on the white horse was written, King of kings and Lord of lords. That the spiritual sense of the Word is to be opened at the end of the church is signified not only by what is said of the white horse and of Him who sat thereon, but also by the great supper to which the angel standing in the sun invited all to come, and to eat the flesh of kings, and of captains, of mighty men, of horses and of those that sat upon them, and of all, both free and bond. All these expressions would be empty words and without life and spirit unless there were something spiritual within them, as the soul is in the body.

[10] In Revelation, chapter 21, the Holy Jerusalem is described:

In her was a light like a stone most precious, like a jasper stone, clear as crystal; and had a wall great and high, and had twelve gates, and at the gates twelve angels, and names written thereon which are the names of the twelve tribes of the Children of Israel. The wall was a hundred and forty and four cubits, according to the measure of a man, that is, of the angel. And the building of the wall of it was of jasper; and its foundations of all manner of precious stones, of jasper, of sapphire, chalcedony, emerald, sardonyx, sardius, chrysolyte, beryl, topaz, chrysoprasus, jacinth, and amethyst. The gates were twelve pearls. The city itself was pure gold, like clear glass; and it was four-square, the length, breadth and the height being equal; twelve thousand furlongs [Revelation 21:11,12, 16-21 with many other particulars]. That all these things are to be understood spiritually may be evident from this, that by the Holy Jerusalem is signified a new church which is to be established by the Lord, as is shown in "The Doctrine of the Lord," Num. 62-65. Since the church is here signified by Jerusalem it follows that all things said of it as a city, of its gates, its wall, the foundations of its wall, as well as their measures, contain a spiritual sense; for the things which relate to the church are spiritual. What the particulars signify is explained in the work on "THE NEW JERUSALEM," published in London in the year 1758, No. 1; and I therefore refrain from any further explanation of them here. It is sufficient to know from that work that there is a spiritual sense within all the particulars of the description, like a soul in the body,; and that without this sense nothing relating to the church would be understood in the things there written; as, that the city was of pure gold, its gates were of pearls, its wall of jasper, the foundations of its wall of precious stones, that its wall was a hundred and forty and four cubits, which is the measure of a man, that is, of an angel; that the city was in length, breadth, and height, twelve thousand furlongs, and so on. Anyone however, who has a knowledge of the spiritual sense from the science of correspondences understands those things, as for instance that the wall and its foundations signify doctrine from the literal sense of the Word, and that the numbers twelve, one hundred and forty four, and twelve thousand have a like signification, namely the sum total of all the truths and goods of the church.

[11] In Revelation chapter 7 it is said:

That there were sealed one hundred and forty and four thousand, twelve thousand of each tribe of Israel; the same number of the tribe of Judah, of Reuben, of Gad, of Asher, of Naphtali, the tribe of Manasses, of Simeon, of Levi, of Issachar, of Zebulon, of Joseph and of Benjamin.

The spiritual sense of these words is, that all are saved with whom there is the church from the Lord, for in the spiritual sense, to be marked in the forehead, or sealed, signifies to be acknowledged by the Lord and saved. By the twelve tribes of Israel are signified all of that church; by twelve, twelve thousand, and one hundred and forty and four thousand, are signified all; by Israel is signified the church; and by each tribe something specific of the church. Anyone who does not know this spiritual meaning of these words may suppose that ONLY A CERTAIN NUMBER ARE TO BE SAVED, and these only from the Israelitish and Jewish nation.

[12] In Revelation chapter 6, it is said that:

When the Lamb opened the first seal of the book, there went forth a WHITE HORSE: and He that sat on him had a bow, and a crown was given to Him . . . When He had opened the second seal, there went forth a RED HORSE: and to him that sat thereon a great sword was given. When he had opened the third seal, there went forth a BLACK HORSE: and he that sat on him had a pair of balances (statera) in his hand. And when he had opened the fourth seal, there went forth a PALE HORSE: and his name that sat on him was death (Revelation 6:1-5,7,8). What these things signify can only be unfolded by means of the spiritual sense; and it is fully unfolded when it is known what is signified by the opening of the seals, by a horse, and by the other particulars. By these things are described the successive states of the church from the beginning to its end as to the understanding of the Word. The opening of the seals of the book by the Lamb signifies the manifestation of those states of the church by the Lord. A HORSE signifies the UNDERSTANDING OF THE WORD; the WHITE HORSE the understanding of truth from the Word (in the first state of the church!); the bow of him that sat upon that horse signifies the Doctrine of Charity and Faith combating against falsities; the crown, eternal life, the reward of victory.

2.   The RED HORSE signifies the understanding of the Word destroyed as to good in the second state of the church; the great sword signifying falsity combating against truth.

The BLACK HORSE signifies the understanding of the Word destroyed as to truth in the third state of the church; the pair of balances (statera) signifying the estimation of truth so small as to be hardly appreciable.

The PALE HORSE signifies the understanding of the Word nullified from evils of life and consequent falsities in the fourth or last state of the church; and death signifies eternal damnation.

That such is the signification of these things in the spiritual sense does not appear in the sense of the letter or the natural sense. Therefore, unless the spiritual sense were at sometime opened, the Word as to this passage, and as to the rest of Revelation, would be closed so completely that at length no one would know where its Divine sanctity lay concealed. It is equally so in respect to what is signified by the four horses and by the four chariots going forth from between the two mountains of brass, in Zechariah 6:1-8.

[13] In Revelation 9 we read:

The fifth angel sounded, and I saw a star fall from heaven unto the earth: and to him was given the key of the bottomless pit. And he opened the bottomless pit; and there arose a smoke out of the pit, as the smoke of a great furnace; and the sun and the air were darkened by reason of the smoke of the pit. And there came out of the smoke locusts upon the earth: and unto them was given power, as the scorpions of the earth have power . . . The shapes of the locusts were like unto horses prepared unto battle; and on their heads were as it were crowns like gold, and their faces were as the faces of men. And they had hair as the hair of women, and their teeth were as the teeth of lions. And they had . . . breastplates of iron; and the sound of their wings was as the sound of chariots of many [horses] running to battle. And they had tails like as unto scorpions, and there were stings in their tails: and their power was to hurt men five months. And they had a king over them, which is the angel of the bottomless pit, whose name in the Hebrew tongue is Abaddon, but in the Greek tongue hath his name Apollyon (Revelation 9:1-3,7-11). These things also no one would understand unless the spiritual sense were revealed to him; for nothing here is said without meaning: everything, even to each particular, has a signification. The subject here treated of is the state of the church when all cognitions * of truth from the Word have been destroyed, and consequently man, having become sensual, persuades himself that falsities are truths.

2. By the star fallen from heaven is signified the cognitions of truth destroyed; by the sun and the air being darkened is signified the light of truth become thick darkness; by the locusts which went forth out of the smoke of that pit are signified falsities in ultimates (extremis) such as are with those who have become sensual, and who see and judge all things from fallacies; by a scorpion is signified their persuasive power. The locusts appearing as horses prepared for battle signifies their reasoning's as from the understanding of truth; that the locusts had crowns

like gold upon their heads, and faces like the faces of men, signifies that they appeared to themselves as conquerors and wise; their having hair as the hair of women signifies that they appeared to themselves as if they were in the affection of truth; and their having teeth as the teeth of lions signifies that sensual things, which are the lowest things of the natural man, appeared to them as if they had power over all things.

3. That they had breastplates as breastplates of iron signifies argumentations from fallacies, by which they fight and prevail. The sound of their wings being as the sound of chariots running to battle signifies reasons as from truths of doctrine from the Word, for which truths they were to combat; their having tails as scorpions signifies persuasions; their having stings in their tails signifies craftiness in deceiving by means of their persuasions. Their having power to hurt men five months signifies that they bring into a kind of stupor those who are in the understanding of truth and in the perception of good. That they have over them a king, the angel of the bottomless pit whose name is Abaddon or Apollyon, signifies that their falsities were from hell, where those are who are merely natural and in self-intelligence.

4. This is the spiritual sense of these words of which nothing appears in the sense of the letter; and it is the same throughout the Revelation. It should be known that in the spiritual sense all things cohere in a continuous sequence, to the perfect arrangement of which each word contributes in the sense of the letter, or natural sense. Thus, if the smallest word were taken away the sequence would be broken and the connection would be destroyed. Lest this should happen therefore, at the end of this prophetical book it is added, that not a word should be taken away (Revelation 22:19).

It is the same with the books of the Prophets of the Old Testament. Lest anything should be taken away from these, it was brought about by the Divine Providence of the Lord that each particular in them was counted, even to the letters. This was done by the Masoretes.**

[14] Where the Lord speaks to His disciples about the consummation of the age, which is the last phase of the church, at the end of His predictions concerning its successive changes of state, He says,

Immediately after the tribulation of those days shall the sun be darkened, and the moon shall not give her light, and the stars shall fall from heaven, and the powers of the heavens shall be shaken:

And then shall appear the sign of the Son of Man in heaven: and then shall all the tribes of the earth mourn, and they shall see the Son of Man coming in the clouds of heaven with power and great glory. And He shall send His angels with a great sound of a trumpet, and they shall gather together His elect from the four winds, from one end of the heavens to the other (Matthew 24: 29-31).

2. By these words in the spiritual sense it is not meant that the sun and the moon would be darkened, that the stars would fall from heaven, that the sign of the Lord would appear in heaven, and the He would be seen in the clouds; and also that angels with trumpets would be seen. But by the expressions in this passage are meant spiritual things relating to the church, concerning the state of which at its end these things are said. For in the spiritual sense, by the sun which shall be darkened is meant the Lord as to love; by the moon which shall not give her light (lumen) is meant the Lord as to faith; by the stars which shall fall from heaven, the cognitions of good and truth which will perish; by the sign of the Son of Man in heaven, the appearing of Divine Truth; and by the tribes of the earth that shall mourn the want of all truth which is of faith, and of all good which is of love. By the coming of the Son of Man in the clouds of heaven in power and glory is

* The term cognitiones, here used in the Latin, is translated "cognitions" to distinguish these knowledge's from those that are meant by the Latin scientifica also used in the writings of Swedenborg. Two of the meanings most commonly associated with cognitiones are, (1) A particular species of knowledge, as knowledge's of the Word, of good and truth, or of spiritual things (A.C. 24,3665,9945; N.J.H.D. 51; H.H. 111, 351, 469,474,517,518); AND (2) A higher type of knowledge which is from understanding and perception (A.C. 1486-7; H.H. 353). ** These were Jewish Rabbis whose object was to preserve the integrity of the text of the Hebrew Scriptures. Meant the presence of the Lord in the Word, and revelation; by the clouds is signified the sense of the letter of the Word, and by glory, the spiritual sense of the Word. By the angels with a great sound of a trumpet is signified heaven, whence comes Divine Truth; by gathering together the elect from the four winds from one end of the heavens to the other, is signified that which is new (novum) in the church as to love and faith.

3. That the darkening of the sun and moon, and the falling of the stars to the earth, are not here meant, clearly appears from the Prophets, for in them similar things are said concerning the state of the church when the Lord was about to come into the world. Thus in Isaiah:

Behold, the day of Jehovah cometh, cruel . . . with fierce anger . . . For the stars of the heavens and the constellations thereof shall not give their light: the sun shall be darkened in His going forth, and the moon shall not cause her light to shine. And I will punish the world for their evil (Isaiah 13:9-11; 14:21,23).

In Joel:

The day of Jehovah cometh . . . A day of darkness and of thick darkness . . . The sun and the moon shall be dark. And the stars shall withdraw their shining (Joel 2:1,2,10; 3:15).

In Ezekiel:

I will cover the heavens, and make the stars thereof dark; I will cover the sun with a cloud, and the moon shall not give her light. All the bright lights . . . will I make dark . . . and set darkness upon thy land (Ezekiel 32:7,8).

By the day of Jehovah is meant the Coming of the Lord, which took place when there was no longer any good and truth left in the church nor any rational conception of the Lord.

[15] In order that it may be seen that the prophetic parts of the Word of the Old Testament are, in many places, not intelligible without the spiritual sense, I would adduce a few passages only; as in Isaiah:

Then shall Jehovah stir up a scourge against Assyria, according to the slaughter of Midian at the rock of Oreb: and as his rod was upon the sea so shall he lift it up after the manner of Egypt. And it shall come to pass in that day, that his burden shall be taken away from off thy shoulder, and his yoke from off thy neck . . . He shall come to Aiath, he shall pass to Migron; at Michmash he shall give orders to his arms (A.V. he hath laid up his carriages). They shall pass over Mebarah; Gibeah shall be a lodging for us; Ramah shall be afraid; Gibeah of Saul shall flee. Lift up thy voice, O daughter of Gallim; give ear, O Laish, O poor Anathoth. Madmenah is removed; the inhabitants of Gebim shall gather themselves together . . . As yet shall he remain at Nob that day? He shall shake his hand the mountain of the daughter of Zion, the hill of Jerusalem . . . Jehovah shall cut down the thickets of the forest with iron, and Lebanon shall fall by a mighty one (Isaiah 10:26-34). In this passage only names occur from which nothing can be drawn but by the aid of the spiritual sense; and in this sense all names in the Word signify things of heaven and the church. From this sense it is gathered that by these things is signified that the whole church was devastated by natural knowledge (scientifica) perverting all truth and confirming falsity.

2. Elsewhere in the same Prophet: In that day . . . the envy also of Ephraim shall depart and the adversaries of Judah shall be cut off: Ephraim shall not envy Judah, and Judah shall not vex Ephraim. But they shall fly upon the shoulder of the Philistines towards the sea (A.V. the west) they shall spoil the children of the east together: Edom and Moab shall be the laying on (emissio) of their hand. Jehovah shall utterly destroy the tongue of the Egyptian sea; and with the vehemence of His spirit shall He shake His hand over the river; and shall smite it in the seven streams, and make it a way for men to go over dry-shod. And there shall be an highway for the remnant of His people, which shall be left, from Assyria (Isaiah 11:11, 13-16). Here also no one would see anything divine unless he knows what is signified by each of the names mentioned; although the subject treated of is the Coming of the Lord and what shall then come to pass,

as is clearly manifest from verses 1-10 of the same chapter. Who then, without the aid of the spiritual sense, would see that by these in their order is signified that they who are in falsities from ignorance, and have not suffered themselves to be led astray by evils, will approach the Lord; and that the church will then understand the Word; and that falsities will no longer harm them?

3. The case is similar in those passages where names do not occur, as in Ezekiel:

Thus saith the Lord Jehovih; Thou son of man, speak unto the fowl of every wing, and to every beast of the field. Assemble yourselves and come; gather yourselves on every side to my sacrifice that I do sacrifice for you, even a great sacrifice upon the mountains of Israel, that ye may eat flesh, and drink blood. Ye shall eat the flesh of the mighty, and drink the blood of the princes of the earth . . . Ye shall eat fat till ye be full, and drink blood till ye be drunken, of my sacrifice, which I sacrifice for you. Thus ye shall be filled at my table with horse and chariot, with the mighty man and with every man of war . . . Thus I will set my glory among the nations (Ezekiel 39:17-21). He who does not know from the spiritual sense what is signified by a sacrifice, by flesh, and blood; and what by a horse, a chariot, a mighty man, and a man of war, would not know otherwise that such things were to be eaten and drunk. The spiritual sense however, teaches that eating the flesh and drinking the blood of the sacrifice, which the Lord Jehovah will give, upon the mountains of Israel, signifies appropriating to oneself Divine Good and Divine Truth from the Word. For the subject treated of here is the calling together of all to the Lords kingdom, and in particular, the establishment by the Lord of the Church among the nations. Who cannot see that flesh is not meant by flesh, nor blood by blood? Such as where it is said that they should drink blood till they should be drunken, and that they should be filled with horse and chariot, the mighty man and every man of war? So likewise in a thousand other places in the Prophets.

[16] Without the spiritual sense no one would know why the prophet Jeremiah was commanded:

To buy himself a girdle, and put it upon his loins, and not to draw it through water, and to hide it in a hole of the rock by the Euphrates (Jeremiah 13:1-7).
Why the prophet Isaiah was commanded:
To loose the sackcloth from off his loins, to put off the shoe from his foot, and to go naked and barefoot three years (Isaiah 20:2,3).
Why the prophet Ezekiel was commanded:
To pass a razor over his head and over his beard, and then to divide the hairs, to burn a third part in the midst of the city, to smite a third part with the sword, and to scatter a third part to the wind; but to bind a little of them in his skirts, and finally to cast them into the midst of the fire (Ezekiel 5:1-4).

Why the same prophet was commanded: To lie upon his left side three hundred and ninety days, and upon his right side forty days; to make himself a cake of wheat, and barley, and millet, and fitches, with cows dung, and eat it; and in the meantime to cast a trench and mound against Jerusalem, and lay siege to it (Ezekiel 4:1-15).

Why the prophet Hosea was commanded twice:

To take himself a harlot to be his wife (Hosea 1:2-9; 3:2,3). And many more things of a like nature.

Moreover, without the spiritual sense, who would know what is signified by all the things of the tabernacle, as by the ark, the mercy seat, the cherubim, the candlestick, the alter of incense, the shewbread on the table, the veils and its curtains? Without the spiritual sense who would know what is signified by the holy garment of Aaron, by his vest, his robe, the ephod, the Urim and Thummim, the mitre, and the many other things associated with him? Who also, without the spiritual sense, would know what is signified by all those things commanded relating to burnt—offerings, sacrifices, meat offerings, and drink offerings? And also by those relating to Sabbaths and Feasts? THE TRUTH IS THAT NOT THE LEAST OF THESE THINGS WAS COMMANDED WHICH DID NOT SIGNIFY SOMETHING RELATING TO THE LORD, TO HEAVEN AND TO THE CHURCH. From these few examples it may be clearly seen that there is a spiritual sense in all things of the Word in general and in particular.

[17] That the Lord when He was in the world spoke by correspondences, and thus both spiritually and naturally at the same time, may appear from His parables, in which every single expression contains a spiritual sense. Take for example, the parable of the ten virgins. He said:

The Kingdom of the heavens is like unto ten virgins, who took their lamps, and went forth to meet the bridegroom. Five of them were wise, and five were foolish. They that were foolish took their lamps, and took no oil with them: but the wise took oil in their vessels with their lamps. While the bridegroom tarried, they all slumbered and slept. And at midnight there was a cry made, behold, the bridegroom cometh; go ye out to meet him. Then all those virgins arose, and trimmed their lamps. And the foolish said unto the wise. Give us of your oil; for our lamps are gone out. But the wise answered, saying (A.V. Not so); lest there be not enough for us and you; but go ye rather to them that sell, and buy for yourselves. And while they went to buy, the bridegroom came: and they that were ready went in with him to the marriage: and the door was shut. Afterwards came also the other virgins, saying Lord, Lord, open to us. But he answered and said; Verily I say unto you, I know you not (Matthew 25:1-12).

2. That in every part of this parable there is a spiritual sense, and consequently a Divine holiness, none can see but those who know tat there is a spiritual sense, and are acquainted with the nature of it. In the spiritual sense by the Kingdom of God is meant heaven and the church; by the bridegroom the Lord; by the wedding, the marriage of the Lord with heaven and the church by means of the good of love and of faith. By the virgins are meant those who belong to the church; by ten are meant all, and by five a certain part; by lamps are meant the truths of faith, and by oil the good of love. By sleeping and waking are meant the natural life of man in the world, and his spiritual life after death. By buying is meant to procure for themselves; and by going to those that sell, and buying oil, is meant to procure for themselves after death the good of love from others. Because this can no longer be acquired after death, therefore, although they came to the marriage door with their lamps and the oil they had purchased, still the bridegroom said to them, "I know you not." This is because man, after his life in the world, remains such as he had been in the world.

3. From these things it is evident that the Lord spoke by pure correspondences, and this because He spoke from the Divine that was in Him and was His own. That the bridegroom signifies the Lord, and the Kingdom of the heavens, the church; that the wedding signifies the marriage of the Lord with the church by means of the good of love and of faith; that virgins signify those who belong to the church; that by ten are meant all, and by five a certain part; that SLEEPING MEANS A NATURAL STATE, and buying, procuring for themselves; that the door means entrance into heaven, and not to know, when spoken by the Lord, not to be in His love; all this may appear from many passages in the prophetic Word, where these expressions have a similar signification. Because virgins signify those who belong to the church, therefore in the prophetic Word, is there such frequent mention of virgin, and daughter of Zion, of Jerusalem and of Israel; and because oil signifies the good of love, that all the holy things of the Israelitish church were anointed with oil. The case is the same with the other parables, and with all the words spoken by the Lord and recorded in the Evangelists. For this reason the Lord declares that His words are spirit and life (John 6:63).

4. It is the same with all the Lords miracles. These were Divine because they signified the various states of those with whom the church was to be established by the Lord. Thus, when the blind receive sight, it signified that those who were in ignorance of truth should receive understanding; when the deaf received hearing, it signified that those who had previously heard nothing concerning the Lord and the Word, should hear and obey; when the dead were raised, it signified that those who otherwise would have spiritually perished, should become alive; and so on. This is meant by the Lords reply to the disciples of John when he sent them to inquire whether it was He who should come:

Go and tell John those things which ye do hear and see:

The blind receive their sight, and the lame walk, the lepers are cleansed, and the deaf hear, the dead are raised up, and the poor have the gospel preached to them (Matthew 11:3-5). Moreover, all the miracles recorded in the Word contain within them such things as relate to the Lord, to heaven, and to the church. On this account these miracles are Divine, and are distinguished from miracles not Divine. These few examples may serve to illustrate what the spiritual sense of the Word is, and to show that it is present in the whole of the Word, in general and in particular. (The Doctrine of Sacred Scripture will continue on page 62.)

The falsified smile!

Can a Christian be loving, or good anytime he or she pleases? Can an angel of God be loving or good anytime they please? Is there a man, spirit, or angel ever created, or ever to be created that can be loving or good anytime they please? If you are a God fearing person, or someone who is very loving, you may say yes to this question. But just because we can feel love, or even wish to love others almost always, I am sure you have noticed times in your life when you just didn't feel like being bothered by anyone, and you are slightly irritated when company shows up. Whatever the case may be, no one ever stays in a good and loving mode for the duration of his or her life. Therefore, our moods, or daily states in life must be controlled by God; so that he allows us to be good at times, and does not remove our evil, or disturbing thoughts at other times, which causes us to sin, or to offend someone, sometimes. For no man is good, in and of himself, as we have many times discussed. So as far as when each of us is found to be in good, that is all up to God. Now you may say to yourself that if God hates sin and evil, why would he allow his children to sin, or to be found in evil? If he can remove evil from us every time we think it, why would he not do so? Well, that is a very in depth subject, of which we will only skim the surface. Now we know that God says he is not a respecter of persons, right? So in order for this statement to be true, everything you learn from God, or the Word must fall within the perimeters of this statement. Therefore, everything God requires of man, he must in turn require of woman. If he did not do so, he would be a respecter of one or the other, would he not? Therefore there are two types of affections which every man and woman must possess till forever. These affections are good and truth, or love and wisdom, or faith and charity. For these all represent the affections of the Lord, and mankind. But this is a state that mankind must eventually reach, and he or she is not in at first. When however man is in his natural state, he represents the truth, and woman represents the good. Or he represents the wisdom, and woman represents the love for his wisdom. In order for man to be saved he must take on her love; and in order for woman to be saved she must join herself to his wisdom, or truth. And as the Lord spoke to his disciples, woman must become man, in order to be saved. This does not mean a physical man, but that she must seek out, and find truth from the Lord, and then make it a part of her everyday life. Man, because he does not have the maternal instinct, as a woman does, must find how to truly love, and he only finds this when he is in childlike faith. Therefore a man must find innocence and humility, which comes from truly conjugal love, and join these to his truth that he has received from the Father. But whereas one has to find good, and the other truth, they both are joined as one, and go hand in hand in the Lord. When a man or woman become an angel, they are actually two who become one. And whereas the woman used to represent good, the order is now reversed, and she now represents truth. And whereas the man used to represent truth, the order is as well reversed, and he now represents good. And this is how woman becomes man. Far away an angel is seen as one angel, but up close he is seen as one man and one woman, or husband and wife. But they both share a single soul in the spiritual world, with their own separate bodies. For just as man comes to be with a woman in the material realm, so to does he does so in the spiritual world, with the exception that no children are ever born in the spiritual world. Have you heard the phrase "With much wisdom comes much sorrow?" This statement not only includes Godly wisdom, but worldly wisdom as well. For with much Godly wisdom we come to learn that we cannot ever be good all the time; if we are ever to help our fellow man. For we must be all things to all people (1 Corinthians 9:19-23), at any given point in time. Sometimes we must be merciful, so as to win those who seek mercy. We must be blunt so as to win those who are stubborn, or proud. We must be gentle so as to win those who are timid or shy, as well as simple minded. We must be patient so as to win those who are not yet ready to receive the truths of the Word. We must be firm, and even harsh at times so as to win those who are stuck believing they are good in and of themselves. But this will hurt those people who wish to always love all people. For it is impossible to love all people all the time. And so we must at times sacrifice ourselves, or our love for our neighbor, so as to teach them the right way. Worldly wisdom works in the same manner. For if we are wise according to the worlds standards, and we are seeking God before we have actually been called and this is possible), or before we have been regenerated by God, we become frustrated and alone at times. For no one can come to the Lord until they are called, and so if you are having hard times in your life because you are living for the worlds ways, and you go to God for help, you will find that he will not answer. We must be seeking God for the right reasons, and not to satisfy our fleshly desires, or fantasies. For you will not be able to understand the ways of God, according to the wisdom of the world. No matter how wise you may appear to those in the world, if you are seeking God, you must first become as a child before you will ever find him. For to live for, or in God, you must give up your worldly wisdom, no longer putting your faith and trust in your physical senses, and begin to completely live a life in faith in the Lord; believing everything that God teaches, or provides in your everyday lives from now on. Because before, we understood things as though they were at least mostly, or partially true, but now, in the Lord, we shall see things as they truly are. Jesus said something to Peter that really caused me to think, hey! Are we really supposed to be letting men teach us for the rest of our lives, or just until we receive the wisdom to realize that God has been teaching us all along, and now we must totally lean on him; and receive all our teachings from him from now on. For the Lord said to Peter: I tell you the truth, when you were younger you dressed yourself and went where you wanted; but when you are old you will stretch out your hands, and someone else will dress you and lead you where you do not want to go (John 21:18). The Lord told Peter this to show him what type of death he would glorify God by. In other words he would die to his flesh, and no longer be lead by his own desires, but by the will of God. He would now begin to do things he never would have done before, because he wished to truly love all of his friends and neighbors, while at the same time living his life as a good example to them all. But what did Jesus do when he entered the temple, and found them exchanging goods for money and what not? He overturned the tables in anger, and rebuked them all. But he did this to teach them, by his rebuke; but it was done because of the love he had for all of mankind. He gained nothing for his flesh because of this, and he meant no ill will to his friends and neighbors; he only wished to set things straight, and to teach them what was right. And so with Jesus, as with all righteous men, we will be called to do many things that we do not wish to do, simply because we must learn how to truly love our neighbor. Mostly all Christians today would not agree with this type of teaching, for the true way that is taught in the churches of today is to always act in love, with a smiling face. But that is just what it is; an act, and we have all done it at some point in our lifetimes. For no one has learned to act more loving than today's Christian, and I should know, I am as guilty as the rest. Even to this day I find myself acting out the role of a good, smiling, loving Christian; while at the same time harboring ill feelings for someone. No brothers, I am not good all the time, as no one else is either, for we are human, and are not God. However, as often as the Lord permits me to love, be in good, and to have a true smile on my face, I am more than happy to oblige the Lord; but remember, it can only be done through the Lord. For with mankind, to always be good, to always be loving, and to always wear a smile would be a lie on our part, for man can do nothing on his own. For man was created to enter into different states throughout his lifetime, so as to never become bored with his life of being good to others at all times, if that were possible. Only God can actually be the good guy all the time, and that is because he doesn't have to actually live among the evil of this material world. Yes we have to live according to his will, but he does not have to live according to ours. And so, to be completely pure, and in perfect love, you cannot physically dwell among evil beings, but can only teach them, and lead them from their minds. For as I have stated, God cannot ever be directly connected with evil, at any level. Therefore he dwells within a world that exists within another world, but neither actually coming into contact with the other, in a material sense. We are human beings only in appearance, but in reality we are a part of God, and therefore are god. We reside within the heavens when we are in good, or love; but we are in a state of sleep when we are not in good, and are being disobedient to our Father, and are therefore in our own hell. Yes we will reside within the heavens till forever, but when disobedient, we will lose all true knowledge of where we actually are. FOR God cannot allow us to be a part of reality, and to help him rule over his creation, if we are not at each moment in love to him and our neighbor. So if we cannot be trusted at any point in time, we are chastised until we come back around to reality. So even though we are god because we are a part of God, we will forever submit to his will because we are finite beings, and he is infinite. We will forever share our lives with human beings, who are also bound midway between good and evil. We will always remain midways between good and evil so as to remain in free will, always being permitted to choose good or evil for ourselves. Yes! Human beings, or fleshly material beings are actually little gods, as is said in the Word, who were created in Gods image. They, or we, rule our own little world from within, just like all of creation dwells within the Lord as his heavenly kingdom, and he is the ruler of that kingdom. We are little atmospheres of all different affections or loves, and as we grow or mature in life we learn more and more about actual love, and the evil human beings we share our life with learn about love from us as well, and they also go on one day to enter life as another spirit or angel, once they put off their flesh. So do not ever accept the belief that you are a fleshly human being, for you are not. For this material world, along with all its different fleshly creatures, man included, is temporary, and nothing more than fantasy. It does not truly exist, but only exists within the accumulated thoughts of affections from the Lord, as well as mans fantasies created from these thoughts of affections. For the real beings live within these fleshly bodies we carry around, and the evil beings are those who serve as a shell, or base for us spiritual beings, good or bad. All evil beings and affections are derived from the fantasies of those who live for self, or this material world. For because everything in creation must have an opposite, we live out our lives within these fleshly forms of our opposite images, or persons. For the inner or higher is good and it is real, as the outer or lower is evil, and it is fantasy. To be good at all times, night and day, twenty four-seven, would be to abandon our opposite image, or opposite self, in which case they would be spirits who are doomed to eternal damnation forever; simply because we did not truly love our enemies, as the Lord has plainly told us all to do. I mean, why do you think he said to love our enemies? Because he knew that one day every man would come to learn that his true enemy is himself, or his opposite self. If you can live with your own evil thoughts, which we all have at some point in our lives, then you should have no trouble loving and forgiving your enemies in the material realm. But even though it is true that "With much wisdom comes much sorrow," we will truly all be blessed in the long run, as long as we finish the race; and we will all finish the race, for this is Gods predestination for us all. So what we have so far is a firm understanding (According to our faith) that we are good when we are the actual affection that God created each of us to be. But when we are in fantasy, which will be the case every time we live for self, or the ways of the world, we are in direct disobedience, and therefore separate from God. It is very possible to live in the world, but not of the world, or self. When we achieve this state in our lives, we are actually being prepared for the heavens, and will then go on to be the angel we were created to be. But let me explain for you why we cannot ever be good at all times, so that you may see why human beings need us angels, and we need them as well. "Spare the rod spoil the child." Every mother and father who does not fully understand the importance of this statement is cheating his or her child out of a better life in years to come. If you give your child everything they ask for just to keep them quiet, you are doing that child a disservice. If a child does not at first fear, and therefore respect you, that child will go on to lash out at you later in life. And when you go to love them over and above this they will turn away from you. For it is a truth that you must first teach fear, and then comes love later on. When the child is a baby, or an infant, of course the mother is to love and nurture that child. But when the child reaches a point so as to know the difference between right and wrong, that child should be taught by the father, and the mother should now take a back seat to the father. And so now the father in charge of rearing the child, and teaching them respect for others, as well as their parents. He must teach the child respect by instilling fear in the child, without actually harming the child. But there will be times for spankings, and the father should carry this out as needed. Of course a parent must use good judgment when deciding to spank a child. For a child should not be spanked for minor things, but only when they are continuously disobedient when it comes to certain situations. You should never receive enjoyment from spanking a child, but must do so because it has been used as a last resort for chastisement. If the mother does not learn to let go however, and there is a constant battle between the parents, the child will learn to use this against the parents, in which case they have failed in their Childs upbringing. Just as once you teach a child young, that they will in adolescent years continue in the manner in which they were taught, if they are not taught early on in life, it will be too late to change them later in life. So teach the child young, and do not let your love for that child stand in the way of rearing them according to Gods plan of parenting. There will be times your decisions will seem a bit harsh, but you must do what seems right, according to the love you have for that child. Just as the mother has to let go of the child when the father takes over, such is the way of Gods church. The church is the mother, who nurtures and teaches the new born babe; and then later on is supposed to let that child go, so that the Father (or God), can now teach that child. But just as the mother of a family in our world is no longer willing to let go of the child, so as to permit the father to teach it, so too is the state of the church today, which teaches new Christians to continue to follow the teachings of the church, and to go no where else to seek the truths of the Kingdom of heaven. And because the churches today are in this state, this is the cause of the families falling apart, and the fathers no longer have a say in the Childs upbringing. Yes there are exceptions to this statement, as there are exceptions to every rule, but I do not have to tell you the condition that families are in today, as well as the state of the church. Today's church has lead as an example to the rest of the world, how a family truly acts once they have closed the church doors on Sunday, and they then go home to be with their families. Families have not been taught the true meaning of love for God, or their neighbor. A man goes home from church and he begins ruling his household, and this is by no means Gods way. The mother goes home from church and she either listens to her husband, doing everything he tells her, or she lashes out, and goes and does her own thing. Then the children watch every move they make, and listen to every word they say, and this is the type of upbringing the children receive. So too, do they grow up to be the same type of parents, and so on down the line, from one generation to another. And if the father is not one who rules his household (which is wrong), then the mother does, and the children are taught from all love and no truth, or wisdom. For the woman represents good or love, and the man represents truth or wisdom. And no family will raise proper, respectful children without these two forming as one in a marriage. You can say, or pretend as you please, but God is never wrong. So the less we have good and truth in our churches and families today, the more this generation is doomed to do it all over again, until they get it right. Am I saying that we are reincarnated, or that I even teach reincarnation? No, I am not, but something similar, which is called Transmigration. For we cannot ever return to this world as a single person, for we never were a single person in the first place, but share our lives with many within this human body, which is actually a little world. Why do you think we have so many different thoughts within a single mind? But as I was saying, the church, as well as the mothers out there need to let go. The fathers on the other hand need to live up to their responsibilities as well as a parent, and play the role of a father. Mothers were created to love and nurture, fathers were created to chastise, and to teach the child the way in which to walk in life. And because a father cannot ever represent love like a mother, he must retain the understanding that it takes to know when to back off and allow the child to be loved by the mother. This all takes teamwork, and most of all love from every member of the family. The children must of course learn love from their parents; that is of course if they truly know love themselves. To truly know love is to truly know God. And you cannot truly know God if you are not seeking love. If you are seeking love, you will always find it. If you want to know how to love your spouse, and your children as well, it is simple to do, but you must give up self. You must put your spouse, as well as the good of your children before your own wants or needs, and this will serve in teaching you love. If you are not willing to put self-last in life then you will never achieve love in your life, and will return to do it all over again, until you get it right. So as far as my statement in the beginning goes, you cannot always be good in life because sometimes fear has to be instilled in a child or person, so as to get them motivated, or on the right track. Many of the unlearned in the world, as well as the church today are set in their ways, or they are just plain lazy in their walk with God, and you sometimes have to give them a little shove, or coaxing. This however will not work if a person has to be coerced every time, not taking over in their responsibilities to seek truth for themselves. But it will sometimes help to get them started in the right direction. So if you are attempting to live for God, and are trying to be good all the time, just keep doing what you are doing, and God will gradually point you in the right direction. But remember this; just as a parent cannot always be good to their child, if they wish to teach them the right way in life, neither can we always be good to a brother or sister, if we are truly wishing them to achieve salvation. More on this subject will be told as these pages unfold, but for now this will suffice to show you that no man can or will ever always be good, and even to be good requires God in your life, acting as your will.

CHAPTER 3

Bound forever!

Is man destined to live in this material realm till forever? Will some go to be with God in heaven, and some to be with Satan in hell for an eternity? Or will we all eventually go to the same place, so as to spend our days repeating our lives until we become perfect? Now it is true that I have stated many times in the past that man, upon death in this material world, will enter the spiritual world, to live forever either in heaven or in hell. But if you recall, I also stated that death is not real, but is actually sleep, and only for a short time. But if we go to sleep at the end of our days in this world, that means we are awake in this world, right? Well, not exactly. We think we are awake in this world when we are actually in a deep sleep, and how much we are asleep depends on how uneducated, or how mature we are. For God controls the life of every man by his state of sleep in life. And if you reflect on your state when you supposedly dream at night, you will see that sleep can appear to be very real. As a matter of fact, it can appear as real as God wishes for it to be, depending on how much a person is living in fantasy, or living for themselves or the world. This is how it is decided whether you will be in heaven or in hell at any given time in your life. If you draw on affections that are good, you are allowed into the heavens, but if from evil, you take yourself to the hells. For God sends no one to hell, but they go there of their own free will. And so everyone is permitted into the heavens whenever they are in good. And because of this, even evil people can enter the heavens as often as they please, just by being good. But being good and acting good are two separate issues, and God is never fooled. So if you act good you still enter the hells of your own free will, because you chose deception, which originates from the hells. Remember when it was said that Satan masquerades as an angel from heaven at times? We are the Satan's that do so when we attempt to deceive others into believing we are really good, when in fact we are evil. So if a human being is evil this means they are drawing on mostly evil spirits from the hells, and they are always punished by the laws of the material, or natural universe, set up by God in the beginning. For there is a set punishment for every sin ever committed, or ever to be committed. And because no human being will ever be good at all times, even till forever, these laws will be used to educate every human being. Angels on the other hand do not need to be educated, they only need to wake up and realize who they are, eventually. For an angel is given all the things they can receive from God, as they are prepared to receive them. But all must be according to their own free will, and according to their love, or affection in life. Where we see it as educating the angel, the angel is actually being used by God to educate evil beings, who will also one day share a part in the Lord with us. Why? Because love wishes nothing more than to share all that it is or has with all others. Love also wishes nothing more than to become one with all others, including especially the uneducated, or evil. For what profit does the good receive by loving itself. Because when a spirit is good, it is a part of God, and is God. And god does not receive pleasure by loving himself. So, we must learn to love those who do not know how to love, or who do not have love; so that they can one day become one with us, and God. Remember what the Lord Jesus said to the disciples? "I will not leave you as orphans; I will come to you. Before long, the world will not see me anymore, but you will see me. Because I live you also will live. On that day you will realize that I am in my Father, and you are in me, and I am in you. Whoever has my commands and obeys them, he is the one who loves me. He who loves me will be loved by my Father, and I too will love him and show myself to him." So you see, until you come to realize whom you really are, you must love God of your own free will; and then, when you come to know love you will know God, and will once again return to God. But love does not ever teach to love self before another, so we must love others, and put self last at all times. When you put self first this will tell you that you are in the flesh, or living for the flesh. So when you are in good, you are one with the Lord, but when you are disobedient, you are separated from the Lord, and are in hell. I said angels do not have to learn to be good, but this can be misunderstood by some. Angels are from God and are already good, but they lay dormant in man if he never calls on good in his life. So angels are not bound to a single human being, ever. Since they are from God, they are life, and must be a part of life at all times. But when man is living for self or the world he is dead, for he resides in the hells. And so an angel must retreat, and share the life of a human being who is in good. For just as those from the hells cannot stand the presence of angels, neither can angels stand the presence of those from the hells. But the angels will permit those from the hells to remain in their presence for as long as they can stand it; and then if they do not leave of their own free will, they are removed by force. But not because the angels are in pain, but because they do not wish to see the evil suffer any longer. So as I said, when a human being is living for self, or the world, they are already dead. So how can they die in this lifetime if they are already dead? You may ask. This is a misconception by all men who have not been regenerated by God. For there is no fear in love; which means only those who are not in love can fear death, or even believe in death. God receives no pleasure by the death of any man. This is in the Word, for He means exactly what He says. We are already dead if we are living for the fleshly self, or the ways of the world. To live for God is always to live in CHILDLIKE FAITH. For when we have been regenerated in this life we automatically know it, and everything God gives us from thereon is all truth. So we no longer have to doubt as to whether what we think, or read is truth or not, because we are now guided by the spirit. But if you are not yet regenerated, or in the process of regeneration, you will not believe nor understand these things. As well, if you are being regenerated by God then you are ready to receive the new wine, and you are a new wineskin; and you will know this with all your heart. For every man in the church lives in doubt all of his life, as long as he depends on man, or his physical senses. For to live for God is to by all means live in faith, childlike faith. Do you know what childlike faith is? Childlike faith is when a child will put his whole life into his parent's hands, with no fear of injury or death. Childlike faith is when a child will stand on the kitchen counter, his parent tell him to jump into their arms, and that child just knows they will catch him; that is childlike faith, and very few Christians actually have it today. But there always comes a time in every mans lifetime (a lifetime is till forever), when he receives that childlike faith as a gift from the Lord, and he immediately knows he has it. I knew when it was not there, and even wondered if I would ever receive it, because it is such a wonderful thing to have; but as soon as I received it from God, I knew I had it, and I look forward to exercising it every day of my life. So, if you want to be truly good in life you must have childlike faith, so as to trust that every move you make, and every decision you make, is of the Lords will, when you are seeking good. But remember that the good does not come from you or any angel, but from God. If you are in a state of good then you should trust your decisions, according to childlike faith, and know that your decisions have either been chosen by God, or permitted by God, so as to be for the good of mankind. He knows what is best for everyone, and he guides our every thought or action in the direction, which best fits for the overall good of man. Now, jumping back on subject, do we die, and if not what actually happens? This is a long subject, and I will attempt, according to the Lords will, to stay on this subject until it is finished. Here we go: Man is born into the material world as a spirit, but he is not who or what he thinks he is. He is a spirit formed from a good affection from the Father, and an evil affection from the mother, or the flesh. Now do not get all bent out of shape women, for I am not saying women are evil, and men are good, or loving. For in this world women actually represent good, or love, and man represents truth, or wisdom. But what I am actually saying is that the Father is the Lord from the beginning, and he provided the very first seed, or soul. And it is a fact that he provides every spirit or soul to come from eternity to eternity. So every human being ever born, or ever to be born receives their spirit from the Father, or God if you will. So he is the soul of ever man, but the inner man and not the exterior, or fleshly man. The flesh is always provided by the mother, or nature. And nature is dead in reality, and so is evil, or hell, or fantasy; whichever you wish to call it. So God takes his affections, and mixes them with mans affections, and basically creates a whole new affection in man. And this affection is born into the material world as a child, later to become an angel when the child becomes reborn, or regenerated by God. So because we are born into a world which is really dead in the first place, we as angels must live out our lives as all angels and spirits do, sharing the life of a human being, while teaching that human being; and at the same time teaching ourselves, even though we are not really learning these things for the first time, but are waking up as we mature in life. So we live out our life in this world and when we leave it we go from one world to another by entering sleep once again. But whereas it is sleep to us, it appears as a death to those still in the material world, which is why they experience such a loss when a loved one passes on. And depending on how much evil is actually in a person, that is how badly they take the death of a loved one from this world. For you must remember, there is no fear in love. So what we see in a person's passing is not what everyone else sees, but we experience a persons passing on from within ourselves. If you see a child, or person dying in a car that has caught on fire, and you actually see them burning, do you really believe a loving God would allow any human being to suffer in this apparent manner? All that is left in that person at the time they are burning, or apparently suffering, is the evil spirits that belong to this world. For nothing of this world can enter into the heavens. Flesh and blood shall not enter the kingdom of heaven. But what we don't understand today, is that flesh and blood are from this world of fantasy, and so are all the spirits from hell. So when a person is about to leave this world, everything that belongs to this world stays in this world, and everything that belongs to God goes back to God. Therefore, no one ever suffers death but the evil, for God snatches away the good spirits, or his own. The screams we hear are from the hells, and by those who live in the hells. So if you ever see someone experiencing a horrible death, just remember, the ones experiencing this death are no one you ever knew, but are those who are their opposites in hell. I cannot say these things to most men because I cannot put it all in one short statement. And all men like a short, or fast response to their questions in life. This is why many do not enjoy reading books that much, in which case they cannot learn these type of things, for there are many details to every truth there is, and man does not like a lot of details. So for me to just state a quick response to a question such as, "Why do good people die young, or why do they die such horrible deaths?" would simply cause a person to wish to stone me to death, or something similar. For no one wishes to accept the fact that none of us are good. No one wishes to believe that people do not actually feel the horrible pain from such horrible deaths as we have mentioned. But the truth is every evil spirit in the vicinity of such a horrible death as we have spoken of, will see horrible things, because the evil are in fantasy, and so they see what they most fear in life. So when you see someone die, anything negative you receive from the experience is seen through the eyes of evil spirits who live within you. For we all, no matter how good we may think we are, have evil spirits living within us. Evil spirits cannot see good, but good spirits can see evil spirits. This is because when spirits from lower realms in the spiritual world go up to the higher realms, they cannot see these spirits or angels, because they live in another atmosphere. This is also why we cannot see other beings on other planets, for we come from different atmospheres, and atmospheres are what allow us all to see things in our own atmosphere. This can change however, but only if the Lord permits it, and only at certain times. So because we only go to sleep when going from this world to the spiritual world, we wake up in the spiritual world. But as long as we live in this world, we remain asleep, or simply appear to wake up the next day in this material world again. So going from this world to the spiritual world is going from death to life. However, even when we wake up in the spiritual world we still think we are in the material world, for all things appear to be and look the same to us. And this is the way it will remain until we have gone through our vastation process. The vastation process is where we are a good spirit being purged of all evil affections, or we are an evil spirit who is purged of all good affections. This is how vastation is explained in the Word: "Whoever has will be given more, and he will have an abundance. Whoever does not have, even what he has will be taken from him" (Matthew 13:12). So vastation in the World of Spirits, which is where we go immediately after we pass on from this world, simply means that those who think they possess some good, if they are truly evil spirits, will be separated from all good they possess, and given to those who are worthy. After this process has taken place in the World of Spirits, each begins to enter different societies, until they have found a society, which agrees with their affections, or until they find the society they were in while in the world. And once they find the society that agrees with them they are guided to that society, whether it be in the heavens or the hells. Either way no one is forced to enter where they do not wish to go. So all spirits who enter the hells, do so of their own free will. For the Lord is a loving God, and sends no one to hell, but permits all to enter the heavens if they wish to do so. But whether you enter the heavens or the hells is all decided by you, according to your similar affections of love. Now, does everyone still remember what our original subject is; "Do we die, or what actually happens to us?" I think you can now see that we do not actually die, as well as what really happens to all men when they pass on from this world. But there's more, so stay with me and ill try and keep it as simple as possible for everyone, including myself. Now when we pass on from this world and enter the spiritual world we either end up in heaven or in hell. But this does not happen so quickly, for God is a patient God. Sometimes we are permitted to spend a while in the World of Spirits, living within our own heaven, for the time being. But those who are evil go immediately to the hells. So as I was saying, those who are good spirits remain in the World of Spirits for a short time, or sometimes for an extended time, even up to about thirty years, but never beyond thirty years. At this day however men never remain in the World of Spirits any longer than about twenty years. There is still one exception to this rule, and that is that those who are permitted to form their own personal heavens in the World of Spirits are permitted to remain this way sometimes up to several centuries, (or a few hundred years). Now lets not forget brothers and sisters, that God can allow exceptions to his rules at any time he pleases, of which he reserves the right to do so. Therefore, because God is man, and man is God, man will always have a part in creating new laws and other things that are in the perimeters of the created universe. Yes God is the same yesterday, today, and forever, but that simply means his personality remains the same. He will always be a loving God, and even though we, or man, may at one time or another see something that appears to be new, there is never anything new with God, for as it is said in the book of Ecclesiastes, "There is nothing new under the sun." So if it has not happened in this lifetime, you can rest assured that it has happened in a past lifetime. One thing that we can be sure of however, that will never change, is that God will always remain a God who is not a respecter of persons, whether you are a man or woman. Now as I was saying, we are permitted to remain in the World of Spirits for an extended period of time, but only if we are waiting for the arrival of a family member, or members. For who does not know that when an elderly person passes on in our world, the other usually grieves for a year, two years, and sometimes for even several years before they pass on, and their sole wish is to be with their spouse on the other side. And God permits this to happen, for those who wish it to be this way. There is always the possibility that a person can change affections while in the World of Spirits, and wish to no longer wait for their consort, or spouse; in which case the Lord will select a new one for them if they wish, and they can move on to the heavens above, where they will spend eternity together. Some people believe when they leave this world that they will enter their last judgment, and afterwards return to this world in their bodies, but that is not how the last judgment works. As man, after passing from this world, goes on to take on a spiritual body, which he will enjoy in the spiritual realm until forever, or to eternity. Those in the spiritual world will also have spiritual bodies, and all will see one another as we see one another in this world, even though they do not actually have bodies in the first place. I say they have bodies because in the spiritual world, no one actually has their own body, but they take on a body as needed, such as when they are speaking to another spirit or angel. But when they are alone, they have no need of a body, and they only feel as though they possess on. This is similar to how we feel in this world; for the only way a person knows they possess a body is by them reflecting on the fact that they possess one, but if we do not reflect, do we really possess a body? Remember, this world only appears real to us because we are provided with senses that lie to us and tell us we can see, hear, touch, taste, smell, or speak. When all along, it is the spirit within us, which possesses these senses, and acts them out through mans fleshly body. So there are two worlds that live together simultaneously in man. We think we are real, and that this material world is real as well. Then, on the other hand, those in the spiritual realm believe they are real, and they see man as we see them, as someone who is actually them. For it is a truth that spirits believe that they are actually the man whose body they possess. Angels on the other hand are much more wise, and they have knowledge of both worlds, even though they cannot enter our world, without the Lord first permitting them to do so, and only from time to time. For angels are permitted to help men at times, according to the Lords good pleasure. This is one of those things that is always an exception to the rule, and is only permitted because of the Lords mercy, as well as it being predestined before time began. So where will you be when you pass on from this lifetime? Lets think about it for a moment. There are plenty of people in the world, but not all are good, so as to go to heaven when they pass from this world. As a matter of fact, whether you wish to believe it or not, the amount of good people in the world compared to the evil is probably about one in a thousand. That means that out of every thousand people in the world today, one is righteous, and actually living for God. Now of course we all think the number of those who are righteous is much higher, based on the amount of people we see attending churches today. But do you really think all those people are righteous, or that they even try to be good, once they have left church on Sunday and have returned home? And yes, many go to church as much as three times a week, and still it is all an act, so as to appear righteous to those around them. How do I know? Because the Lord let me be one of them by joining their circle, before he removed me from the circle of organized religion. Organized religion is only permitted by God because this is how the babes are taught and given the basics as to how to live a good, clean, honest life, and to teach them the bible before God takes over as their teacher. But before God will take over as your teacher, you must give up the worldly church, which lives for the flesh and the ways of the world. So as long as you hold on to worldly things God cannot intervene in your life. But he does tell each and every one of us who have ever read the bible that he will be your teacher, and that a man will no longer teach his brother. So why don't we listen to what he says? Because it is not comfortable for our flesh. When I was a member of organized religion I use to believe that I was a good person, and that the good actually came from myself. I even thought I could earn my salvation by doing all sorts of good works, and so I would search for people to help, or charities to donate my time or money to. This is what organized religion taught me, causing me to believe I was a righteous man, and that I would enter heaven before others who were not members of any church at all. So there you have it, one group that didn't attend a worldly church would not be saved; and even though they would not come right out and tell a person they were going to go to hell, they sure made it clear behind the pulpit. And God allows this damnation and hellfire type of preaching in the world for exactly the reason I stated earlier. You must teach a child fear (which teaches respect as well), before you can truly teach them love. This is why the Word is written in the manner it is written, and not a jot or tittle will be removed from it to eternity. God loves each and every one of us, good and bad, but we are children, just like we see our children in the world. We however do not live by childlike faith as our children do, but we live according to our physical, worldly senses. This is because we live in fantasy while we are children, but when we mature as angels living by faith alone; the babysitter will slowly be taken away. As it says in Galatians: But after that faith is come, we are no longer under a schoolmaster (Gal. 3:25). What this is telling us is that the Law was written as a schoolmaster to all men, to teach them to live properly, in a moral and civil manner, until they each receive faith in Christ from God, and no longer need the guidance of the law in their life, therefore continuing on to learn the things of love, or faith grounded in our works of charity. But the works we now do will be the evidence that we are living in true faith. For faith without the works of charity is no faith. Whereas on the other hand, faith that is backed up by the works of man is no faith as well. For any works to be done in life are to be from the Lord, and acted out through man. So how do you know if your works are from you or God? Because the works of God are out of love, and they put the neighbor first, or love first. So if you do a work, and that work is done so that there arises self-gain or recognition because of this work, it is probably from you. For we are to do our good deeds expecting nothing in return, but to please the Father, who is the Lord. If you loan anything to a man, you are not to expect it to be returned. If a man asks you to go a mile with him, you should go two miles, and not do only what is asked or expected of you. And when you do a good deed, expecting nothing in return, do not announce it to the public, or a friend; otherwise you have expected recognition, and you have already received your reward. Do you know of any church that does all of its giving in secret? Do you know of a church that collects tithes and offerings in secret, or do they do it out in the open where those who do not give are embarrassed? Do churches only sell books when the funds are needed for the church to continue in a modest fashion, or do they sell books, take collections, have bake sales, and even go on television to get more money to build larger churches, instead of remaining just a modest assembly? For which do you think God prefers? Larger churches, or more churches so as to cover a larger area of spreading the Word? The whole point I am making is that we are to give and not take. The Word of God is to be free to all of those who cannot afford to give, or pay. And those who do give should never be coerced into giving but giving should always be done in secret. That way those who are poor will not be embarrassed because they cannot give. All things of today's church are done backwards because they act according to the needs of the flesh. If we were to act according to faith, grounded in our works of charity, the church would take on a totally new look. And it will take on a totally new look, for those who learn what the true church is. The true church is the New Church, and it is about to make itself known in the world. The old church is at its end, which is a church based on mans senses, which teaches according to the ways of the flesh. For the Lord is not returning so he can bless your flesh, but so that he can teach you how to put off your flesh, and its evil ways. As we read in Luke: Do you think I came to bring peace on earth? No, I tell you, but division (Luke 12:51). So you see, the Lord does not return to bless your flesh, but he returns to teach those who are chosen at that particular time, to mortify the deeds of the flesh, and to begin their life living in faith in him and his ways. And his ways are totally different from mans. For where we think the Word was written about this material world, it actually has nothing to do with this material world. For what the Lord is about to teach each and every human being is that we are all angels, and that when we each awaken to reality, we will receive our inheritance. For right now we are nothing more than the Prodigal Son. Now, from what I have said, do you see that no man is good, and that we all go to heaven at our own predestined time? For if none are good, and we are only good when the Lord allows us to be good, this means that we are all equal in Gods eyes, and that he will regenerate every man in his own time. But time is not as man sees it, for we all live much longer in the flesh than we truly know. We also live much longer in the spirit than we truly know. For who can imagine what forever is like, owing to the fact that we look at everything according to time and space. But forever cannot be measured as we measure time. Neither can God be measured as we measure space. For God is all time and space rolled into one, which causes him to be infinite. But getting back to the subject, no man is good, and therefore no man can be comfortable in saying he will go to heaven when he passes on from this world. So would you like for me to tell you my theory, which I have received from the spiritual world? I simply call it theory, because nothing I speak, or teach is a confirmed truth, for when you confirm a truth, it becomes a lie. Why? Because there are more details to each truth than can ever be stated, and therefore each truth is an open book, so to say. Therefore, everything I say and teach is as an open book, which will never actually end, and is always open for further additions. So confirm nothing I say, but simply consider everything I say as part of the actual truth, with other parts soon to come. This is another mistake those of the church make, for because every church represents a religion or doctrine, they confirm their truths, and therefore cause them all to be lies. Do not continue to make this mistake, for God cannot teach you in faith without you considering all things you see, read, think, hear, dream, feel, or live. And all of these things teach a man who is a New Church, by him living in faith, true Godly faith. So as I was saying, here is how we find our way into heaven, each and every one of us. We are born as an affection, which is created by the joining of a man and a woman in our world. The affections combined from this man and woman mix, and cause the creation of another affection, or spirit. And as they mix in this material world, so to do their spirits mix in the spiritual world, both being in the same spiritual society at the same time during conception. When each child, or spirit is born into this world they begin life with at least two heavenly angels, and two spirits from hell. This is done because man is created with free will, and is living at all times in a place called equilibrium. Equilibrium is what is known as midway between heaven and hell. And every man remains midway between heaven and hell all his life, in the material world. Now when we are first born we are in pure innocence as a baby, drawing only on the angel's affections from within. And these angels remain with us all through our childhood to protect us. This does not mean that children are never meant to come to harm. For as long as man has free will, which he will always have, children, as well as adolescents, young adults, adults, and the elderly will all fall into harm at some point or another. As we read in Ecclesiastes: I have seen something else under the sun. The race is not to the swift or the battle to the strong, nor does food come to the wise or wealth to the brilliant, or favor to the learned; but time and chance happen to them all (Ecclesiastes 9:11). Now many would think that because God is a loving God that he would not allow time and chance to happen to every man, but he does and he must. And understand that what I mean by time and chance is basically anyone can fall into a hole, or get caught in a snare. Anyone can get hit by a bus, or win the lottery for twenty million dollars. Anyone can find God, simply by chance, not even expecting it to happen, or not even seeing it coming in his or her life. Anyone can curse out of anger, or strike a friend because of a momentary weakness, or temporary insanity from anger. Anyone can kill, and anyone can love. And for my final example God has created this universe so that: There is a time for everything, and a season for every activity under heaven: A TIME TO BE BORN AND A TIME TO DIE, A TIME TO PLANT AND A TIME TO UPROOT, A TIME TO KILL AND A TIME TO HEAL, A TIME TO TEAR DOWN AND A TIME TO BUILD, A TIME TO WEEP AND A TIME TO LAUGH, A TIME TO MOURN AND A TIME TO DANCE, A TIME TO SCATTER STONES AND A TIME TO GATHER THEM, A TIME TO EMBRACE AND A TIME TO REFRAIN, A TIME TO SEARCH AND A TIME TO GIVE UP, A TIME TO KEEP AND A TIME TO THROW AWAY, A TIME TO TEAR AND A TIME TO MEND, A TIME TO BE SILENT AND A TIME TO SPEAK, A TIME TO LOVE AND A TIME TO HATE, A TIME FOR WAR AND A TIME FOR PEACE. What does the worker gain from his toil? I have seen the burden God has laid on men (Ecclesiastes 3:1-10). Now I have used capitals for a reason, so that this section may easily be found. As you can see, all things will happen to all men, but each in its own season. And childhood is a season just as young adulthood, adulthood, and old age. Just as morning, noon, evening, and night. And just as spring, summer, autumn, and winter. And as long as there is a created universe, which there will be to eternity, all men will endure seasons in their lives, so as to learn all things that God has in store for each of us. Now when we are children, if the angels living within each child were not present, every child would pass on from this life at a very early age. For out of every hundred mothers and fathers in the world, none are ever truly prepared for parenthood, and will therefore make mistakes; and you can count on it. Therefore God has thought of this ahead of time, and provided each child their own babysitters you could say. Of course people of the world are not aware of this, and most would never even believe it if you were to tell them. However it is true, and this is why babies and young children do not come under harm more often than they do. And as I said, yes children do get hurt, sometimes badly, but they heal, and the parents learn a great lesson from it. But do not think God takes it out on the children, for they do not feel the pain that grownups believe they do, for God can easily remove pain, or even hold it back. For as I have already stated, children are innocent until adolescence, and are therefore protected from evil as well as severe pain, because God will not allow evil, or harm to come to the good. But you must understand what harm is, for I do not speak of physical harm, because we all endure physical harm, just at different levels of pain.

And the levels of pain in life are controlled, believe it or not, by the level of evil in a person; and children are not actually ever evil. So even though a child may appear to be harmed, God does not allow pain beyond what a child can easily stand. Yes that child will cry, or scream, or even go crazy sometimes, but this is for the parents good, and the child will not suffer any ill affects because of it, at least not while they are a child. But as they become older, this does not mean they will not suffer consequences from their childhood, because they are bad or evil at some point in their adulthood. But it is always the evil that are punished, and never the good. You will find this hard to accept, this I know, because most people want to believe they are good, and do not understand why they suffer such things in life. Now you are probably saying to yourself by now: Hey! Is he saying that children never suffer really bad circumstances, or never become badly hurt? No! I am not saying that at all, for if you remember, man has free will, and because of this children even get hurt very badly, and even suffer death at all different extremes. If God were to stop every bad situation, which harms children, the world would become over populated, plus the fact that God is not a respecter of persons; and what he does for one he has to do for another, right? If he stops a child from dying he may allowing that child to live longer than he is supposed to, or longer than he was predestined to live. For God removes much future evil from this world, simply by permitting mans free will to take place. He does not allow the unlearned of the world to know this however, for they live for the flesh, and will accept no harm that comes to their children, or that is even permitted by God. Of course this is because they do not see, nor understand the big picture. Look at it this way: If you are truly a loving Christian, and you knew your child was going to grow up to be a murderer and a rapist, would you stop someone from ending their life in this world, especially if you knew they would go to a place where they would be raised by angels, and would never even see the evil that would have caused them to become the person they would have become, if he had remained in this world? If I were to guess, I would say you still would not wish to allow that child to be taken from this world, because you are flesh, and cannot think like a loving spiritual being. But you must one day come to understand why and how God can allow this, for it is necessary. For this material world, with its fleshly beings was put here for the simple reason that we are to populate the heavens with angels. This world is the seedbed for the heavens to come. So, because we are the seedbeds, we can be removed from this world whenever the Lord so chooses for us to do so. And he loves each and every one of his children the same, whereas you love your worldly, fleshly children more than all others. And because of this, we cannot yet be trusted with the things of God, at least until we have been regenerated by God, and so come to understand his ways. There are many things to consider when deciding when a person is to leave this world, and then go on to be with the angels in heaven. I know I am not ready to be trusted with this decision yet, and don't know if I ever will be, but that is okay with me for now. But I have another piece of information for you, which I have not yet mentioned. You would be happy for your child because he died at a young age, if you knew the ways of God, and if you could truly know where your child goes from here. For when a child dies young it is a given that he enters the heavens, whereas when they are older, such as adolescents, young adults, adults, or elderly, there is no guarantee where they are headed. But just because they are in heaven does not mean they are not still living among fleshly human beings. For they are living within a fleshly human being, such as yourself, and will continue to do so till forever, or to eternity. Yes, losing a child is hard for anyone, but we all must continue on, doing what God intended for us to do in the beginning. For every human being is created as an affection, so as to forever serve as a use to mankind. And even though we may lose a child or loved one we still must go on, doing for mankind as we always have been doing. And for all of you who may have lost a child or loved one, I can assure you that you will be with them again, and can even spend eternity with them, if that is at all your wish. So when we are children, we are protected by God, one way or the other. It may not appear to the parents as though we are protected, but we are. For however you look at it, we are in the presence of angels, who are nurturing us, teaching us, and protecting us as children. As we grow older however, things change, and we begin to draw from the evil affections from within. Every child inherits the evil that is within their parents, and can therefore choose these evils as their own. But they also have the free will to not accept their parent's ways as their own. For this reason, no man can blame his mother or father for any bad habits, or evil ways he may have in life, for he is always his own person. However, as you have probably noticed throughout life, many people inherit, and keep as their own, their parents evil ways, or traditions. For because of mans foolish pride, he believes he must hold onto his Family Traditions, and follow in his or her parents footsteps. Now because this happens many times in a generation, it usually takes up to many, many generations in a family before change, or good is brought about in that bloodline. For someone must break the string of evil in that spirit, or family. For each family is a spiritual society in the spiritual world. Now we read in the Word: You shall not bow down to them or worship them; for I, the Lord your God, am a jealous God, punishing the children for the sin of the fathers to the third and fourth generation of those who hate me (Deuteronomy 5:9). Now whereas we may look at this statement and take it literally, the numbers third and fourth do not mean third and fourth, but these numbers mean something else other than actual numbers. For three or third in the word mean completion, according to truths, and four, or fourth means completion as far as goods are concerned. The number four in the Word also signifies conjunction of goods and truths. So a family will be visited by their families past evils until goods and truths are completed in that family line, or until there is no more goods or truths found in that family line, in which case a New Church is born in that family line, and so a new beginning for that family. When this is completed in each family generation, or spiritual society, morning has then come, or spring, or childhood, or a new birth. This is when the conjunction of goods and truths has taken place, and a New Church formed. For it is a new season for that generation. This is when the Last Judgment takes place in a spirits life, or in a family line, and all things are put back into order, that being goods and truths. When this happens, which the actual material physical rarely recognizes, the Lord enters the world again, and forms a New Church in place of the old one. So you can usually study a person for a short time, and you should be able to, if you are a regenerated New Church member, at what state that person is in their present lifetime. State being either spring, summer, autumn, or winter. Morning, noon, evening, or night. Childhood, young adulthood, adulthood, or old age. But you cannot see these things in the flesh, only in their spirit, or inner man. And to be able to recognize the state of a person's spirit requires you to be in the spirit at that time. And God only allows us to do so when he chooses, and only for a persons good, not to judge anyone. For we are not here to judge, but to love, and accept, and to show mercy when the Lord leads us to do so. So if you cannot see any of these things in your life, it just hasn't become your time yet. However, if you are reading these words, more than likely, it is your time. But we must all enter into, and pass through four seasons in our complete lifetime in this material world, which will take more than the lifetime of a single human being. So we go from Dad, to son, to grandson, to great grandson, and so on, until we have completed our four seasons, and then go on to become a new church. And when we reach that point, we sometimes are given the awareness that it has happened, before we leave the material world for the last time. But even though we may not return to this material world again, as far as actually living life in this world, we will still live within human beings, as angels. And angels live forever within human beings, and cannot survive for an extended period of time outside of a human being. On the other hand, human beings could not live for a single second, without the presence of angels and spirits. So when we leave this world as either a New Church, being aware that we are a new church, or not being aware that we are a new church, we enter the World of Spirits, and then soon after go directly to our corresponding heaven, or we sometimes enter our corresponding heaven immediately upon entry into the spiritual world, all according to the Lords decision. For at this point in our lives, some of us are so easily seen as angels upon entry into the spiritual realm, that the Lord will send us directly to our heaven, with no vastation process at all. And when we are on the other side for our final appearance, we go on to live within the heavens to eternity. But even though the heavens are now our home does not mean we will never sin, or be disobedient again. For we are still men, with free will, simply living in another world. We still have a connection with the material world, but we have no recollection of what is going on there at any given time. That is unless the Lord so chooses to allow us as angels to see, or temporarily appear in the material world. And how we appear as angels in the material world is very simple. A human being sees the angel from within himself, with his own eyes. So if you are ever to actually see an angel in this world, you are simply seeing them from within yourself, but you cannot see angels from their own substance unless you are seeing them from your spirit as well. And when this happens, God opens up the sight of your spirit in this material world, or in the spiritual world, for both can be done. But you cannot ever see an angel in truly material flesh, as you yourself are. You can even see the Lord, while in this world, but only as an angel, and not actually as he truly is. For it would be like looking straight into the sun, that is a thousand times brighter. Do you now see how you go from one world to another, and still you remain a man, just as though you were still in this material world? The only difference is that spirits believe themselves to be the fleshly human being they possess, and angels know they are not the person they possess. Therefore if you are now reading this work, and think you are that fleshly human being that you reside within at this time, you are a spirit. But if you know that you are not that fleshly human being which you now live within and possess, you are no longer a spirit, but an angel, who is simply waiting to enter the other life, so as to remain an angel in heaven forever. God will now do many wonderful things from you alone, with you acting out, only what he leads you to do from now on. There will still be times when you are not sure if your actions are from the Lord or from yourself, and this is where faith comes in. Always remain in faith to the Lord, trusting that he will guide you into all things; and if you mess up from time to time, he will not only forgive you, but he will cover over your mistakes with things which are still for the good of all mankind. Remember, you are still in a material world, where there is still much evil around you, and Satan will do his very best to continue to trap you, and lead you astray, so remain faithful to the Lord and he will forever continue to lead you not into temptation, as well as forgive you for your evil ways while in this world. And even though I can assure you of all these things, you will still continue to reap that which you sow in this world, or lifetime; so do your very best to sow in love.

(Continuation of The Doctrine of Sacred Scripture)
(This number 3. follows number 2.—which coincides with [9].)

[18] 3. BECAUSE OF THE SPIRITUAL SENSE THE WORD IS DIVINELY INSPIRED, AND HOLY IN EVERY WORD.

It is asserted in the Church that the Word is holy, and this because Jehovah God spoke it. However, as its holiness is not apparent from the letter alone, therefore, he who once has doubts about its holiness on that account, when he afterwards reads the Word, confirms his doubts by many things in it. For he then reflects, Is this holy? Is this Divine? Therefore, lest such thoughts should flow into the minds of many and ultimately prevail, and thereby conjunction of the Lord with the Church where the Word is should perish, it has pleased the Lord now to reveal its spiritual sense in order that it may be known where in the Word that holiness lies concealed. Some examples may be given to illustrate this.

(2) The Word sometimes treats of Egypt, sometimes of Assyria, sometimes of Edom, of Moab, the children of Ammon, Tyre and Sidon, and Gog. He who does not know that by those names things relating to heaven and the Church are signified, may be led into the error that the Word treats much of nations and peoples, and but little of heaven and the Church; thus much of earthly and little of heavenly things. When, however, he knows what is signified by these nations and peoples, or by their names, he may come out of his error into the truth.

(3) In like manner, when it is observed that in the Word frequent mention is made of gardens, groves and woods; and also of their trees, as the olive, the vine, the cedar, the poplar and the oak; and also of the lamb, the sheep, the goat, the calf and the ox; and also of mountains, hills, valleys, and the fountains, rivers and waters in them; and much more of a similar nature; he who knows nothing of the spiritual sense of the Word cannot believe otherwise than that only these things are meant. For he does not know that by a garden, a grove and a wood are meant wisdom, intelligence, and knowledge; by the olive, the vine, the cedar, the poplar and the oak are meant the good and truth of the Church, celestial, spiritual, rational, natural and sensual; by the lamb, the sheep, the goat, the calf and the ox are meant innocence, charity and natural affection; by mountains, hills and valleys are meant the higher, lower, and the lowest things of the Church. Moreover he does not know that by Egypt is signified knowledge; by Assyria, reason; by Edom, the natural; by Moab, the adulteration of good; by the children of Ammon, the adulteration of truth; by Tyre and Sidon, cognitions of truth and good; and by Gog, external worship without the internal. When however, a man knows these things, he is then able to consider that the Word treats only of heavenly things, and that those earthly things are only the subjects (subjecta) in which are heavenly things.

(4) An example from the Word may illustrate this also. We read in the Psalms:

The voice of Jehovah is upon the waters: the God of glory maketh it to thunder: Jehovah is upon great waters. The voice of Jehovah breaketh the cedars; yea, Jehovah breaketh in pieces the cedars of Lebanon. He maketh them also to skip like a calf; Lebanon and Sirion like a young unicorn. The voice of Jehovah divideth as a flame of fire. The voice of Jehovah shaketh the wilderness; the Lord shaketh the wilderness of Kadesh. The voice of Jehovah maketh the hinds to calve, and discovereth the forests: and in His temple doth everyone speak of His glory (Psalms 29:3-9).

He who does not know that the particulars in this passage, even to every single word, are Divine and holy, may say within himself, if he is a merely natural man: What is this? That Jehovah sits upon the waters, by His voice breaks the cedars and makes them to skip like a calf, and Lebanon like a young unicorn, and makes the hinds to calve? And much more. He does not know that the power of Divine Truth, or of the Word, is described by these things in the spiritual sense.

For in that sense by the voice of Jehovah, which is here called thunder, is meant Divine Truth, or the Word, in its power; by the great waters upon which Jehovah sits are meant the truths of the Word. By the cedars and by Lebanon, which He breaks, and breaks in pieces, are meant the falsities of the rational man; by the calf, and the young unicorn, the falsities of the natural and of the sensual man. By the flame of fire is meant the affection of falsity; by the wilderness and the wilderness of Kadesh, the Church where there is not any truth and good. By the hinds which the voice of Jehovah makes to calve are meant the Gentiles who are in natural good; and by the forests which He discovers are meant the knowledge's of natural and spiritual things which the Word opens up to him. The passage therefore continues, that in His temple everyone speaks of His glory. By this is meant that in all the particulars of the Word there are Divine Truths; for the temple signifies the Lord, and consequently the Word, and also heaven and the Church; and glory signifies Divine Truth. Hence it is manifest that there is not a word in this passage which is not descriptive of the Divine power of the Word against falsities of every kind among natural men, and of the Divine power in reforming the Gentiles.

[19] There is in the Word a sense still more internal, called the celestial, concerning which something was said above in No. 6; but this sense can be explained only with difficulty, for it does not fall so much into the thought of the understanding as into the affection of the will. There is within the Word a still more internal sense called the celestial because from the Lord proceed Divine Good and Divine Truth, Divine Good from His Divine Love, and Divine Truth from His Divine Wisdom. Both of these are in the Word, for the Word is the Divine. Proceeding, and because both are there, therefore the Word imparts life to those who read it reverently. Something however, will be said on this subject in the chapter where it will be shown that in all the particulars of the Word there is the marriage of the Lord and the Church, and consequently the marriage of good and truth.

[20] 4. THE SPIRITUAL SENSE OF THE WORD HAS HITHERTO BEEN UNKNOWN.

That all things in nature, both general and particular, and also all things in the human body, correspond to spiritual things is shown in the work "Heaven and Hell, Nos. 87-105. What correspondence is however, has hitherto been unknown; yet in most ancient times it was very well known, for to those who lived then the science of correspondences was the science of sciences, and was so universal that all their treatises and books were written by correspondences. The Book of Job, which is an ancient book, is full of correspondences.

[2] The hieroglyphics of the Egyptians and the myths of antiquity were of a like nature. All the ancient Churches were representative of heavenly things; and their ceremonies and also the statutes, on which their worship was founded, consisted of pure correspondences. Of a like nature were all the things of the

Church established among the children of Jacob; their burnt offerings and sacrifices with all the things connected with them were correspondences. So also was the tabernacle with everything in it; and likewise their feasts, as the feast of unleavened bread, the feast of tabernacles, and the feast of the first fruits; and also the priesthood of Aaron and the Levites, and the holy garments of Aaron and his sons; and, moreover, all the statutes and judgments relating to their worship and life.

[3] Now because Divine things manifest themselves in the world in correspondences, therefore, the Word was written by pure correspondences. Therefore, also the Lord, since He spoke from His Divine, spoke by correspondences. For whatever proceeds from the Divine manifests itself in nature in such things as correspond to what is Divine; and these things then have stored up within them Divine things called celestial and spiritual.

[21] I have been informed that the men of the Most Ancient Church, which existed before the Flood, were of so heavenly a genius that they conversed with the angels of heaven; and that they had the power to do so by correspondences. Consequently, their wisdom became such that, whatever they saw on earth they thought of not only naturally but also spiritually, thus also in conjunction with the angels. I was further informed that Enoch, who is mentioned in Genesis verse 21-24, and his associates collected correspondences from their speech, and transmitted this knowledge to posterity. As a result of this the science of correspondences was not only known but was also cultivated in many kingdoms of Asia, particularly in the land of Canaan, Egypt, Assyria, Chaldea, Syria, Arabia, and in Tyre. Sidon and Nineveh. It was thence communicated from places on the coast to Greece; but it was there changed into fable, as may be seen from the literature of the oldest Greek writers.

[22] When however, in the course of time the representative things of the Church, which were correspondences, were turned into idolatry and also into magic, by the Divine Providence of the Lord the science of correspondences was gradually obliterated, and amongst the Israelitish and Jewish nation was completely lost and became extinct. The worship of that nation consisted indeed of pure correspondences, and consequently was representative of heavenly things; but the people themselves did not understand the representation of a single thing. For they were all together natural men, and therefore they did not wish, nor indeed were they able, to know anything of spiritual things, nor therefore, anything of correspondences.

[23] The idolatries of nations in ancient times arose from a knowledge of correspondences because all things that appear on the earth have a correspondence, as trees, cattle and birds of every kind, also fishes and all other things. The Ancients who had a knowledge of correspondences made for themselves images corresponding to heavenly things, and they took delight in them because they

signified things of heaven and consequently of the Church. These images, therefore, they set up, not only in their temples but also in their homes, not to worship them but that they might remind them of the heavenly thing which they signified. Thus, in Egypt and elsewhere there were effigies of calves, oxen, serpents, also children, old men and virgins; because calves and oxen signified the affections and powers of the natural man; serpents, the prudence of the sensual man; children, innocence and charity; old men, wisdom; and virgins, affections of truth; and so on. When however, the knowledge of correspondences was lost, their posterity began to worship as holy, and at length as deities, the images and likenesses set up by the Ancients, because these were in and about their temples.

[2] So too, with other nations; as with the Philistines in Ashdod, where Dagon was worshipped, concerning which see 1 Samuel verse 1 to the end. This image in the upper part was like a man, and in the lower part was like a fish, and was so devised because a man signifies intelligence and a fish knowledge; and these make one. On account of their knowledge of correspondences also the ancients worshipped in gardens and groves, according to the different kind of trees growing in them, and also on mountains and hills; because gardens and groves signified wisdom and intelligence, and every tree something that had relation to these. Thus, the olive signified the good of love; the vine, truth from that good; the cedar, rational good and truth; while a mountain signified the highest heaven, and a hill, the heaven beneath it.

[3] The knowledge of correspondences remained among many eastern nations even until the coming of the Lord. This may be seen from the story of the wise men from the East, who came to the Lord at his nativity.

A star went before them, and they brought with them gifts; gold, frankincense and myrrh (Matthew 2:1,2,9-11).

For the star which went before them signified knowledge from heaven; gold, celestial good; frankincense, spiritual good; and myrrh, natural good; and from these three all worship proceeds.

[4] Still there was no knowledge whatever of correspondences among the Israelitish and Jewish nation, although all the particulars of their worship, all the judgments and statutes given to them through Moses, and everything contained in the Word were pure correspondences. The reason of this was that they were at heart idolaters and of such a nature that they were not even willing to know that any part of their worship had a celestial and spiritual meaning; for they desired that all those things and things connected with them should be holy of themselves. If, therefore, the celestial and spiritual things had been revealed to them, they would not only have rejected, but would even have profaned them. For this reason heaven was so closed to them that they hardly knew that there was a life eternal. That such was the case is very evident from the fact that they

did not acknowledge the Lord, although the whole Sacred Scripture prophesied concerning Him, and foretold Him. They rejected Him for the sole reason that He taught them about a heavenly and not about an earthly kingdom; for they desired a Messiah who should exalt them above all the nations in the whole world, and not one who should make their eternal salvation His chief regard. Moreover, they declare that the Word contains within itself many Arcana, * which they term mystic; but they have no desire to know that these related to the Lord. They are however, willing to know when it is said that they relate to gold.

[24] The science of correspondences, by means of which the spiritual sense of the Word is communicated, was not disclosed at that time because the Christians of the primitive Church were extremely simple men, so that it could not be revealed to them; for if it had been revealed it would have been of no use to them, nor would it have been understood. After that time darkness came upon the whole Christian world, in consequence of Papal dominion; and those who are subject to that, and have confirmed themselves in its falsities, are not able, nor are they willing, to entertain anything spiritual, nor consequently to apprehend what is the correspondence of natural with spiritual things in the Word. For thus they would be convinced that by Peter is not Peter, but the Lord as the rock; and they would also be convinced that the Word even to its inmost things is Divine, and that a decree of the Pope is a matter of no account in relation to the inmost things of the Word. Moreover, after the reformation heavenly truths were hidden from men because they began to separate faith from charity, and to worship God under three persons, and thus three Gods whom they supposed to be one. For if these truths had been revealed, men would have falsified them and applied them to faith alone, applying not one of them to charity and love. Thus they would also have closed heaven to themselves.

[25] The spiritual sense of the Word has at this day been disclosed by the Lord because the doctrine of genuine truth has now been revealed; and this doctrine, and no other, agrees with the spiritual sense of the Word. This sense also is signified by the appearing of the Lord in the clouds of heaven with glory and power (Matthew 24:30,31); and this chapter treats of the consummation of the age, by which is meant the last phase of the Church. The opening of the Word as to its spiritual sense was promised also in Revelation. It is there meant by the White Horse and by the Great Supper to which all are invited (chapter 19:11-18). That for a long time the spiritual sense will not be acknowledged, and that this is owing entirely to those who are in falsities of doctrine, especially concerning the Lord, and who therefore do not admit truths, is meant in the Revelation by the beast and by the kings of the earth who were about to make war with Him that sat upon the White Horse (Rev. 19:19).

*   Arcanum (plur. Arcana), what is shut up, enclosed, from arceo to shut up, and
        arca, an ark, chest, or box. Usual connotation, hidden things.

        By the beast is meant the Roman Catholics, as in Revelation 17:3; and by
the kings of the earth are meant the reformers, who are in falsities of doctrine.

[26] 5. HENCEFORTH THE SPIRITUAL SENSE OF THE WORD WILL BE
MADE KNOWN ONLY TO THOSE WHO ARE IN GENUINE TRUTHS
FROM THE LORD.

        This is because no one is able to see the spiritual sense except from the Lord
alone, and unless he is in Divine Truths from the Lord. For the spiritual sense
treats only of the Lord and of His Kingdom; and in the understanding of that
sense are His angels in heaven, for that sense is the Divine Truth there. Man
can violate Divine Truth, if he has a knowledge of correspondences and by it
proceeds to explore the spiritual sense of the Word from his own intelligence;
since by a few correspondences known to him he may pervert the spiritual sense,
and even force it to confirm what is false. This would be to offer violence to
Divine Truth, and also to heaven. Therefore, if anyone desires to discover that
sense from himself and not from the Lord, heaven is closed to him; and when
heaven is closed he either sees no truth, or becomes spiritually insane.

[2]   This is also because the Lord teaches everyone by means of the Word. Moreover,
       He teaches from those truths, which a man already possesses: He does not directly
       impart new truths. Therefore, if a man is not principled in Divine Truths, or
       if he has only acquired a few truths as well as falsities he may by their means
       falsify the truths. This is done by every heretic with regard to the sense of the
       letter of the Word, as is well known. Lest therefore anyone should enter into the
       spiritual sense of the Word, and pervert genuine truth, which belongs to that
       sense, guards are placed over it by the Lord, and guards in the Word are meant
       by the Cherubim.
[3]   That guards were so placed were represented to me in the following manner:
       It was granted me to see large money bags, in appearance like sacks, in which
       silver was stored up in great abundance; and as these were open, it seemed as if
       anyone might take out, or even steal, the silver deposited there; but near those
       bags sat two angels as guards. The place where the bags were laid looked like a
       manger in a stable. In an adjoining room were seen some modest maidens, in the
       company of a chaste married woman. Near the room were standing two children,
       who, I was told, were not to be played with as children but as wise persons.
[4]   Then there appeared a harlot, and a horse lying dead. When I had seen these
       things, I was informed that they represented the sense of the letter of the Word,
       within which is the spiritual sense. The large money-bags full of silver signified
       cognitions of truth in great abundance. The fact that they were open and yet
       guarded by angels, signified that everyone might take from them cognitions

of truth, but that care must be taken lest anyone should violate the spiritual sense, in which are pure truths. The manger in the stable in which the purses lay signified spiritual instruction for the understanding. This is the signification of a manger, for a horse that eats from it signifies the understanding. The modest maidens who were seen in the adjoining room signified affections of truth; the chaste married woman, the conjunction of good and truth; and the children signified the innocence of wisdom therein. They were angels from the third heaven, who all appear like little children. The harlot, with the dead horse, represented the falsification of the Word by many at the present day, by which all understanding of truth perishes; a harlot signified falsification, and a dead horse, an understanding dead to all truth. * * This passage is in quotation marks in the original, and repeated elsewhere. (See T.C.R. 277; A.R. 255; AND S.D. 3605a.)

[27] III

The sense of the letter of the Word is the basis, the containant and the support of the spiritual and celestial senses. In every Divine work there is a first, middle and a last; the first passes through the middle to the last, and so exists and subsists; consequently, the last is the basis. Again, the first is in the middle, and by means of the middle in the last, and thus the last is the containant; and because the last is the containant and the basis, it is also the support.

[28] It will be comprehended by the learned that these three may be called end, cause and effect; also being, becoming and existing: the end is being, the cause is becoming, and the effect is existing. Consequently, in everything that is complete there is a Trine, called the first, the middle and the last; also the end, the cause, and the effect; as well as being (esse), becoming (fieri), and existing (existere). When one understands these things then also does one understand that every Divine work is complete and perfect in its last; and also that the whole is in the last, which is a trine, because the prior things are simultaneously therein.

[29] For this reason by three in the Word, in its spiritual sense, is understood what is complete and perfect, and thus all inclusive; and because this is the signification of that number it is used in the Word when such a meaning is intended, as in the following places:

Isaiah walked naked and barefoot three years (Isaiah 20:3). Jehovah called Samuel three times, and Samuel ran three times to Eli, and Eli understood the third time (1 Samuel 3:1-8). Jonathan told David to hide himself in the field three days. Jonathan then shot three arrows at the side of the stone, and finally David bowed himself three times before Jonathan (1 Samuel 20:5,12-41). Elijah stretched himself three times on the widow's son (1 Kings 17:21). Elijah commanded them to pour water on the burnt offering three times (1 Kings 18:34). Jesus said, The Kingdom of heaven is like unto leaven, which a woman took and hid in three measures of meal, till the whole was leavened (Matthew 13:33). Jesus said to Peter that he would deny Him thrice (Matthew 26:34).

Jesus said three times to Peter, Lovest thou me (John 21:15-17)? Jonah was in the whales belly three days and three nights (Jonah 1:17). Jesus said that they should destroy the temple, and that He Himself would build it in three days (Matthew 26:61). Jesus prayed three times in Gethsemane (Matthew 26:39-44). Jesus rose again on the third day (Matthew 28:1). There are many other passages where the number three is mentioned; and it is used where a work finished and perfect is treated of because this is the meaning of that number.

[30] These things are stated to introduce what follows, that this may be comprehended intellectually; and now, at this point, that it may be understood that the natural sense of the Word, or the sense of the letter, is the basis, the containant and the support of its spiritual and celestial sense.

[31] It was stated above in Nos. 6 and 19, that there are three senses in the Word; also, that the celestial sense is its first sense, the spiritual its middle sense, and the natural its last or lowest sense. Hence, the rational man may conclude that the first of the Word or the celestial, passes through its middle or the spiritual, to its last or natural; and that thus its last is the basis. Also, that its first or celestial is in its middle or the spiritual and by means of this is in its last or the natural; and consequently that its last or the natural, which is the sense of the letter of the Word, is the containant, and because it is the containant and the basis, it is also the support.

[32] But how these things are brought about cannot be stated in a few words. They are moreover, Arcana, which engage the angels of heaven, and they will be explained as far as possible in the treatises mentioned in the preface to "THE DOCTRINE OF THE LORD." These will be explained from angelic wisdom, concerning Divine Providence, Omnipotence, Omnipresence, Omniscience, Divine Love, Divine Wisdom, and also Life. It is sufficient for the present that we may conclude from what has been said above that the Word, which is an essentially Divine work designed for the salvation of the human race, as to its lowest or natural sense, called the sense of the letter, is the basis, the containant and the support of the two interior senses.

[33] From this it follows that the Word without the sense of its letter would be like a palace without a foundation, a palace in the air instead of on the ground, a mere shadow which would vanish away. Again, it would be like a temple, containing many sacred things, whose central shrine had no protecting roof or dividing wall, which are its containants. If these were wanting, or were taken away, its holy things would be carried off by robbers, and violated by the beasts of the earth and the birds of the air, and thus destroyed. It would be like the tabernacle (in the inmost of which was the Ark of the Covenant, and in the center the golden lamp stand, the golden alter upon which was the incense, and the table upon which was the shewbread, which were its holy things), without its outermost things, namely, the curtains and the veils. Indeed, the Word without the sense of its letter would be like the human body without its coverings, called skins,

and without the support of its bones: without these all the inward parts would fall asunder. It would also be like the heart and lungs in the thorax without their covering, called the pleura, and their supports, called the ribs; and like the brain without its covering, called the dura mater, and without its general covering, containant, and support called the skull. Thus would it e with the Word without the sense of its letter. Therefore, it is said in Isaiah that Jehovah will create upon all the glory a covering (Isaiah 4:5).

[34] The case would be similar with the heavens where the angels are, without the world where men are. The human race is the basis, the containant and support of the heavens; and the Word is with men and in them. For all the heavens are distinguished into two kingdoms, called the celestial kingdom and the spiritual kingdom: and these two kingdoms are founded upon the natural kingdom in which men are: likewise also the Word, which is with men and in men. That the angelic heavens are distinguished into two kingdoms, the celestial and the spiritual, may be seen in the work on "Heaven and Hell," Nos. 20-28.

[35] It was shown in "THE DOCTRINE CONCERNING THE LORD" No. 28, that the prophets of the Old Testament represented the Lord as to the Word, and thereby signified the doctrine of the Church from the Word: and that they were therefore called Sons of man. From this it follows that by the various things which they suffered and endured they represented the violence inflicted by the Jews upon the sense of the letter of the Word; as that: The Prophet Isaiah was commanded to put off the sackcloth from his loins and his shoes from his feet, and to go naked and barefoot three years (Isaiah 20:2,3).

Likewise: The Prophet Ezekiel was commanded to draw a barbers razor upon his head and upon his beard, to burn a third part [of the hair] in the midst of the city, to smite a third part with the sword and to scatter a third part to the wind; and to bind a little from these in his skirts, and finally to cast it into the midst of the fire and burn it (Ezekiel 5:1-4).

2. Because the Prophets represented the Word, and consequently signified the doctrine of the Church from the Word, as was said above, and because by the head is signified wisdom from the Word, therefore, by the hair of the head and by the beard is signified the ultimate of truth. In consequence of this signification it was a mark of deep mourning, and also a great disgrace, for anyone to make himself bald, and also to appear bald. For this reason and no other the prophet was directed to shave off the hair of his head and his beard, that he might thereby represent the state of the Jewish Church as to the Word. For this reason and no other: The forty-two children who called Elisha bald head were torn in pieces by two she—bears (2Kings 2:23,24); for the prophet represented the Word, as was observed before, and baldness signified the Word without its ultimate sense.

3. The Nazirites represented the Lord as to the Word in its ultimates, as will be seen below, No. 49; and therefore, it was a statute for them that they should

let their hair grow and shave off none of it. Moreover, the term Nazirite in the Hebrew tongue signifies the hair of the head. It was also a statute for the high priest that he should not shave his head (Leviticus 21:10). Similarly for the head of a family (Leviticus 21:5).

4. Hence it was that for them baldness was a great disgrace, as may be evident from the following passages:

On all their heads shall there be baldness, and every beard cut off (Isaiah 15:2; Jeremiah 48:37). Shame shall be upon all faces and baldness upon all their heads (Ezekiel 7:18). Every head was made bald, and every shoulder was peeled (Ezekiel 29:18). I will bring up sackcloth upon all loins, and baldness upon every head (Amos 8:10). Make thee bald, and poll thee for thy delicate children; enlarge thy baldness . . . for they are gone into captivity from thee (Micah 1:16). Here by putting on and enlarging baldness is signified falsifying the truths of the Word in its ultimates; and when these are falsified, as was done by the Jews, the whole Word is destroyed. For the ultimates of the Word are its stays and supports; indeed, every word is a stay and support of its celestial and spiritual truths. As the hair signifies truth in its ultimates, therefore, in the spiritual world all who despise the Word and falsify the sense of its letter appear bald; but those who honor and love it appear with becoming heads of hair. On this subject see also below, No. 49.

[36] The Word in its ultimate or natural sense, which is the sense of its letter, is also signified by the wall of the holy Jerusalem, the structure of which was jasper; and by the foundations of the wall, which were precious stones; and also by its gates, which were pearls (Revelation 21:18-21). For by Jerusalem is signified the Church as to doctrine. However, more will be said of these things in a subsequent article. From what has been stated it may now appear that the sense of the letter of the Word, the natural sense, is the basis, the containant and the support of its interior senses, namely, the spiritual and the celestial senses.

[37] IV

Divine Truth, in the sense of the letter of the Word, is in its fullness, its sanctity, and its power. The Word, in its sense of the letter, is in its fullness, its sanctity, and its power, because the two prior or interior senses, called the spiritual and the celestial, are simultaneously in the natural sense, which is the sense of the letter, as was said above, No. 31; but how they are present simultaneously will now be told in a few words.

[38] In heaven and in the world there are two kinds of order, a successive and a simultaneous order; in successive order one thing succeeds and follows after another, from the highest to the lowest; but in simultaneous order one thing exists side by side with another, from what is inmost to what is outmost. Successive order is like a column with steps from highest to lowest; while simultaneous order is like a work coherent in concentric circles from the center even to the

last surface. We will now state how successive order becomes in the ultimate or last form simultaneous order. It becomes so in this manner. The highest things of successive order become the inmost of simultaneous order, and the lowest things of successive order become the outmost of simultaneous order, just as if a column of steps were to sink down and form a coherent body in a plane.

[2] Thus, the simultaneous is formed from the successive; and this is so in all things both in the natural and in the spiritual world, in general and in particular. For everywhere there is a first, a middle and a last; the first passing through the middle and proceeding to the last. Apply this now to the Word. The celestial, the spiritual and the natural proceed from the Lord in successive order, and in the ultimate or last form they are in simultaneous order; thus, then, the celestial and the spiritual senses of the Word are simultaneously in its natural sense. When this is understood it may be seen how the natural sense of the Word, which is the sense of the letter, is the basis, the containant and the support of its spiritual and celestial senses; and also how the Divine Good and the Divine Truth are, in the sense of the letter of the Word, in their fullness, their sanctity and their power.

[39] From this it may be evident that the Word is the Word itself in its sense of the letter, for within this there reside spirit and life; the spiritual sense in its spirit, and the celestial sense in its life. This is meant by what the Lord says: The words that I speak unto you, they are spirit, and they are life (John 6:63). The Lord spoke His words before the world, and in the natural sense. The spiritual and celestial senses are not the Word, without the natural sense, which is the sense of the letter; for they are like spirit and life within a body; and they are as has been said above in No. 33, like a palace which has no foundation.

[40] The truths of the sense of the letter of the Word are, in some cases, not naked truths, but appearances of truths, being, as it were, similitude's and comparisons taken from such things as are in nature, accommodated and adequate to the apprehension of simple people and children; but because they are correspondences, they are the receptacles and abodes of genuine truth. They are like vessels, which enclose and contain, as a crystal cup holds noble wine, or a silver dish nourishing food. They are like garments, which serve as clothing, like swaddling clothes for an infant, and comely robes for a maiden. They are also like the knowledge of the natural man, which comprises the perceptions and affections of truth of the spiritual man. The truths themselves unveiled, which are included, contained, clothed and comprised, are in the spiritual sense of the Word, and goods unveiled are in its celestial sense.

2. This however, may be illustrated from the Word:
    Jesus said: Woe unto you Scribes and Pharisees . . . for ye make clean the outside of the cup and of the platter, but within they are full of extortion and

excess, Thou blind Pharisee, cleanse first the inside of the cup and the platter, that the outside of them may be clean also (Matthew 23:25,26).

In this passage the Lord spoke by ultimate things, which are containants, and used the words "cup and platter." By the cup is meant wine, and by wine, the truth of the Word; by the platter is meant food, and by food the good of the Word. To cleanse the inside of the cup and of the platter signifies to purify the interiors, which relate to the will and thought, and thus to love and faith by means of the Word. That the outside may be clean also, signifies that the exteriors may be purified; and the exteriors are deeds and words, for these derive their essence from the interiors.

3.   Again:

Jesus said: There was a certain rich man, who was clothed in purple and fine linen, and fared sumptuously every day; and there was a certain beggar, named Lazarus, who was laid at his gate full of sores (Luke 16:19,20).

In this passage also the Lord spoke by natural things, which were correspondences, and contained spiritual things. BY THE RICH MAN IS MEANT THE JEWISH NATION, called rich because they possessed the Word, which contains spiritual riches. By the purple and fine linen with which the rich man was clothed are signified the good and truth of the Word, by the purple its good, and by the fine linen its truth. By faring sumptuously every day is signified the delight of the Jewish nation in having the Word and reading it. By the beggar Lazarus are meant the Gentiles, who do not possess the Word. By Lazarus lying at the gate of the rich man, full of sores, is meant that the Gentiles were despised and rejected by the Jews.

4.   The Gentiles are meant by Lazarus, because the Lord loved the Gentiles as He loved Lazarus, who He raised from the dead (John 11:3,5,36); who is called His friend (John 11:11); and who reclined at the table with Him (John 12:2).

From these two passages it is evident that the truths and goods of the sense of the letter of the Word are like vessels, and like the clothing of unveiled truth and good, which lie concealed in the spiritual and celestial senses of the Word.

[41] Since this is the nature of the Word in the sense of the letter, it follows that those who are principled in the Divine Truths, and who believe that the Word is interiorly holy and Divine, and especially those who believe that the Word is of this nature by virtue of its spiritual and celestial senses, see Divine Truths in natural light, while they read the Word in a state of enlightenment from the Lord. For the light of heaven in which is the spiritual sense of the Word, flows into the natural light in which is the sense of the letter of the Word, and enlightens mans intellectual faculty, called the rational, enabling him to see and acknowledge Divine Truths, both when they are manifest and when they are concealed. These truths, together with the light of heaven, flow into the minds of some men, even when they are unaware of the fact.

[42] Our Word in its inmost depths is from its celestial sense like a gentle flame which burns, and in its middle recesses is from its spiritual sense like a light which illumines; consequently the Word in its ultimate form from its natural sense, within which are the two interior senses, is like a ruby and a diamond. Since this is the nature of the Word in the sense of the letter from its transparency, therefore, the Word in this sense is meant by the following:

(1) The fountains of the wall of Jerusalem.
(2) The Urim and the Thummim on Aaron's ephod.
(3) The Garden of Eden, in which the king of Tyre has been.
(4) Also the curtains and veils of the tabernacle.
(5) And the external things of the Temple at Jerusalem.
(6) But in its glory, the Lord when He was transfigured.

[43] (1) THE TRUTHS OF THE SENSE OF THE LETTER OF THE WORD ARE MEANT BY THE FOUNDATIONS OF THE WALL OF THE NEW JERUDSALEM (Revelations 21).

This follows from the fact that by the New Jerusalem is meant a New Church as to doctrine, as was shown in "THE DOCTRINE OF THE LORD, Nos. 62-63." Therefore, by its wall and by the foundations of the wall, nothing else can be meant but the external of the Word, that is, the sense of its letter; for it is this sense from which there is doctrine, and by means of doctrines, the Church; and doctrine is like a wall with its foundations, that surrounds and secures the city. The following things are recorded in Revelation concerning the wall of the New Jerusalem and its foundations:

The angel measured the wall of the city Jerusalem, an hundred and forty-four cubits, which was the measure of a man, that is, of the angel . . . and the wall had twelve foundations, garnished with all manner of precious stones. The first foundation was jasper; the second, sapphire; the third, a chalcedony; the fourth, an emerald; the fifth, sardonyx; the sixth, sardius; the seventh, chrysolyte; the eighth, beryl; the ninth, a topaz; the tenth, a chrysoprasus; the eleventh, a jacinth; the twelfth, an amethyst (Revelation 21: 14, 17-20). By the number one hundred and forty-four are signified all the goods and truths of the Church from doctrine derived from the sense of the letter of the Word. The same is signified by twelve. By a man is signified intelligence; by an angel, Divine truths from which this is derived; by measurement is signified their quality; by the wall, and by its foundations, the sense of the letter of the Word; and by the precious stones, the truths and goods of the Word in their order, from which is doctrine, and by means of doctrine, the Church.

(Doctrine of Sacred Scripture will be continued on page 92.)

CHAPTER 4

Your Day of Judgment!

So what is the duration of every mans life? We are born into this material world as the Most Ancient Church. This Church was before the flood in the Word. We can communicate with the angels at this time in our life by correspondences. For everything a man does and says corresponds to an affection in the spiritual world. And since every child is in innocence, they are at all times in contact with the angels, and are actually at this period in their life being taught by God from within. They are also considered very wise at this time, though they have not learned to communicate with the people of this world yet, but still are wise as far as their spiritual society is concerned. At this time they worship an invisible God, for their spiritual society is still a child as far as knowing their God is concerned, or being ready to be entrusted with heavenly truths. This is because their wisdom comes totally from the heavens and the angels, or the Lord, and he cannot yet allow them to give truths to those of the material world. Plus everyone knows that the angels are very wise from the Lord alone, compared to man in this world, who is wise in his own eyes. So as long as man is in innocence, having childlike faith, he is wiser than all other men, for he seeks his wisdom from the Lord alone. And when we speak of the Most Ancient Church, we speak from the spiritual world in a man, not the material. For the Church does not actually exist in the material world, but is a representative Church at best. So we are born as "The Most Ancient Church," which is also childhood, morning, spring, and if you can accept it, at each of these stages we, or our spiritual society, is either in the Northern, Southern, Eastern, or Western quarter within the spiritual world. The reason we are in one of these or the other is because when these four quarters are spoken of in the Word they never pertain to the material world, but to the spiritual world alone, and represent the level of connection we each have at any given time to the Lord, who is the Sun in the spiritual world. Therefore East represents the Lord, and being in the good of love to the Lord in the spiritual world, from our interior man, or spirit; West represents being in love to the Lord as well, but in the exterior sense, or in an obscure sense; South represents being in truths from that love or good, in the interior sense; and North represents being in truths from that love or good, but in an exterior sense, or obscure sense.

So while a man is still a child, he is in all of these states or seasons, you could say. But all of these examples form one person, or state, or spiritual society. Next we have the Ancient Church, which comes after the flood. It runs all during adolescence, and on into young adulthood. And these as well worship an invisible God, but more of the material world is now a part of their life, and they have begun to form images of God, using them to represent Godly, or heavenly things. And God does appear at times to them in the form of an angel, such as he did to Abraham. But no one calls God by the name Jehovah at this time. Still they are in good, but in an exterior sense alone. And they can no longer communicate with God and the angels through correspondences, at least very few can, at this time in their life. And so this church in their life is only representative. This state is also noon and summer, and this adolescent will go from north, south, east, and west in his daily life; but only as far as his spirit is concerned. This is the second state in a mans life, two more are to come. The third Church to come is the Israelitish or Jewish Church, whichever you wish to call it, for it is only representative in our life. This Church is the third Church in line and they are totally representative, and have no truths either at this time. This is the time during the Prophets, where God speaks to the Prophets as well as sometimes shows himself to them in the form of an angel. This group still worships idols and performs sacrifices to other gods, but those who worship the true God now call Him Jehovah, who is no longer an invisible God, but he is now worshipped in human form. This human form is representative of the Lord who was to come. And because the Lord was representative, so were all other things of this Church. This Church as well does not possess truths. Now they worship God as a man because of the Messiah to come, but still they live by their senses and not in faith, and therefore have no conjunction with God as of yet. When the Lord comes, which is at the end of the fourth church, all sacrifices as well as things pertaining to sacrifices are abolished. This state, or season is what is also known as evening and adulthood. Still going through the four quarters in the spiritual world throughout their day. The fourth, and last Church on the list is The Christian Church. This Church is the final stages in the Church, in a mans life, or his Day of Judgment. This is the day before the coming of the Lord. This Church did indeed acknowledge one God with the lips, but in three persons, each one singly, or by himself God. Therefore they say one God but think three. Still they teach of an invisible God, and therefore can have no conjunction with him yet. They do not yet realize that God came into the world, and assumed a human, so as to have conjunction with man. This state in life is also known as night, and old age. This is where man has matured to his fullest, and is ready to be regenerated by God. Therefore, the old Church, which consisted of a total of four representative Churches, is at its end, or consummation. The Lord now returns in His spiritual sense of the Word, and teaches the man what it is time for him to know. A Last Judgment now takes place and a vastation process before the New Church is brought in his life. Evil is totally separated within his Church, and they are sent to their corresponding hells. While those of the true

Church, who are left, form to create a New Church, from a society in heaven called Michael. For all New Churches are formed by the Gentiles in the world, but also by the society called Michael. The Gentiles are those who have not been corrupted by falsities, and were not a part of the old Church, but outside it. These are the spirits who always felt that they never fit into that Church. So now the fourth Church, called the Christian Church, has reached its end. Judgment has been assessed, and all things are now back in order. The Lord brings in the New Church in the mans life, and He begins giving truths to the man, or Church. The man now begins living life in faith in the Lords teaching, and leading in his life. No longer is there fear of death, or of not finding truth. All truth is now provided, only according to the truths the man has. For the Lord does not add new truths, but teaches the man from the truths he already has in life. For we are taught according to our love, in our spiritual society. But believe me, you know much, much more than you think you know. As far as the number three being the number of completion, this is also completion in the material realm, where man has conjunction with the Lord, and is now body, soul, and spirit. Or Father, Son, and Holy Spirit. Father is the soul, Son is the body, and Holy Spirit is the spirit. And together they make the Lord, of which we are images of the Lord. And as I have said before, it takes three to make all things, whatever it may be. For everything needs a body, a soul, and a spirit; including a rock, if you can believe it. Now the only reason we do not leave this world immediately after becoming a New Church, or new being is because our days in this material world have not been completely fulfilled yet, and there is still more to do. For God has designed it so that you leave this material world at the exact moment he wishes you to leave it, and you will not be taken a moment sooner. For you must remember, you never actually die, but everyone lives forever. You also do not enter, and pass through all four seasons, or churches in a single lifetime in the material world, but it takes several, each mans days being different of course. Therefore, even though you go from being a baby, to adolescence, to young adulthood, to adulthood, and on into old age in a single lifetime in this world, does not mean that you have entered into, and passed through four Churches in that course of time. This is why there are so many different levels of maturity, and ignorance in the world today, because each of us are at a different season, or Church, or state in our lives, in which we are not all in our final state of regeneration by God. And as a matter of fact, very few are in that state or season; which is why the Word says: Enter through the narrow gate. For wide is the gate and broad is the road that leads to destruction, and many enter through it. But small is the gate and narrow the road that leads to life, and only a few find it (Matthew 7:13). So you see when the Word speaks of the number of people who enter the heavens, it speaks of those whose spirits have been prepared, or regenerated each moment, or hour, or day, or week, or month, or year. But in reality, time is not even involved, and the Word is not speaking of the material realm at all. For at the consummation of the seasons, or the Church in any mans life, a Last Judgment then takes place, and few within that human beings spiritual society actually make it to the heavens, and the rest go to the World of Spirits, or the hells. As far as the material world is concerned, we will have no recollection of these things, but only we who actually make it into the heavens, in our spiritual society. For a mans spiritual society consists of the bad as well as the good, but all are still separated by atmospheres in the spiritual world, which also protects the good from the evil, as well as the evil from the evil. So is this all there is to Gods plan of creation and salvation? No, for we have only scratched the surface. Do you now wonder why the Lord allows the good and the evil to live together in the spiritual realm? Yes the evil do live outside, on the perimeters of a society in heaven, and the most evil live on the outside, or perimeter of a society in the hells. For the heavens and the hells are all arranged according to the level of good and truth found in each society, and then the least perfect are situated at the exterior, or the perimeter of each society. And as the good advance upward or inward in a society, so too do those below who are more evil, advance inward or upward in theirs, or another society. The Lord is always willing for a spirit to change societies, and it is up to the spirit as to whether he remains in that society, for the others of that society cannot cause him to leave, and neither do they wish it. Spirits and angels advance in their levels of good and truth until forever, and continue to advance in societies for this reason. This means that all spirits and angels will reach the same destination in the spiritual world; at least eventually. For we all continue to grow in wisdom and maturity until eternity. So when you are talking or looking, and watching another persons actions, do not assume that you know what they are thinking or going through in their life, for we do not even come close to understanding all the different scenarios which can be applied to every affection or situation in a persons life. Just because you see a person crying or laughing does not mean they are necessarily sad or hurt if crying; and happy or just heard a funny joke if they are laughing. Just because a man robs a liquor store, with what could be a toy gun, and only takes food, does not mean he wishes to hurt, or steal from someone. His family may have not eaten in a week, in which case he has now become desperate, and only wishes to feed his family. If you are a concerned citizen, does this mean you should shoot this person down in cold blood, if you happen to have a gun at the time, should you mind your own business; jump the person, hoping they don't shoot you; or should you call the police and let them handle it? If you are a police officer, should you shoot this person; wait them out; try and physically retain them; attempt to arrest them; call for backup; or simply try and talk them out of it? All these scenarios play a part in a persons thoughts during a situation such as this, and man always has a choice as to how he actually deals with it. Things are not always as they seem, and this is usually the case, more often than not. Should a man die for trying to feed his family, even if he breaks certain laws? Should a man be willing to shoot a man over food, or because he has a gun in his hand, but is just trying to get out of the store? I think you know that with the given state of our world today, a police officer would more often than not shoot this man; even though I am not picking on police officers, or any certain man.

But the truth is, mercy is not a qualification for making the police force. And because there are so many different kinds of people in the world, and because everyone thinks differently, and has free will to do so, most men as police officers would not risk their life to save another. Therefore they would shoot, and ask questions later. But just as we are all forgiven for our mistakes, bad decisions, and even our bad decisions that were made on purpose; men will continue to kill for the wrong reasons. People will harm others, lash out at them at the wrong time, judge them in all different circumstances, and usually be wrong in their judgment of them. We will always continue to be cruel at times, laugh at others mistakes, put others down, or talk behind their back, not even knowing their true situation. The whole point I am making is that you should learn to live and let live, judging no one for his or her actions or mistakes. For if you have not read what I have said about this before, listen now; "All men eventually walk in all other men's shoes, and will experience everything another man experiences, so as to one day have the ability to have compassion for all other men." You don't remember all the things you have experienced because you are now in another human being, but God allows you to feel the effects when they are needed in a certain situation; such as having mercy for another, even though you don't understand why you should have mercy. We must learn mercy before we will ever see the gates of heaven. Remember that that guy you were just talking to is either not matured as far as you, or he has matured beyond where you are at this time; but either way, we continue to come back to this world until we get it right, and are completely prepared for our life in the heavens. No man is where every other man will not end up eventually, once his regeneration by the Lord is complete. Where my children and grand children are in their state in life, at this moment, is where I was also at one point in time; and where I am at this moment is where they will one day be as well; if not in this lifetime in the material world, then in the next, or the one to follow. But one thing is sure, they will live out their days as physical human beings, will enter into and pass through four complete seasons in their life, become a New Church or being, and will go on to enter the heavens as an angel, as all men before and after them will, or did do. This happens because every single human being ever born is an extension of the life, and representative life of every affection, or life the Lord has ever lived, or will live. We are all one in the Lord, as He is one in us, and so we are an extension of our brothers, neighbors, friends, sisters, mothers, fathers, enemies, or children. We are all the next stage, or life of another man, and so we are one. My grandson is me, my daughter is me, my father is me, my grandfather is me; my great, my great—great, and my great—great—great grandfathers are me; on down the line until we reach the first man ever created, who is by the way, the Lord. You may think two people were created at the same time in the beginning, but this is not the case. One was created after the other, and they were just as we will once again all be. The Father provided the Soul, and the mother provided the form, or body. And this was the case with the first male and the first female. Both share the same soul in the Lord, but different bodies in the mother, or nature. Therefore, every man or woman ever born, or ever to be born have the same soul, just at a different state in the Lord, or in creation. We appear to have our own existence, and consciousness in our life, but we all share a single existence, or consciousness in the Lord. So in creation the Lord is divided up into different heavens, different societies, different affections, and different thoughts. Outside the Lords body, in darkness, in fantasy, or in sleep we have the hells, and as they come to awaken in life they are permitted to be included in life and in the Lord. All these different hells are where man resides while he lives in and lives for, the material world. As he lets go of certain things of the material world, he is raised higher, or more inward in the spiritual world, so as to eventually totally give up the material world, and its pleasures, He is then permitted into the heavens, but in the natural heavens. He is not allowed into the upper heavens until he actually passes on from this material world, and has completed his regeneration. A man, or woman can know they have completed this regeneration, and are now being prepared for eternal life in the spiritual world, within the heavens, when he or she has begun to give up the things of the flesh, and are continuously giving up more as each day, week, month, and year continues to pass by. So that by the time they leave this world this last time, they will have been separated from all desires of the flesh, things such as jealousy, revenge, lust for the naked body, ruling over others including your mate or spouse, material gain, the love of money or riches, the need to win all the time, the need for recognition over others, and many, many more things of the flesh. Holding on to these things is what keeps us in this material world. When we no longer require them in our life, we can then enter a better, more loving world, and so go on to live forever in love. Yes we will be one in the Lord, but we will all get to share in the overall consciousness of his thoughts, as we are mature enough to receive, and live them. If you are still a child, you will only be trusted with childish things in his everyday thoughts. Still you will retain your own consciousness. The more mature you have become, the more of the overall thoughts and decisions you are permitted to make, as though they were your own. But whatever your love is, or whatever affection you represent in the Lord, these are the thoughts you will always be a part of living, and these are the areas you will be helping to make decisions on. You may say well, how can that keep me busy? Because you will be providing these affections to every human being of which your spiritual society resides within, at any given time. And so you will at all times be sufficiently busy, and will have no slack time that you do not wish to have. For out of all the people living in the world right now, as well as those on all the other planets, as well as those in the past, you are them, and provide the affection you represent, or love you represent, to every human being alive, or that ever was alive. For remember, the past is alive and well, in the Lord. Now, listen to this, the human being you are residing in right now is not you, but his spirit is you or an extension of you, and you are providing only the affection of thought that your spirit represents in that human being. Lets say you represent the love for throwing snowballs, and yes I know that is a weird love, but bear with me. Only when that human being is throwing snowballs will you be providing his thoughts of affections, and at all other times you will be in the perimeters of his spiritual society, always there to be called on once again. But as far as how much your love and his love truly have in common, this will decide how often this human being calls on your thoughts of affections. Now, because we all have consciousness as long as we are awake, we are used in societies of other human beings, because the spiritual world overlaps in the Lord, and is in all men who call on each and every affection or man, ever created. So if your affection is to help others, so that this is all you can think of most of the time, your affection will be a part of the life and everyday thoughts of every human being who is in the love of helping others, at any given point in time, or in a day. And because the Lord is always with every man, and because you are with more men than any other is, you would be closest to the Lord, and would be an angel who is highest in the heavens over all. But this is considering the fact that you are the most called on angel. The more our affection of good is called on by humans, the closer we are to the Lord; because we actually make up more of the Lords body. The more your evil affections are called on by human beings, the more you make up the hells, and the farther you are away from the Lord. Now if it is hard for you to make sense of all this, I ask that you back, and slowly read all this again, for it is very important that you get it. Our level of connection, or conjunction with the Lord all depends on how much our affection of good is used for mankind's thoughts in his everyday life. For because every man ever created is different than any man ever created, or ever to be created, this means we each represent an affection, or love, and that love stays with us for the rest of our days, unto eternity; for we are that affection in the Lords life. And so we are the Lord because we are of the Lord; and what is of the Lord is the Lord. This is very hard for man to accept if he has not read my earlier books, for all that I have written up to this point serves as proof to these statements I am here providing. So do not attempt to confirm any of this by itself, but get all the details I have given first, and then things will make much more sense to you all. I realize there are those who wont even consider what I am saying, but that is okay, for these words are for the chosen generation, or uncorruptable generation. So as I was saying, each of us is an affection of the overall man, who is actually the Lord. We become more of the Lord and our love expands in size, as we grow and mature, and as we receive more Godly wisdom. And in turn we provide, or become more and more a part of the good thoughts of affections within mankind. And this means our heavenly society grows larger and larger every moment, every hour, every day, year, and so on. Do we ever completely become the Lord? No! Because He is infinite, and we will always remain finite, and dependent on Him for our life. We do remain an angel to eternity, and grow continuously in wisdom and knowledge, but we will never match the Lord in these areas, or any others. The fact that you become an angel simply means you have reached a certain point in your life where you no longer require the things of a material world, and now choose wisdom and knowledge, or good and truth as your loves. As well you no longer require a body all the time, or form in order to live, but are happy just providing the thoughts of affections for mankind till forever. But what you are really doing is loving mankind, and allowing mankind to love you back, in the Lord, whenever they choose to do so, and according to their given free will. For if you truly love your neighbor, you wish to share all that you are, or possess with them, as well as become one with them. And how do you become one with your neighbor? By becoming one in the Lord, and making all that you are or have available to all others. Making your wisdom their wisdom, as well as your knowledge theirs. And this is the same as sharing all good and truth with your neighbor, so that they can one day learn to do the same. Now, does this mean the when you become an angel in the heavens that you will no longer have a body, or even enjoy the things of the body any longer? No, it does not! You will not require a body at all times, for you will only need a body for a limited number of things, at which time the lord will provide a human body immediately. You see, in this world we need a body at all times to survive and live, and so our bodies as well as all other things of this world are set, and permanent. However, in the heavens the angels just think of what they want, or where they wish to be and it appears, or they appear where they wish to be. But when the angel is no longer thinking of said object, or of where they are, the object disappears or they leave the place they are immediately. So as you can see, all things are instant in the heavens; for the Lord provides them instantly. Now because all things in the heavens appear as the angel wishes them, the same goes for a body. But many things in a mans life can be done completely without a body. For even in our world, and even as I sit here, my body is for the most part not required. But still it is here because this is a world where all things are fixed in place. But as far as my spirit is concerned, I am sitting here typing on a keyboard, and all that I possess is a hand and a forearm, as far as my reflection is concerned. The rest is there in the material realm, but only a hand and a forearm are present in the spiritual realm. If I wished to see the rest of my body, it would appear immediately in my sight. But in the heavens not many things actually require a body because an angel's love is wisdom and knowledge, or good and truth. We will no longer require material food, and so we will not need lips or a mouth. We don't have to have actual ears to see, but we need only believe that we have ears, and we will hear. Do you see your ears without a mirror? We also will not need legs, arms, hands, feet, torso, or head. For none of these things are needed in the heavens to carry out our everyday lives. Most of the bodily things or parts can be drawn from the material realm, and so used in the spiritual realm without even possessing them, actually. For the spiritual world is a world of appearances while this world is a world of actualities. To put it into more simpler terms I would say this: The one inside you right now who is doing the thinking is your spirit, and it is either in the heavens or in the hells at this moment. But mostly in the middle, within the World of Spirits. You can see, smell, hear, taste, and touch; and yet you do not require a physical body to do these things, but only the human you possess requires a body. The sight, touch, taste, smell, and hearing actually originate from the spiritual world, and the body parts used to allow them to be able to do all these things from the spiritual world are only seen in our world. For instance a spirit within you can be looking at something right now through your eyes, thinking they are actually you, when they really are in another world. They even believe that their memory is yours, or your memory is theirs. They see what you see, but in correspondences. So where your life is lived according to your love, theirs is lived according to theirs. Angels however cannot see things of this world through mans eyes because they know they are not human beings in a material world. So when angels see through your eyes they see the spiritual world all the time, and can go from one place to another, or one man to another in an instant. As long as a man is a spirit he believes he is the man he possesses. He sometimes dwells in the spiritual world and sometimes in the material world; but he never remains within the spiritual world for good because he covets the things of the material world still. But once he learns who he really is, and he gives up the things of the material or physical world, he has become an angel of the Lord. He is still bound by the material world until his set time because he is still in the natural heavens while in the material world as an angel. I will give a diagram to show you what I am saying on the next page. This diagram will show you exactly how God sends His influx of good and truth, or wisdom and knowledge down through the heavens, even though it appears on my drawing as sideways, and passes through the heavens until it reaches man in the material realm, or natural world. The smallest point of the vortex shown is the most pure heavens where God dwells at the center of each world as the Spiritual Sun. It acts as a successive order coming from the smallest point or highest heavens, but as a simultaneous order once it (or Gods influx) reaches the natural heavens, or natural world. The natural world and the natural heavens are the same, as long as man is in the heavens while in the world. If we travel in our affections outside this vortex shown, we are now in the hells, but still in the natural world. The difference is we move from reality to fantasy. The right end of the vortex shown is what is called the World of Spirits, and this is where man dwells while he is in the material world. If he is in good he moves farther towards the center of the circle, if he is in evil, he remains on the exterior of the circle, but in a world of fantasy. When a man passes on from this world, and he has completed his full course of his regeneration, he goes on to the world of spirits where he awakens in about three days and he is vastated, if there are evils that have to be removed from his love, or affections. If there are not, he goes straight to his corresponding heavens, where he will remain forever. This means he moves from the first, and largest circle in succession, to the next circle, which is the spiritual heavens, but on to the third circle if he is a celestial angel. Usually whatever circle you are a part of in your material life, which is one of the circles within the first big circle, this is the circle you enter when you wake up in the spiritual world, and after vastation; if you need to be vastated, which most men do. What this means is that a man will usually choose the same heavenly society that corresponds to the society in which he lived while in the material world. This is because that is where our spirit lives while we are in the world, as well as most of our loved ones spirits. So when we pass on, we find the spirits of many of our loved ones in that certain society, if they have passed on before us. For if they still remain in the world we cannot be in their presence for the fact that we would tell them things which they are not yet prepared, or permitted to know. This is why their spirit will remain in the first circle until they pass on from the material realm. This circle represents an atmosphere, which separates those of different spiritual societies, as well as different worlds. For because man cannot ever be trusted until God has regenerated him and allowed him to see who he really is, all beings who are different must be kept separated from one another. This is why we never see life on other planets, and never will, unless there is some reason the Lord sees fit for someone to do so. For every planet has a different atmosphere than its neighboring system, and as man grows closer to finding his way to the system after that he will find that the same rules will apply. For we are never to interfere with other civilizations, as we are in the habit of always doing on our own planet. But just as spirits and angels dwell among all men, so to do they dwell on other planets among all citizens of such planets. But as I have stated, where there is a spirit there is a human being, or man. Not all men on every planet looks the same, but there are many varieties out there, just as we have supposed for ages. However, same will always live among same, as all citizens in our world are more the same than we realize. There may be blacks, whites, Indians, Hispanics, Jews, Greeks, Chinese etc;

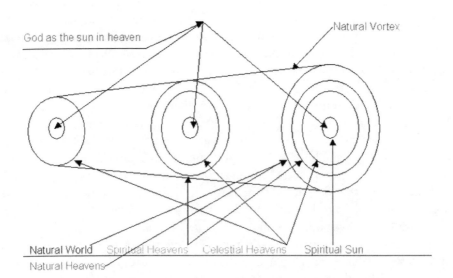

(From above), but these are minor differences compared to those that societies from other planets have with us. And because we have not, and may not, ever learn to even love those who are different from us on our own planet, God will not allow us to see those who reside on other planets. However, once we become angels, and have not only learned of who we really are, but have learned to love unconditionally as well, we will then be permitted to coexist among the occupants of all other planets and galaxies. This is why we are permitted certain little tidbits of proof in this world, that there may be life in other worlds out there, and that maybe there is hope after all that we can all co-exist among one another one day, and actually learn to love our neighbor, no matter what his faults or ways. But the Lord also knows that we must all come to the same conclusion about ourselves eventually, which is that we are hopeless when relying on our own wisdom or decisions in life, for we want nothing more as human beings than to always please our flesh, and usually could care less about our neighbors needs or wants. When we all get to this point in our lifetime, then the Lord can do something with us, in which case he will then regenerate each man who reaches this state in life. But we must leave this world, and enter the next, before we can extend our reaches beyond this planet. Now you may be one of those who does not even believe there is life on other planets, but I say to you, if you are one of these, do you really think an all powerful God would create a single measly planet for His creation to live on, such as ours is, and then create all those other moons, suns, and earths; just so they could sit out there doing nothing? If God is everywhere, and He fills all space, then he has access to all space. That being the case, why would He limit His creation to one civilization, when He could create an infinite number of planets with people on them. And the proof is already out there that He has done so, we just need to mature to the point that we realize that this is exactly what He has done. But He did not create man to fill the universe with human beings; he created angels to do so. For no angel exists that was not first born a material man. And so the Lord will gradually fill the cosmos with angels and heavens, and the number of fleshly beings will be regulated, for flesh is evil, and the Lord does not wish to fill the cosmos with evil beings. He wishes to fill the cosmos with beings that do not die, and not ones that are already dead. So each planet was designed to handle a certain number of men, women, and children, and the laws of nature were designed to regulate this number accordingly. In order for this to be accomplished some people appear to die before their time, but this is not the case. God stops the death of many children who would otherwise have died from their parent's negligence, but He will allow the death of certain children if that Childs death was meant to be, according to the law of Divine Providence, or predestination. Because some children are actually saved much physical pain, grief, and days of despair by being taken out of this world early, and the parents have no idea that these things would have come in their Childs life. And yes, even though a child will return to this world several times in total through a new childbirth, they still go to heaven when they die in this world; although death is not real death, but sleep. For every man, woman, or child experiences the same seasons in their lifetimes, on up to the day they are regenerated by God and then move on to live as an angel in the heavens. However you look at it, when a child is taken from this world early in life, it is actually a blessing to that child. The parents will suffer hardship, but that will pass in time, and they all will one day understand that it was for the best that their child was taken. I tell you all these sad things so that you may understand that what we understand as cruel acts of God are actually acts of mercy. Now this is only one example of how Gods laws of nature control population, and regulate the life and death of the good and evil of the world. I have mentioned these issues many times in my books in hopes of providing all of mankind with a much better understanding of how their God is patient, merciful, just, a good teacher, and a good Father. When we come to mature to the level He intends for us all to reach, we will then understand all things, and realize God is not an evil, unjust God; but a loving, fair, and merciful God. You who fear death only fear it because you do not understand it, and so you do not wish it to come upon your children, family members, or self. But since you live in a world that is already dead, with you as life alone living in these bodies of flesh, to experience death in this world is actually to enter into life, in the real, spiritual world. Yes you are life, because you came from life, and all things of the material world are all dead. But since I have stated that death is not real, what do I mean by dead? All things of this material world are the fantasies that were given their own appearance of reality, from the thoughts of affections of men, spirits and angels. All things of this world are nothing more than a dream that man has come to know as his life; when in fact it is the sleep state of spirits and angels. But angels know it is the sleep state, and therefore are not affected by it any longer. It serves only as dreams to the angels, of such things as they no longer desire in their life. While we live in this world we only have a present, and know nothing of what is to come, and eventually forget the things that have taken place in our past. In the heavens however, where we live as angels; we live in the past, present, and the future all at the same time. For because we are connected to the Lord when we are angels our spirits dwell in the past, present and the future as the Lord does. This is how we have conjunction with the Lord. So when our spirit is in the future, it is there waiting on us while we are being recreated in the past. For our spirit feeds our past, as well as feeds our future. In other words in the Lord are these three; end, cause, and effect. As with the heavens are end, cause, and effect. As is shown on the diagram above, the Celestial heavens (the end), on the left are inwardly in the cause, the cause being the Spiritual heavens in the middle; and by means of the cause or spiritual heavens the end is in the effect; the effect being the natural world on the right. And so the end joins with the cause in order to create the effect. The end is not the cause, but it produces the cause; the cause is not the effect but it produces the effect; consequently, these three things follow one another in order. The end with a man is the love of his will; for what a man loves, this he proposes to himself and intends: the cause with him is the reason of his understanding; for by means of reason the end seeks for middle or efficient causes: and the effect is the acts or operation of the body, from and according to the end and the cause. So there are three things in man, which follow one another in order, in the same manner as the degrees of altitude follow one another. But I will not dive too deep into this subject at this time, as it is a lengthy one. Just keep in mind the number three, as it applies here as well. So as I was saying, we all live in the past, present, and future as far as our spirits are concerned, but we are not given understanding of this until we become angels. There's that number three again: Past-present-future! And so our past feeds the present, and the two move on so as to combine forces and feed the future together. And so the combined forces of all three; end, cause, and effect again feed the end, which is the past. As I said earlier, our future is there waiting on us while we are being recreated in the past, so that we can both meet up in the present. Where do you think mans memory would come from if he were not still connected with the past? Where are past experiences stored up, so that man can retain them at a moments notice? They are stored up in the Lord, and exist in your spiritual world. And so the Lord decides which memories a man may draw from, and not man; even though it appears you are the one who decides. But memories aside, why do we even need to have access to the past if God has control of our future? Because without the recreation of the past, there would be no present; and without the recreation of the past and present together, there would be no future. And without the recreation of the past, present, and future together, there would be no mankind, no spirits, and no angels. All would cease to exist, because they would have no foundation in which to dwell. Are we the past? No! But we were the past yesterday to those who lived today. And tomorrow we will be future to those who live today. And while all this is going on, the past is being recreated by the future. So before a man can once again visit the past he must pass on from the material world, enter the spiritual world, and become an angel. When he becomes an angel he is permitted to visit the past, but only so as to provide truths. Once he becomes a celestial angel he can fully visit the past, providing goods mostly, and sometimes truths when he is in a lower sense. But celestial angels wish to love others, and not so much teach. For they do not like to argue over truths as those in the spiritual heavens have to sometimes do in order to teach. Would you believe it if I told you the past cannot die, and neither can the present or the future absorb it, or

Celestial heavens _____
Spiritual heavens _____
Natural heavens _____

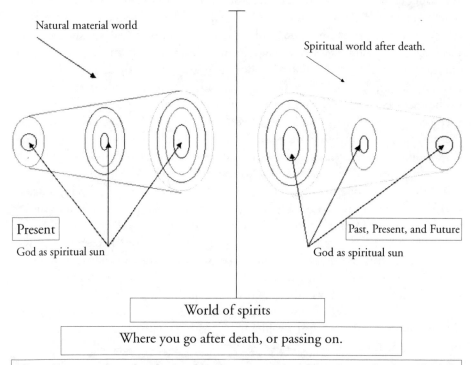

Natural material world

Spiritual world after death.

Present

God as spiritual sun

Past, Present, and Future

God as spiritual sun

World of spirits

Where you go after death, or passing on.

If you have not completed your four seasons or churches, you go back to the left side when you pass on.

(Cont. from above)

—take the place of it. For the past is alive and will always remain alive by itself, as well as being conjoined with the present and the future. But the past will never end, and will not become the future but will only create the future, or help to cause it. For as end does not become the cause but only helps create the cause, so too does cause not become effect, but only works with ends so as to help create the effect. Therefore all things exist in threes together as well as separately. Remember this when thinking of the heavens, for the celestial help create the spiritual but do not become the spiritual. As well the celestial and the spiritual work together to create the natural, but they do not become the natural. And all three then work together to once again create a new life in which case all things begin all over again. But remember, the past does not exist in our material world but only in the spiritual world. So the past is recreated in the spiritual realm, in the heavens. What is the past other than the beginning of each man? So in the heavens we are permitted to share our lives with all of mankind, which includes those who were born in the past. It's like raising children all over again, but this time you get to provide their thoughts of affections. Now you may ask, when we become angels do we have access to all of the past and all of the future? No we do not, only the Lord has this privilege, for all dwells within the Lord already; past, present, and future included. We on the other hand only have connection to the past and future as far as our knowledge of good and truths takes us. For every man or angel is wiser, and more knowledgeable than another. From the most ignorant all the way up to the oldest, and most knowledgeable angel in existence. But does this mean that if you are the oldest you are the most knowledgeable? No, because all men from the beginning of creation have had free will; and that includes the free will to ask any question we wish, believe any facts we wish, and dream of as crazy, or unimaginable a subject as we choose in life. And because of this some men have advanced farther than others in wisdom and knowledge, even though they may be a younger spirit or angel. But angels are always wiser than spirits, and so you would have to compare angels to angels and spirits to spirits. But if you don't ask questions in life from other human beings, as well as to yourself, you are bound to be less wise than an angel who asks questions all the time. So where do the answers come from if man does not have many of them? For we must remember, much of what man believes is fantasy, and is based on his senses in this material world. So where do the answers come from? They come from God, and are given to man in many forms. We can read and learn things from the Ancients, as well as God. We can dream, and learn things from God through angels and spirits. We can hear different preachers, although most of this teaching will be elementary teachings. And we can see visions at any time of day, or night, which are provided by God to those who diligently seek Him, and His kingdom. So as I was saying, God allows angels to live among those of the past and future all according to their maturity level, and knowledge. And as angels grow in these things more and more unto eternity, they can have connection with the past and future more and more as their lives continue on into the future. But the future never ends either, for it is connected on both ends to the past and the present. What this all boils down to is that every human being ever born is sole heir to the throne of God. But he is also joined to many others who are sole heirs as well, and we all form one life, which is the Lord. Because in this material world we choose to work against one another, we do not have any recollection that we are all one. However, as people learn to work together, putting all their assets or possessions together, and dividing them evenly among all those included in the group, peace and joy is experienced. As well ways of the flesh, or the world have begun to be done away with. For in a society such as just mentioned there is eventually no jealousy, envy, hatred, backbiting, violence, or theft. For all learn to work for the good of all in the group, and to keep things as even as possible. They learn that having more no longer pleases them, but seeing others around them happy, instead of the depressed states we see citizens in our country reflect every day. To live in this manner can only be accomplished through the Lord and love. Therefore, anyone who is not truly in love to God and their neighbor would immediately be spotted and removed from the group. For that matter they would not even be happy being a part of such a group, and would eventually leave on their own. What I am describing as a scenario in this material world is exactly how the live in the heavens, and was once the ways of those in our world, until became corrupt, living for self, and depending on his own wisdom, or proprium: (Proprium meaning of self). So as we learn to follow the heavenly pattern on earth, we begin to change, and eventually have conjunction with the heavens as a whole. But seldom is this accomplished in our world because few have any interest in testing the theory, for we all seek our own comfort in life, at least for the time being. So we will all see our day of judgment, but it will be in the spiritual world, not in this world. Your day of judgment will come for all of you, separately, and at the time when your angel realizes that you have entered into and passed through four seasons, and four churches in life. With three representing the full period, or duration of your regeneration, and your complete conjunction with the Lord. But remember, the number three in the Word does not actually represent the number, but all numbers in the Word represent things; whereas three represents completion of the conjunction of goods and truths with the Lord. So when your judgment comes you will not know of it until it has passed, otherwise you may attempt to sway it, or interfere with the process. But you will know when it is accomplished, for this process rings in the beginning of a New Church in you. But fleshly human beings do not experience the Last Judgment according to self, but for many men who have lived in the past. For you are a society, and even represent a society when you are under the Last Judgment, for a society is what controls the life of a human being throughout his whole lifetime, and is to be judged for it; however, not after its first lifetime but after a total of several. For it all depends on how many lifetimes within a human being it takes for that spiritual society to become an angel, which is what each society does in the end. And when we are judged in that day, we simply fall under a vastation process where the evil are separated, and sent to their corresponding hells, and others to the world of spirits. For only the good in that society will actually be sent to the heavens. When this happens a new heaven, and a New Church is born from the old. The society still exists, but it is put back in order; and this continues to happen with a society until forever, continuously perfecting the heavens and the angels. So let me ask you, how many times do you think you have been in this material world as a physical human being? Answer: Every time! For you, representing an affection that is unique, and is a single affection, has been a part of every human being ever born in the world; past, present, or future. You are put with the ignorant, so as to experience ignorance; you are put with the shy, so as to experience timidity; you are put with the cruel, sneaky, proud, pushy, loud, soft, or any other affection you may think of, so as to experience all these things, and some affections more than others. When you experience death in this world you will experience many deaths, and from both sides. What I mean is that you will die many times, and you will see others in death many times, so as to one day, after regeneration, learn to understand what death is. But out of all these experiences and lives, you will know no better than that you have only lived a single lifetime in this material world. For God is a God of mercy, and would not permit a man to remember the pain of experiencing many, many deaths; even though they are only apparently death, but are really sleep. But in any lifetime in this world you can draw off of all the experiences you have ever been through, which is every experience, and can live a live according to the one laid out by your own spirit, or love. For we create life, but an apparent life; because it exists in a world of fantasy. Nonetheless, we create it, from our own minds, or spirits; so as to have a human body that completely represents the spirit within us. This spirit, as I have many times said, is created from our parents at first, but changes throughout our lives when our own thoughts of affections are now in control of our life and body. Even if your parents are cruel and evil people, still you do not ever have to be as they are, but can choose a whole different life for yourself. And even if you don't realize it, or because the people around you may see you as worse off than your parents, still you are a more perfect version of your parents, and just don't know it yet. For you see things in life differently than them, and therefore you may deal with issues in a way that the world around you does not agree; and they may even see you as more evil than your parents. But life is a learning experience, and we are given chance after chance to change until we actually do eventually change, and we all even go on to be angels one day. And where the world may have seen your parents as very good people, they could have been acting their whole life, and no one ever knew any better. This is why we cannot trust our senses in life, and this is why many of us are seen as good, when all along we are actually evil, to some extent. For it is a truth that many of the evil pretend to be good, and many of the good are fighting life, trying to figure out why they do such horrible things sometimes, and as they grow up they slowly give up, or give into the temptation, until the Lord comes along and rescues them. But until then, the world sees them as the evil ones, and the actual evil ones as good, because of their play-acting, you might say. This is also why Jesus said this: "It is not the healthy who need a doctor, but the sick. But go and learn what this means: I desire mercy, not sacrifice. For I have not come to save the righteous, but sinners (Matthew 9:12)." And so whereas the Lord says He came to save sinners, we must admit that we are sinners, and that no good comes from us. And even though He says He didn't come to save the righteous, does not mean that the others are righteous; but that they believe they are. And in another place: There is not a righteous man on earth; who does what is right and never sins (Ecclesiastes 7:20). And for my final example: There is no one righteous, not even one; there is no one who understands, no one who seeks God. All have turned away, they have together become worthless; there is no one who does good, not even one (Romans 3:10). Now from these verses I think it is safe to assume that you now know there is no righteous man on earth; until he has conjunction with the Lord, which comes when he is regenerated, and becomes a New Church. So when the Lord said He came to save sinners, what He was saying was that He came to save those who truly knew they were sinners, and have now stopped trusting in their flesh, as well as their physical senses; which told them they were good. The Lord knows who is truly good, and who is not. If you put yourself above others you are not in good; if you believe yourself more righteous than another then you are not good; and if you believe that God wishes to save some, and allow the others to burn in hell then you are not good. If you were good, which only comes from the Lord; you would be seeking the salvation of every human being, and not yourself. For once you truly come to know yourself, you will then realize that you are already saved. But no one is saved until they know that all men will be saved. But as we are straying off the subject, let me repeat the immediate subject at hand: The fleshly human being is not the one who is undergoing a Last Judgment in life, but the spiritual society, which is actually an angel, is the one being judged. And so only those who end up being sent back to the hells within that angelic society have anything to fear. For there is no fear in love but only in fantasy, which creates evil. Therefore no man by himself is ever judged, for no man is ever truly by himself. You as a human being in this world have many lives going on within you, or your spiritual world, which is your mind in this world. Every possible thought you may ever have is in and by itself a single life, or man, or affection. And no single affection is ever under judgment by itself, but all are judged together within a society. This Last Judgment must come at the consummation of the old Church because those who are good no longer have any control over the society, and evils and falsities now have all rule. And so there must come a Last Judgment so as to put all things back in order, and the good to be given their place back in the heavens, whereas the evil all go their proper place, as before stated. So now a new heaven and a New Church are formed from those who are good in this society. This new heaven, as well as the New Church cannot ever become worse than they now are in the spiritual world;

but can only grow in wisdom and knowledge, or love and truth. They can only become less in the material world, where those who are evil continuously join themselves to them, and continuously attempt to gain control over the heavens, the Church, and the angels all around them. But the angels do not despair because they are there to teach the evil of the world about love, sacrifice, and mercy. And the angels know that there is no fear in love, and that the Lord will always protect them. So the human being I am sharing life with at this point has no idea who or what he is. He has become totally confused as to who he is because the angel sitting here typing claims to be the life ruling his body at this time. So when this body, which I am residing in, passes on, or sleeps its final sleep in this world, where do I who am the angel from within, go from here? Answer: I will simply wake up tomorrow in another human being, knowing only that I am myself as an angel, living in either the spiritual heavens or the celestial heavens. I will have the knowledge of who I am, where I am, and what my purpose in life is. I will know what my love in life is, and will retain all memory, subjected to the Lord however, of all things, which pertain to my love. I will have no recollection of bad things, or sad memories, for these do not exist in love. All that I remember will be things according to good and truth. When I do find myself recalling bad, or disturbing memories I will be in my natural state within the natural heavens. But when I am at home in my own heavens, I will have no bad thoughts, or regrets. I will have my own home in the heavens that will resemble closely the home I had in the world; and this home will appear immediately, as I reflect on it, or wish it. And my home will change as I change in affections; or as my spiritual society changes. I will have an occupation just as I did in the world, but slightly different in that heavenly things, whether spiritual or celestial, differ from material earthly things. But I will perform a use, as all angels in the heavens do, on a daily basis (though days are not measured in time in the heavens, but states). When I am done performing my use, or occupation, I go home as I did in this world, and do similar things as I did in this material world. For in the heavens there are very similar things as there are here, such as; gardens, groves, forests, valleys, lakes, museums, aquariums, community centers, and more. And so life in the heavens is all so similar to that of this material world, with the differences being that all things are either spiritual, or celestial; and appears in an instant. However, there are many wonderful things in the heavens, which are not in the world, for they could not even comprehend their splendor. But remember I said angels are wiser than man or spirit, and they know that they are not the human beings they reside within. Therefore an angel cannot be permitted to exist within this material world. They do not even know the goings on of this world, but only have a connection with it through correspondences. So an angel lives within a human being providing the thoughts, which correspond to the angel's affections, but thoughts that take on a material meaning for the material world, or spirit, or man; a spiritual meaning for the spiritual angels, and a celestial meaning for the celestial angels. So the man can be thinking of fishing, while he is sipping on a glass of iced tea at home, while the angel is thinking of truths in a natural sense, for this is what fish represent in the spiritual sense. To drink in the spiritual sense represents to appropriate to ones self spiritual truths. And so the angel is at present thinking of natural and spiritual truths, while the man is drinking iced tea, and thinking of fishing. And when a man is in conjunction with the spiritual or celestial heavens while in the world, he can be thinking of spiritual things, or celestial things, as the angels do; and not thinking of the material things that man in this material world thinks of. But just because a man has not become a New Church, or has not been through his four seasons does not mean that he cannot still have conjunction with the heavens; it just means that he will have to continue to fight off the things of the world, and the flesh, while at the same time seeking the Kingdom of heaven. But it gets easier as we are closer and closer to our consummation, or end of our regeneration process in the world. So there you have it, spirits return to the world as men, but angels return to the human as angels, within another world; still providing life and affections to their human. The angels are still in the past, present and future, according to their affections, because they provide the affections of celestial love and spiritual truth to all of mankind. Spirits are the natural man and angels are the spiritual man. A spirit believes he is the man and an angel knows he is not the man, and has no part in the material world. An angel knows he has conjunction with every human being ever born, and that he is a part of, or one with every human being ever born. At this time I am an angelic spirit who has conjunction with the heavens, but I cannot truly become an angel until I leave this world of fantasy. I still live among humans in this world of fantasy because I am still material flesh. When God is finished using me for his set purpose in this world He will allow me to leave this world, at which time I will go to sleep some day or night and will wake up in the World of Spirits. I will then either be vastated, or sent directly to my corresponding heavens, to live my life forever in the heavens as an angel. But I say this in faith, not as fact; for fact has many more details to it, of which I have only a few. So I do not state fact, I state truths based on faith in the Lord, for only He knows facts, which can be confirmed. So until my time comes, I will continue to do what I do best, which is to live for the Lord in faith, grounded in my works of charity, and will continue to provide these revelations to the world, which the Lord has so graciously given me. We will now return to the Doctrine of Sacred Scripture.

(Cont. to The Doctrine of Sacred Scripture)

[44] 2. THE TRUTHS AND GOODS OF THE SENSE OF THE LETTER OF THE WORD ARE MEANT BY THE URIM AND THUMMIM.

The Urim and Thummim were on Aaron's ephod, for by his priesthood the Lord was represented as to Divine Good and the work of salvation. By the garments of the priesthood, or of holiness, was represented Divine Truth from Divine Good. By the Ephod was represented Divine Truth in its ultimate, and thus the Word in the sense of the letter, for this is Divine Truth in its ultimate, as was said above. Therefore, by the twelve precious stones with the names of the twelve tribes of Israel, which were the Urim and Thummim, were represented Divine Truths from the Divine Good in the whole complex.

(2) Concerning these things it is written in Moses:

They shall make the ephod . . . of blue, and of purple, of scarlet double dyed and fine twined linen . . . And they shall make the breastplate of judgment . . . after the work of the ephod . . . and thou shalt set it in settings of stone, even four rows of stones: the first row shall be a ruby, a topaz and an emerald: the second row shall be a chrysoprasus, a sapphire and a diamond; the third row a lapis-lazuli, an agate and an amethyst; and the fourth row a beryl, a sardius and a jasper . . . . The stones shall be according to the names of the sons (A.V. Children) of Israel; the engravings of the signet shall be according to the name of everyone for the twelve tribes . . . . And Aaron shall bear on the breastplate of judgment the Urim and Thummim . . . and they shall be upon Aaron's heart, when he goeth in before Jehovah (Exodus 28:6, 15-21, 29,30).

(3) What the garments of Aaron, his ephod, robe, coat, mitre and girdle represented is explained in the Arcana Caelestia on this chapter of Exodus; where it is shown that by the ephod was represented Divine Truth in its ultimate. By the precious stones upon it were represented truths transparent from good; by the twelve precious stones, all ultimate truths transparent from the good of love, in their order. By the twelve tribes of Israel, all things of the Church; by the breastplate, Divine Truth from Divine Good; and by the Urim and Thummim, the brilliancy of Divine Truth from Divine Good in ultimates: for Urim is a shining fire, and Thummim brilliancy in the angelic language, and integrity in the Hebrew. It is also shown that responses were given by the variegations of light, and at the same time by tacit perception, or by a living voice; with many other particulars.

(4) From this it may be evident that by these precious stones were also signified truths from good in the ultimate sense of the Word; and that by no other means are responses given from heaven, because in that sense is the Divine proceeding in its fullness. That precious stones and diadems signify Divine Truths in their ultimates, such as are the truths of the sense of the letter of the Word, has been made clearly manifest to me from the precious stones and diadems in the spiritual world with angels and spirits there, whom I have seen wearing them; and I have also seen them in their caskets. It was granted me to know that these correspond to truths in ultimates; indeed, that hence also they have their origin and appearance. Because of this signification of diamonds and precious stones they were also seen by John:

Upon the head of the dragon (Revelation 12:3);
Upon the horns of the beast (Revelation 13:1);

And there were precious stones on the harlot who sat on the scarlet beast (Revelations 17:4). These precious stones were seen upon them because by them are signified those in the Christian world with whom is the Word.

[45] 3. THE TRUTHS OF THE SENSE OF THE LETTER OF THE WORD ARE MEANT BY THE PRECIOUS STONES IN THE GARDEN OF EDEN WHERE, ACCORDING TO EZEKIEL, THE KING OF TYRE IS SAID TO HAVE BEEN.

It is written in Ezekiel:

King of Tyre, thou sealest up thy sum, full of wisdom and perfect in beauty. Thou hast been in Eden; the Garden of God; every precious stone was thy covering, the ruby, the topaz and the diamond, the beryl, the sardonyx and the jasper; the sapphire, the chrysoprasus and the emerald, and gold (Ezekiel 28:12,13).

By Tyre in the Word are signified the cognitions of truth and good; by the king is signified the truth of the Church; by the Garden of Eden are signified wisdom and intelligence from the Word; and by precious stones are signified truths translucent from good, such as are in the sense of the letter of the Word. Because this is the signification of those stones therefore they are called his covering; and it may be seen in a preceding article that the sense of the letter covers the interior things of the Word.

[46] 4. THE SENSE OF THE LETTER OF THE WORD IS SIGNIFIED BY THE CURTAINS AND VEILS OF THE TABERNACLE.

Heaven and the Church were represented by the tabernacle; therefore, the pattern of it was shown by Jehovah on Mount Sinai. Consequently, everything that was in the tabernacle, as the lamp stand, the golden alter of incense, and the table on which was the shewbread, represented and therefore signified the holy things of heaven and the Church. The Holy of Holies, where was the Ark of the Covenant represented and therefore signified the inmost of heaven and the Church. The Law itself, written on two tables of stone and enclosed in the Ark, signified the Lord as to the Word. Now, because external things derive their essence from internal things, and both of these derive theirs from what is inmost, which in the tabernacle was the Law, therefore, the holy things of the Word were represented and signified by all things belonging to the tabernacle. It follows, therefore, that the ultimates of the tabernacle, namely its curtains and its veils, thus its coverings and its containants, signified the ultimates of the Word, which are the truths and goods of the sense of the letter. Because such things were signified, therefore, all the curtains and veils were made of fine twined linen of blue and purple, and scarlet double-dyed with Cherubim (Exodus 26:1,31,36).

What was represented and signified, in general and in particular, by the tabernacle and everything in it, is explained in the ARCANA CAELESTIA on this chapter of Exodus. It is there shown that the curtains and veils represented the external things of heaven and the Church, thus also the external things of the Word. Further, that fine linen signified truth from a spiritual origin; blue, truth from a celestial origin; purple, celestial good; scarlet double-dyed, spiritual good; and cherubim, the guards of the interiors of the Word.

[47] 5. BY THE EXTERNALS OF THE TEMPLE AT JERUSALEM WERE REPRESENTED THE EXTERNALS OF THE WORD, WHICH BELONG TO ITS SENSE OF THE LETTER.

This is because the same was represented by the temple as by the tabernacle, namely, heaven and the Church, and thence also the Word. That the temple at Jerusalem signified the Divine Human of the Lord He Himself teaches in John:

Destroy this temple, and in three days I will raise it up . . . But He spake of the temple of His body (John 2:19,21); and where the Lord is meant, the Word also is meant, because He is the Word. Now, since the interior things of the temple represented the interior things of heaven and the Church, thus also of the Word, therefore its exterior things represented and signified the exterior things of heaven and the Church, thus also the exterior things of the Word, which belong to the sense of the letter. Concerning the exterior things of the temple it is written:

That they were built of stone, whole and unhewn, and of cedar within; and that all its walls within were carved with cherubim. Palm trees and open flowers; and that the floor was overlaid with gold (1KINGS 6:7,29,30).

By all these things are also signified the externals of the Word, which are the holy things of the sense of its letter.

[48] 6. THE WORD IN ITS GLORY WAS REPRESENTED BY THE LORD, WHEN HE WAS TRANSFIGURED.

Concerning the Lords Transfiguration before Peter, James and John it is said:

That His face did shine as the sun, and His raiment became like light; And . . . there appeared Moses and Elias talking with Him . . . A bright cloud overshadowed the disciples; and a voice was heard out of the cloud saying, this is my beloved Son . . . hear ye Him (Matthew 17:1-5).

I have been informed that the Lord on this occasion represented the Word. His face, which shone as the sun, represented His Divine Good, His raiment, which became like light, His Divine Truth. Moses and Elias represented the historical and the prophetical Word; Moses, the Word written by him, and in general the historical Word; and Elias, the prophetical Word. The bright cloud, which overshadowed the disciples, represented the Word in the sense of the letter. Therefore, out of this cloud a voice was heard, saying, This is my beloved Son . . . hear ye Him, as all declarations and responses are only made by means of ultimates such as are in the sense of the letter of the Word; for they are made in fullness from the Lord.

[49] Thus far it has been shown that the Word in the natural sense, which is the sense of the letter, is in its sanctity and in its fullness. Something shall now be said to show that the Word in that sense is also in its power. The greatness of the power of Divine Truth, and its nature, in the heavens and also on the earths, may be evident from what has been said in the work on HEAVEN AND HELL concerning the power of the angels of heaven Nos. 228-233. The power of Divine Truth is directed especially against falsities and evils, thus against the hells. These must be combated by means of truths from the sense of the letter of the Word. Moreover, by means of the truths that are with a man, the Lord has the power of saving him; for by means of truths from the sense of the letter of the Word, a man is reformed and regenerated. He is then taken out of hell and introduced into heaven. This power the Lord assumed even as to His Divine Human, after He had fulfilled all things of the Word, even to its ultimates.

(2) Therefore, when He was about to fulfill what yet remained, by the passion of the cross, He said to the chief priest:

Hereafter shall ye see the Son of Man sitting on the right hand of power and coming in the clouds of heaven (Matthew 26:64; Mark 14:62).

The Son of Man, is the Lord as to the Word; the clouds of heaven are the Word in the sense of the letter; and sitting at the right hand of God means omnipotence through the Word; as also in Mark 16:19.

In the Jewish Church the Nazirites represented the power of the Lord from the ultimates of truth. So also did Samson, of whom it is said that he was a Nazirite from his mother's womb; and that his power lay in his hair.

(3) He himself made it clear that his strength lay in his hair when he said:

There hath not come a razor upon mine head: for I have been a Nazirite from my mothers womb: if I be shaven then my strength will go from me, and I shall become weak, and be like any other man (Judges 16:17).

No one can know why the Naziriteship, by which is signified the hair, was instituted, and why Samson's strength was from his hair, unless he knows what is signified in the Word by the head. The head signifies heavenly wisdom, which angels and men have from the Lord by means of Divine Truth. Consequently, the hair of the head signifies heavenly wisdom in ultimates, and also Divine Truth in ultimates.

(4) Because this was signified by hair from correspondence with the heavens, it was therefore ordained as a law for the Nazirites, that they should not shave the hair of their head, because it was the Naziriteship of God upon their head (Numbers 6:1-21).

For the same reason it was also ordained:

That the high priest and his son should not shave their head, lest they should die, and wrath should come upon the whole house of Israel (Leviticus 10:6).

(5) Since the hair, on account of this signification grounded in correspondence, was so holy, therefore the Son of Man, who is the Lord as to the Word, is described even to His hairs, which were white like wool, as white as snow (Revelations 1:14). So also the Ancient of Days is described in Daniel, 7:9.

On this subject something may also be seen above, No.35. In short the power of Divine Truth, or the Word, is in the sense of the letter, because the Word in that sense is in its fullness; and because the angels of the Lords two kingdoms and men are simultaneously in that sense.

[50] V

The doctrine of the Church must be taken from the sense of the letter of the Word, and be confirmed by it. It was shown in the previous article that the Word in the sense of the letter is in its fullness, its sanctity and its power; and since the Lord is the Word, for He is the all of the Word, it follows that the Lord is eminently present in that sense, teaching and enlightening man from it. Proof of this will be given in due order as follows:

(1) Without doctrine, the Word is unintelligible.
(2) Doctrine must be taken from the sense of the letter of the Word.
(3) But Divine Truth, which is to be the source of doctrine, is manifest only to those who are enlightened by the Lord.

[51] 1. WITHOUT DOCTRINE, THE WORD IS UNINTELLIGABLE. This is because the Word in the sense of the letter consists of pure correspondences, so designed that spiritual and celestial things may be simultaneously in it, and that every word of it may contain them and serve as their basis. For this reason in some places in the sense of the letter truths are not unveiled but veiled, and being so, they are called appearances of truth. There are many truths accommodated to the perception of simple people, whose thoughts do not rise above what they see with their eyes. There are, moreover, some things, which appear like contradictions, whereas there is not a single contradiction in the Word, when it is regarded in its own light. In some parts of the Prophets also there are names of places and persons recorded from which no meaning can be gathered, as in the passages quoted above in No.15. Since then this is the nature of the Word in the sense of the Letter, it may be evident that without doctrine it cannot be understood.

(2) Some examples may make this clear. It is said that Jehovah repents (Exodus 32:12,14; Jonah 3:9, 4:2; it is also said:

That Jehovah does not repent (Numbers 23:19; 1Samuel 15:29).
These passages cannot be reconciled without doctrine. It is said:
That Jehovah visits the iniquity of the fathers upon the children unto the third and fourth generation (Numbers 14:18);

And it is said:

That a father shall not die for a son, neither a son for a father, but everyone shall die for his own sin (Deuteronomy 24:16).

In the light of doctrine these passages are not contradictory, but are in perfect agreement.

(3) Jesus says: Ask, and it shall be given you; seek, and ye shall find; knock, and it shall be opened unto you; for everyone that asketh shall receive, and he that seeketh shall find, and to him that knocketh it shall be opened (Matthew 7:7,8; 21:21,22).

Without doctrine it might be believed that everyone will receive what he asks; but from doctrine it is believed that what is given is what a man asks not of himself but from the Lord; for this also the Lord teaches:

If ye abide in me, and my words abide in you, ye shall ask what ye will, and it shall be done unto you (John 15:7).

(4) The Lord says:

Blessed are the poor, for theirs is the kingdom of God (Luke 6:20).

Without doctrine it might be supposed that heaven is for the poor, and not for the rich; but doctrine teaches that the poor in spirit are meant, for the Lord says:

Blessed are the poor in spirit: for theirs is the kingdom of heaven (Matthew 5:3).

(5) The Lord says:

Judge not, that ye be not judged. For with what judgment ye judge, ye shall be judged (Matthew 7:1,2; Luke 6:37).

Without doctrine this might be quoted to prove that it aught not to be said of evil that it is evil, thus that judgment must not be passed that a wicked man is wicked; whereas according to doctrine one may pass judgment, provided it is just, for the Lord says:

Judge righteous judgment (John 7:24).

(6) Jesus says:

Be not ye called teacher (A.V. Rabbi) for one is your teacher (A.V. Master), even Christ. And call no man father upon the earth; for one is your Father, which is in heaven. Neither be ye called masters: for one is your Master, even Christ (Matthew 23:8,9,10).

Without doctrine it might appear that we may not call anyone teacher, father, or master; but from doctrine it is known that we may do so in the natural sense, but not in the spiritual.

(7) Jesus said to the disciples:

When the Son of Man shall sit on the throne of His glory, ye also shall sit upon twelve thrones, judging the twelve tribes of Israel (Matthew19: 28).

From these words it might be concluded that the disciples were also to judge, whereas they cannot judge anyone. Doctrine therefore will explain this mystery (Arcanum) by teaching that the Lord alone, who is omniscient and knows the hearts of all, will judge and can judge; and THAT BY HIS TWELVE DISCIPLES IS MEANT THE CHURCH AS TO ALL THE TRUTHS AND GOODS WHICH IT POSSESSESFROM THE LORD BY MEANS OF THE WORD; therefore doctrine concludes that it is these which will judge everyone, according to the Lords words in (John 3:17,18,12:47-48).

(8) He who reads the Word without doctrine does not know how those things are consistent which are said in the Prophets concerning the Jewish nation and concerning Jerusalem. It is said that the Church is to remain with that nation, with its seat in that city, forever; as in the following passages:

Jehovah will visit His flock, the house of Judah, and shall make them as His goodly horse in the battle. Out of Him came forth the corner [stone], out of Him the nail, and out of Him the battle-bow (Zechariah 10:3,4,6,7).

Lo, I come, that I may dwell in the midst of thee. And Jehovah shall inherit Judah . . . and shall choose Jerusalem again (Zechariah 2:10,12). It shall come to pass in that day, that the mountains shall drop down new wine, and the hills shall flow with milk . . .

But Judah shall dwell forever, and Jerusalem from generation to generation (Joel 3:18,20).

Behold, the days come . . . that I will sow the house of Israel and the house of Judah with the seed of man. That I will make a new covenant with the house of Israel and the house of Judah . . . And this shall be the covenant . . . I will put my law in their inward parts and write it in their heart; and will be their God, and they shall be my people (Jeremiah 31:27,31,33).

In that day . . . ten men, out of all the languages of the nations, shall take hold of the skirt of a man that is a Jew, saying, We will go with you; for we have heard that God is with you (Zechariah 8:23). So also elsewhere, as in (Isaiah 44:24,26; 49:22,23; 65:9; 66:20,22; Jeremiah 3:18; 23:5,1,19,20;Nahum1: 15;Malachi3: 4).

These passages treat of the coming of the Lord, and what would then come to pass.

(9) But the contrary is said in many other places of which this passage will only be quoted:

I will hide my face from them, I will see what their end shall be: for they are a very forward generation, children in whom is no faith. I said, I would scatter them into the uttermost corners, I would make the remembrance of them to cease from among men:

For they are a nation void of counsel, neither is there any understanding in them . . . Their vine is of the vine of Sodom, and of the fields of Gomorrah: their grapes are grapes of gall, their clusters are bitter:

Their wine is the poison of dragons, and the cruel venom of asps. Is not this laid up in store with me, sealed up among my treasures? To me belongeth vengeance and recompense (Deuteronomy32: 20-25).

Such are the things said of that nation; and similar things are said elsewhere; as in Isaiah 3:1,2,8; 5:3,6; Deuteronomy9: 5,6;Matthew12: 39; 23:27,28; John8: 44; and in Jeremiah and Ezekiel throughout.

These passages however, which seem to be contradictory, will appear to be in perfect accord from doctrine. For doctrine teaches that by Israel and by Judah in the Word are not meant Israel and Judah, but the Church in two different senses; in one sense that it is devastated, and in another, that it is to be established by the Lord. There are other passages in the Word similar to these, and from them it is clearly manifest that the Word without doctrine in unintelligible.

[52] It may therefore be evident that those who read the Word without doctrine, or who do not procure for themselves doctrine from the Word, are in obscurity concerning the truth. Their minds are wavering and unsettled, liable to errors and prone to heresies, which they also embrace if these are held in favour and supported by authority, and if their own reputation is not endangered. The Word to them is like a lamp stand without a light, and they see many things, as it were, in the shade, yet understanding hardly anything, for doctrine alone is that which enlightens. I have seen such persons being examined by angels, and they appeared able to confirm from the Word whatever opinion they pleased, and to confirm what pertained to their own self-love and the love of those whom they befriended. But I have also seen them stripped of their garments, a sign that they were destitute of truths; for garments in the spiritual world are truths.

[53] 2. DOCTRINE MUST BE TAKEN FROM THE SENSE OF THE LETTER OF THE WORD, AND BE CONFIRMED BY IT.

This is because the Lord is present in that sense with man, and nowhere else, enlightening and teaching him the truths of the Church; for the Lord never acts except in fullness, and the Word in the sense of the letter is in its fullness, as was shown above; therefore doctrine must be taken from the sense of the letter.

[54] The Word by means of doctrine is not only understood, but it also as it were gives light; because without doctrine it is not understood, and it is like a lamp stand without a light, as was shown above. The Word therefore, by means of doctrine is understood, and is like a lamp stand with its lamp lit. Man then sees more things than he had seen before, and he also understands those things, which he had not understood before. Things obscure and out of agreement he either does not notice and passes over, or he sees and explains them as in agreement with doctrine. The experience of the Christian world testifies that the Word is understood from doctrine, and also that it is explained according to doctrine. For all the Reformers see the Word from their own doctrine and they explain the Word according to it; so too the Roman Catholics see it from their doctrine and they explain it accordingly; and even the Jews do likewise; thus falsities are seen from false doctrine, and truths from true doctrine. Hence it is evident that true doctrine is like a lamp in darkness and a signpost on the way. Doctrine

however, must not only be taken from the sense of the letter of the Word, but it must also be confirmed by that sense. For if not confirmed by it, the truth of doctrine appears as if it were only mans intelligence in it and not the Lords Divine Wisdom; and thus doctrine would be like a house in the air, and not on the ground, and consequently without a foundation.

[55] The doctrine of genuine truth may also be fully drawn from the literal sense of the Word; for the Word in that sense is like a person fully clothed, but whose face and hands are uncovered. Everything in the Word pertaining to mans life, and thus to his salvation, is there unveiled. The rest is veiled; and in many places where it is veiled it shines through as the face appears through a thin veil of silk. Moreover, as the truths of the Word increase from the love of them, and are coordinated by love, they shine more and more clearly through their coverings and become more obvious. But this is also brought about by means of doctrine.

[56] It may be supposed that the doctrine of genuine truth can be acquired by means of the spiritual sense of the Word, which is obtained through a knowledge of correspondences. Doctrine however, is not acquired by such means, but only illustrated and corroborated. For as was stated above in No. 26 no one comes into the spiritual sense of the Word by means of correspondences unless he is first in genuine truths from doctrine. If a man is not first in genuine truths, he may falsify the Word by means of some correspondences he may know, by connecting them together and explaining them to confirm what is firmly held in his mind from some principle, which he has adopted. Moreover, the spiritual sense is not communicated to anyone except by the Lord alone; and he guards it as He guard's heaven, for heaven is within it. It is important then that a man should study the Word in the sense of the letter: from that sense only is doctrine derived.

[57] 3. GENUINE TRUTH, WHICH IS TO BE THE SOURCE OF DOCTRINE, IS MANIFEST IN THE SENSE OF THE LETTER OF THE WORD ONLY TO THOSE WHO ARE ENLIGHTENED BY THE LORD.

Enlightenment comes from the Lord alone and is granted to those who love truths, and who apply them to the uses of life; with others, there is no enlightenment in the Word.

Enlightenment is granted to those who love truths because they are truths, and who apply them to uses of life because they are in the Lord, and the Lord in them. For the Lord is His own Divine Truth; and when this is loved because it is Divine Truth—and this is loved when it is applied to use—then the Lord is present in it with man. These things the Lord also teaches in John:

At that day ye shall know . . . that ye are in me, and I in you. He that hath my commandments, and keepeth them, he it is that loveth me . . . and I will love him, and will manifest myself to him . . . And I will come to him and make my abode with him (John 14:20,21,23).

And in Matthew:

Blessed are the pure in heart: for they shall see God (Matthew 5:8).

These are they who are enlightened when they read the Word, and with whom the Word is lucid and transparent.

[58] The Word is lucid and transparent with them, because there is a spiritual as well as a celestial sense in every part of it, and these senses are in the light of heaven. Therefore, by means of these senses and their light, the Lord flows into the natural sense and into the light of this sense with man. Consequently, a man acknowledges the truth from an interior perception, and afterwards sees it in his own thought. This happens as often as he is in the affection of truth for its own sake; for perception comes from affection, and thought from perception; and thus arises that acknowledgment which is called faith. On this subject however, more will be said in the following chapter, concerning the conjunction of the Lord with man by means of the Word.

[59] With such men the first thing is to procure for themselves doctrine from the literal sense of the Word; thus they light a lamp for their further progress. After doctrine has been procured however, and the lamp has been thus lit, they see the Word from it. But those who do not procure doctrine for themselves first enquire whether the doctrine given by others and generally received, agrees with the Word; and to those things which agree with the Word they assent, but dissent from those which do not agree. In this way their doctrine is formed for them, and by means of the doctrine their faith. However, this takes place only with those who, not being distracted by the affairs of the world, are able to see; and those, if they love truths for their own sake and apply them to the uses of life, are enlightened by the Lord: others whose lives are in some measure regulated by truths can learn from them.

[60] The contrary takes place with those who read the Word from the doctrine of a false religion, and more especially with those who confirm that doctrine from the Word, LOOKING TO THEIR OWN GLORY AND WORLDLY WEALTH. With them the truth of the Word appears as in the shade of night, and falsity as in the light of day. They read the truth but they do not see it; and if they see the shadow of it they falsify it. These are they of whom the Lord says:

That they have eyes and see not, and ears and do not understand (Matthew 13:14,15).

For nothing blinds man but his proprium and the confirmation of falsity. The proprium of man is self-love and consequent pride of self-intelligence; and the confirmation of falsity is thick darkness counterfeiting light. The light of such persons is merely natural, and their vision like that of one who sees specters in the dark.

[61] I have been permitted to converse with many after death who believed that they would shine like stars in heaven because, as they said, they had regarded the Word as holy and had often read it. They had gathered many passages from it by

which they had confirmed the dogmas of their faith. They had therefore acquired the reputation in the world of being learned scholars, and in consequence they supposed that they would be Michaels and Raphael's.

2. Several of these were examined as to the love from which they had studied the Word; and it was found that some had done so from self-love, that they might appear great in the world, and that they might be held in reverence as leaders of the Church; and others from love of the world, that they might acquire wealth. When these were examined as to what they knew from the Word, it was discovered that they did not know a single genuine truth, but only what may be called truth falsified, which in itself is falsity. They were informed that this was because they themselves and the world were the ends in view, or what is the same, their loves, and not the Lord and heaven. For when themselves and the world are the ends in view, while they read the Word their mind is immersed in the things of self and the world, and therefore men constantly think from their proprium, which is in thick darkness respecting everything relating to heaven. In this state man cannot be withdrawn by the Lord from his proprium and so be raised into the light of heaven; and consequently he cannot receive any influx from the Lord through heaven.

3. I have also seen such persons admitted into heaven; when however, they were discovered there to be without truths, they were cast out; but there still remained with them the conceit that they merited heaven. It is different with those who have studied the Word from the affection of knowing the truth because it is truth, and because it is serviceable to the uses not only of their own life but also the life of their neighbor. I have seen these persons raised up into heaven and thus into the light in which Divine Truth is there, and then at the same time exalted into angelic wisdom and its happiness which is life eternal.

[62] VI

By the sense of the letter of the Word there is conjunction with the Lord, and association with the angels. There is conjunction with the Lord by means of the Word because the Word treats of Him alone; and by it the Lord is the All in all things of the Word, and He is called the Word, as was shown in the Doctrine of the Lord. There is conjunction in the sense of the letter because the Word in that sense is in its fullness, its sanctity and its power, as was shown above in its own chapter. The conjunction is not apparent to man; but it is in the affection of truth and in the perception of it, and thus in the love and faith of Divine Truth with Him.

[63] There is association with angels by means of the sense of the letter because within that sense there are the spiritual and the celestial senses, and the angels are in those senses; the angels of the spiritual kingdom are in the spiritual sense of the Word, and the angels of the celestial are in its celestial sense. These senses are unfolded from the natural sense of the Word, which is the sense of the letter, when a man principled in truth is in that sense. This unfolding is instantaneous, and thus also is his association [with angels]

[64]. It has been proved to me by much experience that the spiritual angels are in the spiritual sense of the Word, and the celestial angels in its celestial sense. It has been granted me to perceive that, while I was reading the Word in the sense of the letter, communication was opened with the heavens, sometimes with one society of them, sometimes with another. What I understood according to the natural sense, spiritual angels understood according to the spiritual sense, and celestial angels according to the celestial sense, and this instantly. As I have perceived this communication many thousands of times, I have not any doubt left concerning it. Moreover, some spirits dwelling under the heavens abuse this communication. They repeat some passages from the sense of the letter of the Word, forthwith observing and making a note of the society with which communication is affected. I have frequently seen and heard this being done. Thus by actual experience it has been granted me to know that the Word, as to the sense of its letter, is the Divine medium of conjunction with the Lord and with heaven. Concerning this conjunction by means of the Word see also what is adduced in the work "HEAVEN AND HELL," Nos. 303-310.

[65] I will now also state in a few words how the unfolding of these senses is affected. In order that this may be understood it is necessary to recall what was said above in Nos. 6 and 38 concerning successive order and simultaneous order. It was there explained that the Celestial, the Spiritual and the Natural follow one after another in successive order from the highest things which are in heaven to the lowest or ultimate things which are in the world; that these are in the lowest degree, namely the natural, in simultaneous order, one side by side with another, from what is inmost to what is outmost; and that in like manner the successive senses of the Word, the Celestial and the Spiritual, are simultaneously in the natural. When these things are comprehended, it may in some measure be explained to the understanding how the two senses, the Spiritual and the Celestial, are unfolded from the natural sense, when a man is reading the Word. For the spiritual angel then calls forth what is spiritual, and the celestial angel then calls forth what is celestial; nor can they do otherwise, for the things are essentially the same, and in harmony with their own essential nature.

[66] This may be illustrated first by comparisons from the three kingdoms of nature, namely, the animal, the vegetable and the mineral. From the animal kingdom: When food has been converted into chyle, the blood vessels extract from it their blood, the nervous fibres their juices, and the substances which are the origins of fibres, their animal spirit.

From the vegetable kingdom: A tree with trunk, branches, leaves and fruit is supported by its root, by which it draws from the ground a grosser sap for the trunk, branches and leaves, a purer for the fleshly part of the fruit, and the purest for the seeds within the fruit.

From the mineral kingdom: In certain places in the bowels of the earth, there are mineral ores, impregnated with gold, silver and iron; and from exhalations hidden in the earth gold, silver and iron derives each its own element.

[67] It may now be illustrated by example how the spiritual and celestial angels draw their own sense from the natural sense, in which the Word is with men. For example, let us take five commandments of the Decalogue:

(1) "Thou shalt honor thy father and thy mother." By father and mother a man understands the father and mother on earth, as also all who are in the place of father and mother; and by honouring, he understands holding them in honour and obeying them. But a spiritual angel by father understands the Lord, and by mother the Church; and by honouring he understands loving. A celestial angel however, understands by father the Lords Divine Love, by mother His Divine Wisdom, and by honouring, doing good from Him.

(2) "Thou shalt not steal." By stealing, a man understands stealing, defrauding, and depriving a neighbor of his property under any pretext whatever. A spiritual angel understands by stealing depriving others of the truths of their faith and the goods of charity, by means of falsity and evil. A celestial angel however, by stealing understands attributing to ones self what belongs to the Lord, and claiming for oneself His righteousness and merit.

(3) "Thou shalt not commit adultery." By committing adultery a man understands committing adultery, committing whoredom, indulging in obscene practices, lascivious conversation, and filthy thoughts. A spiritual angel understands by committing adultery, the adulteration of the good of the Word and the falsification of its truth. A celestial angel however, understands by committing adultery the denial of the Lords Divinity and the profanation of the Word.

(4) "Thou shalt not kill." By killing, a man understands also cherishing hatred and thirsting for revenge even to death. A spiritual angel understands for killing, acting like a devil, and destroying the soul of a man. A celestial angel however, understands for killing, hating the Lord and those things, which are the Lords.

(5) "Thou shalt not bear false witness." By bearing false witness, a man understands lying, and defamation. A spiritual angel understands, for bearing false witness, declaring and persuading that falsity is truth, and evil good, and the reverse. A celestial angel however, understands for bearing false witness, blaspheming the Lord and the Word.

(6) From these examples it may be seen how the spiritual and the celestial are unfolded and drawn from the natural sense of the Word, which contains them. And what is wonderful, the angels draw out their own senses without knowing what the mans thoughts are. Still, the thoughts of angels and men make one by correspondence, like end, cause and effect; for ends actually exist in the celestial kingdom, causes in the spiritual kingdom and effects in the natural kingdom.

Conjunction itself by correspondences is such from creation. In this way, then, association with angels results through the instrumentality of the Word.

The association of man with angels is affected by the natural or literal sense of the Word, and because in every man from creation there are three degrees of life, the Celestial, the Spiritual and the Natural. A man however, is in the natural degree as long as he continues in this world. He is also in the spiritual degree only so far as he is in genuine truths, and in the Celestial degree only so far as his life is in accordance with those truths. Still, he does not actually enter the spiritual or celestial degree itself until after death. But more will be said on this subject elsewhere. From what has been said it may be evident that the Word alone, since by it there is conjunction with the Lord and association with angels, contains spirit and life, and the Lord teaches:

The words that I speak unto you, they are spirit and they are life (John 6:63). The water that I shall give you (A.V. him) shall be a well of water springing up unto everlasting life (John 4:14). Man doth (A.V. shall) not live by bread alone, but by every word that proceedeth out of the mouth of God (Matthew 4:4). Labour for that meat which endureth unto everlasting life, which the Son of Man shall give unto you (John 6:27).

[70] VII

The Word is in all the heavens, and is the source of angelic wisdom. That the Word exists in the heavens has hitherto been unknown. Indeed, it could not be known as long as the Church was ignorant of the fact that angels and spirits are men, like men in the world, and that they have things similar in all respects to those, which men have. The only difference is that angels are spiritual, and all things with them have a spiritual origin, while men in this world are natural, and all things with them have a natural origin. As long as men did not know this they could not know that the Word exists also in the heavens, and is read by angels there, as well as by spirits beneath the heavens. Lest this should remain unknown forever, it has been granted me to be in the company of angels and spirits, to converse with them and to see their surroundings, and afterwards to relate the many things, which I heard and saw. This I have done in the work HEAVEN AND HELL, published in London in the year 1758. In that work it may be seen that angels and spirits are men, and that they are surrounded by all things in abundance, which surround men in this world. That angels and spirits are men may be seen in that work, Nos. 73-77, and Nos. 453-456; and that they are surrounded by things similar to those which surround men in this world, Nos. 170-190 (Go to "The Heavenly Doctrines" by Emmanuel Swedenborg). Also that they have divine worship and preaching in their temples. Nos. 221-227; with writings and books, Nos. 258-264; as well as the Word, No. 259.

[71] As to the Word in heaven, it is written in the spiritual style, which differs entirely from the natural style. The spiritual style consists of letters only, each of which

involves a meaning; and there are points above the letters, which exalt the sense. The letters in use among the angels of the spiritual kingdom are similar to the letters used in printing in our world; and the letters among the angels of the celestial kingdom, each one of which also involves a complete meaning, are like old Hebrew letters, inflected variously with marks above and within them.

2. Since the writing of angels is of this nature, there are therefore no names of persons and places in their Word as in ours; but instead of the names there are the things, which these signify. Thus instead of Moses there is the Historic Word and instead of Elias the prophetic Word; instead of Abraham, Isaac and Jacob, there is the Lord as to the Divine and the Divine Human; instead of Aaron, the priesthood; and instead of David, the kingship, both of the Lord. Instead of the names of the twelve sons of Jacob, or of the tribes of Israel, there are the various things pertaining to heaven and the Church; and there are similar things instead of the names of the twelve disciples. Instead of Zion and Jerusalem there is the Church as to the Word and as to doctrine from the Word; instead of the Land of Canaan here is the Church; and instead of the cities there on this side and beyond Jordan there are various things pertaining to the Church and its doctrine; and so with all the other names. It is the same with numbers; these are not found in the copies of the Word in heaven, but instead of them, the things to which the numbers in our Word correspond. From this it may be evident that the Word in heaven is a Word corresponding to our Word, and therefore that they are one; for correspondences make one.

[72] It is a wonderful circumstance that the Word in the heavens is so written that the simple understand it in simplicity, and the wise in wisdom. For there are many points and signs over the letters, which, as was said, exalt the sense. The simple neither regard nor understand these; but the wise pay attention to them, each according to his degree of wisdom, even to the wisest. A copy of the Word, written by angels under the Lords inspiration, is kept by every considerable society in its sacred repository, in case the Word elsewhere should suffer alteration in any point. Our Word indeed is like the Word in heaven in this respect that the simple understand it in simplicity, and the wise in wisdom; but this is effected in another manner.

[73] The angels themselves confess that they derive all their wisdom from the Word, for the light in which they are varies with their understanding of the Word, light with them being Divine Wisdom, which is the light of heaven. In the Sacred Repository, where the copy of the Word is kept, the light is flaming and bright, surpassing every degree of light in heaven outside. The cause is the same as that stated above, that the Lord is in the Word.

[74] The wisdom of celestial angels surpasses that of spiritual angels almost as much as the wisdom of spiritual angels surpasses that of men, because celestial angels are in the good of love from the Lord, and spiritual angels are in the truths of wisdom from the Lord; and where the good of love is, there is wisdom also; but

where truths are, there is no more wisdom than there is also good of love. This is the reason why the Word in the celestial kingdom is written differently from the Word in the spiritual kingdom. For in the Word of the celestial kingdom are expressed the goods of love, and the signs indicate affections; while in the Word of the spiritual kingdom are expressed the truths of wisdom, and the signs indicate perceptions.

[75] From this we may conclude that wisdom lies concealed in the Word, which is in the world; for within it lies all angelic wisdom, and this is ineffable, for the Word is its containant. Into this wisdom after death the man comes whom the Lord makes an angel through the Word.

(The Doctrine of Sacred Scripture will continue on page 134.)

CHAPTER 5

Day of the Angel!

The angels of heaven all have the same senses as men here in the material world do. The only difference being that their senses are of either a spiritual nature or a celestial nature. But both of a more pure nature than the senses of man in the material realm. Now where as spirits and angelic spirits can see things through the eyes of man, that are in the material world, angels cannot. For angels have the most pure senses and they cannot be shared with man. Their senses are not of or from a material nature, but of a spiritual nature. For instance an angel can see another angel just by thinking of them and they appear. But when they appear they do not appear in actuality, but only apparently. For angels are pure thought and they see, hear, taste, touch, and smell from thought alone. Whereas angelic spirits see through the eyes of mankind, as do all spirits. Any contact that the angels of heaven ever have with mankind is through their close connection with the angelic spirits, and these through good spirits. But angels cannot interfere, nor have any contact with the material world in a direct manner, for their world is pure love whereas our world is pure hatred, or evil. Therefore any connection man wishes to have with the heavens he must do so by correspondences, and this through the good spirits, and the angelic spirits. Now I realize we have discussed these issues before, but they now have to do with the details of a completely different subject, and so I must bring them to light once again. The senses which angels possess are quite different than mans for the simple reason that they are of thought and not actually connected to a bodily form. Angels do at times require a bodily form, in which case God will provide them one immediately, if they so wish. For if you were to see an angel close up you would see two people, a man and a woman, who are husband and wife. But when far away, and not very close up, you will see them as one body, and they will represent, and appear as whatever affection they represent in heaven. For instance if an angel were thinking of intellectual or doctrinal things you would see him from far off as a horse, or if he were among similar company, you would see horses. For whatever an angel in heaven represents in their affections that is what is seen from afar. They are only seen as themselves close up, and even though they appear as husband and wife, they share the same soul. Angels live just as they did when they were in the world; with houses with many rooms, gardens, groves, pastures, lakes, shopping centers, libraries etc. They work at their job or trade just as before, but these trades are correspondences, and are not exactly as they are in the world. For there is no need for plumbers in heaven, for God provides all things, as they are needed. There is no need for carpenters, electricians, or any type of builders there. All appears instantly, and only as needed by each angel. Angels have fantasies just as men in our world do, but not of the flesh, and they do not seek their own needs all the time. Angels wish for the good of a neighbor, and so everyone is blessed because everyone wants for the other, as God happily provides. But because celestial angels are in love to the lord, they wish nothing more than to please him, and to put his will in acts of love according to each angel's affection. The spiritual angels are in truths, and love to their neighbor, and so they want nothing more than to help their neighbor by teaching them truths, as well as loving them from what ever affection they represent as well. When angels are finished with their use for the day, as all in the heavens, as well as the hells must perform a use till eternity. And for those who do not wish to perform a use, they are punished, according to the measure of disobedience they are in. But in the end, all spirits eventually give in and perform their use, so as to be provided with their food, as well as all other basic necessities needed for life. But as I was saying, when an angel is finished performing his use for the day he goes home just as man does in our world. And he does all the things that men in our world do, only according to his love, or affection. To give details of these things would serve no true purpose, and so the Lord has caused me to pass that subject by. So basically angels have all the same desires as they had in the world, but desires that are created from correspondences. In other words, a husband and wife will come together in the heavens just as they do in our world, but they will never have children. And they will each be supplied with their own bodies, of which will be at an age acceptable to the man and woman who form the angel. What I mean is that they will appear as young adults when they are intimate, as this needs no explaining. But they will enjoy most learned conversations, and things that only older adults can enjoy, in which case they will be of the age at this time that fits the moment, or state. And then there are times when the angel, who is husband and wife, may wish to play, or wrestle as children do, and they will appear as children to each other. What I am saying is that the word hints that a man and woman, as husband and wife in heaven would appear to each other as young adults, and this is true, but they will have many more appearances to one another as well, for God wishes for his children to continue to play until eternity, and so he will provide all opportunity to do so. But on the other hand, if you are older, then you know there are special times for a man and woman, even in their later years, and they do not wish to lose these times either. And so the Lord once again provides the opportunity for this to happen as well. There are many states in a man and woman's life that give them many moments of pleasure, and God would not take a single one from them, ever. But do not ever think that heaven is a place where you go and sit on clouds all day long eating grapes, and having the company of many different beautiful women. For he has already accounted for the mate of every human being, and one is more than enough, even to eternity. There are certainly times when we will require a body, and we will receive one when that time comes, but you will surely enjoy the time that you need not even reflect on a physical body, for there are wonderful things to know and learn throughout the universe, and a physical body would then just slow us down. But remember, God said the two will become one, and he said so because when two bodies live from one single soul, there is wonderful agreement in all things. The soul, or spirit is the life, but the body is pure fantasy alone; whether in this world or the one to come. Therefore once we become angels we will not wish to be connected with fantasies nearly as often as we do now. Angels enjoy wisdom and knowledge of truths, according to Gods truths and not mans. Their senses are more accurate you might say, because they are based on rationality and not fantasies. Whereas the senses of spirits are still based on things of the world where man dwells, and they are still attached to mans fantasies. Two worlds, two different levels of senses. This is why animal's senses in our world are more keen than our own, because they are distracted by the pleasures of the world, nor the things of the flesh. For the only thoughts animals have are those of necessity or instinct. Such as the things they need in order to survive in life. Man goes far beyond this because he can rationalize, reflect, and covet. And because he can covet, he many times becomes distracted by the things of the world. Angels are not distracted by bodily things, nor are they weighed down by their lusts in life. For angels look to the good of their neighbor before their own good. So where are angels when they are not in a body, and what can they do without a body? Well, they go to work, performing their use every day. For there are periods of time in heaven which appear as days to angels, but they are actually state, and time is never even considered in the heavens. No one is in a rush because they do not have to be somewhere at any certain time since there is no time, but states. And what this means is that when an angel wakes up, their day begins, or that particular state begins. What uses angels serve are such uses as providing loving thoughts to man through spirits, and angelic spirits. And because angels are wiser and more pure than spirits, they form the human body, and all other things in the material world, however, not directly. Angels represent vortical forms, spirits represent spiral forms, and man represents angular forms. Angular forms being geometric forms. Then the spirits in the natural heavens represent forms of a mixture. For there are vortical forms to many different degrees, there are vortical spiral forms to many different degrees, and there are angular forms to many different degrees. There are vortical spiral angular forms to many different degrees, and there is a combination of all these forms to the level of many different degrees. But no angular form is created from itself, no spiral form is created from itself, and no vortical form is created from itself. For all things that are finite owe their existence to something before themselves. And as mentioned earlier, the vortical must continue on through the spiral so as to end up in the angular, or natural world. As does the spiral with the vortical within continue on through the angular in order to create the material world. But everything in creation has three different degrees. These degrees are what are called end, cause, and effect; as we have discussed earlier. With man the spiritual world is the End, or beginning of all things in the material world. The Use is considered the cause, and the form, or what is natural is the Effect. So can you see how the angels must work through the spirits in order to create the material world? The more pure the part of the human body, the more pure the angels must be who create that part of the body. Such as the Cortical or Ceneritus substance in the brain is created by the celestial angels. The blood is also created by angels at different levels in the angelic societies. For there are different levels of purity in the blood, and the most pure is in the brain. The arteries are filled with less pure blood, and the nerves have even less pure blood than the arteries do. And according to purity in our world, this world is created from angels and spirits in the heavens as well as the hells. But no thing that is of evil, or has anything to do with evil in this world was created directly from God, but from the thoughts of affections of man. For God sends influx of love to all beings, and their form, or body is created according to how they use these affections of love from God. If they turn these affections into those of a murderer, thief, rapist, or an adulterer then the person's body will be formed, or changed accordingly. Does this mean that these types of people are ugly all the time? By no means, because this is a world of fantasy, and how we really look is seen from our spiritual man, or inner man. So the personality of these types of people cannot be discerned by their looks in our world, but by their spirit when it is opened up to you. But the Lord only permits the regenerate to see these types of spirits in people, and no one else. For what good would it do for the evil to recognize the evil in our world? So remember, every human being is created from within by his thoughts of affections, and his physical health is very much reliant on his spiritual affections. If you are evil, you may see your life as very pleasant, in your own eyes that is, but life has a way of catching up with us all; so be careful what you wish for, because you do not ever know what form it will come in. Everything evil permitted to remain in this world will serve its purpose, or use, but this does not mean we will not all reap that which we sow. No animals that are evil, or harmful to man were created by God, but at one time or another by man; and they will only be harmful to the evil people in the world, whether we see these people as evil or not. For you cannot fool the laws of nature, and it will call you to account as is all men's destiny. We who are evil in spirit and hide it, think we are getting away with something, but we are only fooling ourselves. But as I said, about evil animals in the world, they cannot at all harm those who are good, when they are in good. For the Lord promises that the evil will never be permitted to harm the good, and the proof is out there for those who are truly paying attention. But as I was saying before I got sidetracked, angels spend their day performing their use, just as spirits, and men do. Angels can perform all their uses without a body because what the do is done in the spiritual world where bodies are not required. But for me to give further details would take too much time and space, and therefore will not be possible at this time. As I am prepared to close this subject, I leave you with this thought. If all good things in this world alone were created by God, just how much of this world is created by mans fantasies, and is not really real? For remember, nothing that is harmful in any way to man was created by God.

The Shrewd Manager!

How should a good Christian act in the world, whatever generation he lives in? Now we read many things that give us many different opinions as to how a good Christian should present himself to the world, and even how he should act when he is alone or at home with his family. One of the most believed fallacies in the church today is that a man is the head of the household, and that his wife is to only submit to him, and not the other way around. But this is not the case, and I will expound on this subject very shortly. We are also miss-led into thinking that a good Christian is to always be very gentle and loving, never showing a touch of anger, or rebuke toward another man. And that we are not to judge, or have harsh words with anyone. Now I know there are those who do not agree on all these points, but this is the basic accepted way of the Christian world. For we are supposed to obey the Ten Commandments, right? And if this is the case we must first love the Lord our God with all our heart and soul and mind and strength, and to love our neighbor as ourself. We must do unto others as we would that they do unto us. And although this is not one of the Ten Commandments, it is commanded by the Lord (Luke 6:31). We are to give to another expecting nothing in return. We are to give a man our coat if he asks for it, and not only our coat but our cloak as well. If he asks us to walk a mile, we should be willing to walk two. Basically what the Lord, as well as the rest of the Word teaches us is that we are to sacrifice our lives for our God and our neighbor. But who has the strength to do this in the present world we live in? Nobody, that's who! For it is told throughout the Word that man can do no good thing of himself. When we leave that church building on Sunday, or Wednesday night, we usually have a smile on our faces, pretending to be good, when the truth is, it is all an act. Why do I say this? Because I have been there, I am one of you, and God has shown me what we all really look like from within, in our spirits. Yes we smile, and sometimes we actually feel good, and do feel like smiling, but it is usually out of habit. For it is easy for a thief to love another thief, and a liar to love another liar, because they have something in common. But let another man look at your wife in church; let someone's son beat your son up after Sunday school; or let the same friend that you have sat next to in Church on Sunday cut you off on the road, and you not know who it really was. You see, it is easy to pretend to be a loving, forgiving, Christian in church on Sunday, but when you leave church it is a whole other story. When you get on the road you scream, or think mean thoughts about some other driver. When you get home you yell at your spouse for you having to do something they wanted you to do, when you just wanted to relax after church. Or you scream at your children because no one is watching now. Or you scream at your spouse because this is normal around your house. Whatever the case may be, we are a different person when we return home from Church, and this should not be. And I know preachers who will agree with me, and simply state that they are not perfect. But God does not expect us to be perfect, he only wants us to attempt to do our best every day, and not keep coming up with excuses as to why we keep messing up. If you keep looking at other women in a lustful manner, and you tell your wife that you will continue to do so until God changes you, he will never change you. For we are to shun all sins as evil, and continuously ask God to remove the urge to do these things from you. But you are not to accept them in your life and wait on God to zap them out of your life, this is not his way. Now many of us would think that the only good Christian is an honest Christian, and one who does everything in life the hard way. You may say that you are meant to be poor for the rest of your life because you cannot wheel and deal like your car salesman friend down the street can. Or you cannot get a job that pays good money because you only have a high school education. And you may say that you would not ever steal a thing because you are a good Christian. And that if any man ever told you it was okay to steal, you would keep as far away from him as possible, right? Well, don't worry, I am not going to tell you it is okay to steal; only that one day you will, and you will be forgiven for it. There is not a totally honest, all out good loving, rich Christian in the world, and there never has been. You would not give your life for another man, or woman, or child because you would fear that you would lose your life. And this is not a trade any human being would make. If you say you would, you are wrong. Now I know there are many people who believe they would give their life for their own child, but this is not so either. You believe that out of your love for your child, but that love comes from God and not you. When the time came for you to give your life for your child God takes over as pure love and he is the one who saves your Childs life by using you to do so. And you may take the credit, as many men or women do, but you are not responsible. No human being is loving, and none will truly sacrifice their life for any other. The love anyone feels for someone else, whether it be a brother, a sister, mother, father, daughter, son, or anyone else we may love; is a love from God, and it only appears to be from us. Not only that but no man can be faithful to his wife without the help of God, and his Divine Providence of Conjugal Love for a spouse. So whether you believe yourself to be a faithful husband, an honest Christian, a loving father who would give his life for his child, or any other Christian, or just a man who can do no wrong in Gods eyes, you are mistaken. All of these qualities are affections provided directly from God, and can be taken away any time we become so self righteous as to need a wake up call. But God is always patient, and gives us ample time to learn these lessons on our own. So you say you would not steal do you? If your child were hungry enough you would easily steal. And do not ever think you have too much family, or resources in which you would never have to stoop as low as to steal to feed your children. There are times God allows us to lose all we have in order to teach us this lesson, just because nothing else worked to allow you to learn it in any other way. For God never just gives us one way out, but several. However, man is impatient, and he usually will not wait long enough for God to bring him out of a tough situation. Now what about lying, would you say that you would never lie? Hopefully not, because you will surely lie many times in your lifetime. The biggest problem however is that a man will steal, lie, or stand on a street corner simply to provide for himself and his selfish needs first. Many do this in place of working a job of some sorts. They of course will be forgiven these things because what we do in this world will not ever erase our eventual salvation. But man today suffers much, simply because he puts his needs before his loved ones or his neighbor. He will steal for himself, but not for a neighbor. He will lie for his own but not for someone else. He will fight with, and yell at his wife and children, but he will pretend to be a loving human being when he sees his church companions on Sunday. Well, I am going to quote a parable of the Lord Jesus, and I will return to comment: Jesus told his disciples: There was a rich man whose manager was accused of wasting his possessions. So he called him in and asked him, "What is this I hear about you? Give an account of your management, because you cannot be manager any longer"

The manager said to himself, "What shall I do now? My master is taking away my job. I'm not strong enough to dig, and I'm ashamed to beg. I know what ill do, so that when I lose my job here, people will welcome me into their houses." So he called in each one of his master's debtors. He asked the first, "How much do you owe my master?" "Eight hundred gallons of olive oil," he replied. The manager told him, "Take your bill, sit down quickly, and make it four hundred." Then he asked the second, "And how much do you owe?" "A thousand bushels of wheat," he replied. He told him, "Take your bill and make it eight hundred." The master commended the dishonest manager because he had acted shrewdly. For the people of this world are more shrewd in dealing with their own kind than are the people of the light. I tell you, use worldly wealth to gain friends for yourself, so that when it is gone, you will be welcomed into eternal dwellings. "Whosoever can be trusted with very little can also be trusted with much. So if you have not been trustworthy in handling worldly wealth, who will trust you with true riches? And if you have not been trustworthy with someone else's property, who will give you property of your own? "No servant can serve two masters. Either he will hate the one and love the other, or he will be devoted to the one and despise the other. You cannot serve both God and money." The Pharisees, who loved money, heard all this and were sneering at Jesus. He said to them, "You are the ones who justify yourselves in the eyes of men, but God knows your hearts. WHAT IS HIGHLY VALUED AMONG MEN IS DETESTABLE IN GODS SIGHT (Luke 16:1-15). Now few men have ever explained this parable, for the explanation is given only when the Lord returns to the world. And so I will give the explanation just as the Lord provides it to me. But be patient for the explanation has some size to it. For there are things I must tell you before I give the explanation. So here goes:

Ones own prudence persuades and confirms the idea that all good and truth originate from and are in man, because mans own prudence is his intellectual proprium* flowing in from the love of self, which is his voluntary proprium; and the proprium cannot do otherwise than make all things its own., for it cannot be elevated above that idea. All who are led by the Divine Providence of the Lord are elevated above their proprium and they see that all good and truth are from the Lord; indeed, they even see that what is in man originating from the Lord is always the Lords and never mans. He who believes otherwise is like one who, having his master's goods deposited with him, claims them for himself or appropriates them as his own. Such a man is not a steward but a thief; and as mans proprium is only evil he immerses those gods in his evil, whereby they are destroyed like pearls cast upon a dung heap or into an acid solution.

EVERYTHING OF WHICH MAN HAS PERSUADED HIMSELF, AND WHICH HE HAS CONFIRMED IN HIMSELF REMAINS WITH HIM AS HIS OWN.

It is believed by many that no truth can be seen by man except from proof; but this is false. In the civil and economic affairs of a kingdom or of a republic what is useful and good cannot be seen unless several statutes and ordinances in force there are known, and in judicial matters unless the laws are known; and in the things of nature, as physics, chemistry, anatomy, mechanics and other subjects, unless one has been instructed in these sciences. But in matters purely rational, moral and spiritual, truths are apparent in their own light, provided man has from a right education become in some degree rational, moral and spiritual. This is because every man as to his spirit, or that, which thinks, is in the spiritual world as one among those who are there; and consequently he is in spiritual light, which enlightens the interiors of his understanding, and as it were dictates.

*Proprium—To come from ones self; to be of self.

For spiritual light in its essence is the Divine Truth of the Lords Divine Wisdom. Hence it is that man can think analytically, form conclusions about what is just and right in judicial matters, can see what is honorable in moral life and what is good in spiritual life, and also can see many truths, which do not become obscured unless by the confirmation of falsities. What is good and true in the spiritual life man sees almost in the same way as he sees the mind (animus) of another in his face, and perceives his affections from the tone of his voice, with no other knowledge than what is inherent in everyone. Why should not a man see in some measure from influx the interior things of his life, which are spiritual and moral, when there is no animal which does not know by influx the things necessary for it, which are natural? A bird knows how to build nests, lay its eggs, hatch its young, and knows its own food; besides other wonderful things which are called instinct. But how mans state is changed by the confirmations of falsities and persuasions derived from them will now be explained in the following order:

[1] There is nothing that cannot be confirmed, and falsity more readily than truth.
[2] Truth does not appear when falsity is confirmed, but falsity appears from confirmed truth. In other words, if you ever confirm a truth, you cause it to now be a falsity.
[3] To be able to confirm whatever one pleases is not intelligence but only ingenuity, which may exist even with the worst of men.
[4] There is confirmation that is intellectual and not at the same time voluntary; but all voluntary confirmation is also intellectual.
[5] The confirmation of evil that is both voluntary and intellectual causes man to believe that his own prudence is everything and the Divine Providence nothing, but not the confirmation that is only intellectual.
[6] Everything confirmed by both the will and the understanding remains to eternity; but not what has been confirmed only by the understanding.

2.   With respect to the first: There is nothing that cannot be confirmed, and falsity more readily than truth. What couldn't be confirmed, when it is confirmed by atheists that God is not the creator of the universe, but that nature is the creator of her self; that religion is only a restraining bond, and for the simple and the common people; that man is as a beast, and dies like one; and when it is confirmed that adulteries are allowable, likewise secret theft, fraud and treacherous devices; that cunning is intelligence and wickedness is wisdom? Everyone confirms his own heresy. Are there not volumes filled with confirmations of the two heresies prevailing in the Christian world? Formulate ten heresies even of an abstruse nature, and tell an ingenious person to confirm them, and he will confirm them all. If you then regard them only from their confirmations will you not see falsities as truths? As every falsity shines clearly in the natural man from appearances and fallacies, and truth shines only in the spiritual man, it is evident that falsity can be confirmed more readily than truth.

3.   In order that it may be known that every falsity and every evil can be confirmed even to the point that falsity appears as truth and evil as good, take this as an example:
       Let it be confirmed that light is darkness and darkness light. May it not be urged, "What is light itself?" Is it not only something that appears in the eye according to its state? What is light when the eye is closed? Have not bats and owls have such eyes that they see light as darkness and darkness as light? I

have heard it said of some persons that they see in this way; and that infernal spirits, although they are in darkness, still see one another. Has not man light in his dreams in the middle of the night? Is not darkness therefore light, and light darkness? But it may be answered, "What of this?" Light is light as truth is truth; and darkness is darkness as falsity is falsity.

4. Take another example: Let it be confirmed that a crow is white. May it not be said that its blackness is only a shade that is not the reality? Its feathers are white within, and so is its body; and these are the substances of which the bird is formed. As its blackness is only a shade, therefore, the crow becomes white when it grows old, and some such have been seen. What is black in itself but white? Grind down black glass and you will see that the powder is white. Therefore, when you call a crow black you speak from the shadow and not from the reality. But it may be answered again, "What of this?" At this rate it may be said that all birds are white. These examples, although they are contrary to sound reason, are set forth to show that it is possible to confirm falsity that is directly opposite to the truth, and so confirm evil that is directly opposite to good.

5. Second: Truth does not appear when falsity is confirmed, but falsity appears from confirmed truth. All falsity is in darkness and all truth in light; and in darkness nothing is seen, nor indeed is it known what anything is unless by touching it; but it is not so in the light. For this reason in the Word falsities are called darkness; and consequently those who are in falsities are said to walk in darkness and in the shadow of death. On the other hand, truths are there called light, and consequently those who are in truths are said to walk in the light, and are called the children of light.

6. From many things it is evident that when falsity is confirmed, truth does not appear, and that from confirmed truth falsities appear. For example, who would see any spiritual truth if the Word did not teach it? Would there not be merely darkness which could not be dispelled, unless by means of the light in which the Word is, and only with him who desires to be enlightened? What heretic can see his falsities unless he accepts the genuine truth of the Church? He does not see them before this. I have conversed with some who have confirmed themselves in faith separated from charity, and who were asked whether they saw the many things in the Word concerning love and charity, about works and deeds, and about keeping the commandments, and that he is blessed and wise who keeps them, but foolish who does not. They replied that when they read those things they only saw them as matters of faith, and so passed them by as it were with their eyes shut.

7. Those who have confirmed themselves in falsities are like those who see streaks on an inner wall in a house; and in the shades of evening they see in their fancy the marked part like a man on horseback or simply as a man, a visionary image which is dispelled by the light of day when it pours in. Who can perceive the spiritual defilement of adultery but one who is in the spiritual purity of chastity?

Who can feel the cruelty of revenge but one who is in good arising from love of a neighbor? Who that is an adulterer, or who is revengeful, does not sneer at those who call the delights of such things infernal, and who, on the other hand, call the delights of marital love and the love of a neighbor heavenly? And so on.

8. Third: To be able to confirm whatever one pleases is not intelligence but only ingenuity, which may exist even with the worst of men. There are some very skillful in confirming who know no truth and yet can confirm both truth and falsity. Some of them say, "What is truth?" Does it exist? Is not that true which I make true? Yes these are considered intelligent in the world, although they are only plasterers of the wall. None are intelligent but those who perceive truth to be truth, and confirm truth by individual truths continually perceived. These two classes of men are not easily distinguished, because it is not possible to distinguish between the light of confirmation and the light of the perception of truth. There is the appearance that those who are in the light of confirmation are also in the light of perception of truth, when nevertheless the difference between them is like that between illusive light and genuine light; and in the spiritual world illusive light is such that it is turned into darkness when genuine light flows in. There is such illusive light with many in hell; and when these are brought into genuine light they see nothing at all. Hence it is evident that to be able to confirm whatever one pleases is only ingenuity that may exist even with the worst of men.

9. Fourth: There is confirmation that is intellectual and not at the same time voluntary, but all voluntary confirmation is also intellectual. Take these examples by way of illustration. Those who confirm faith separate from charity and yet live the life of charity, who in general confirm falsity of doctrine and yet do not live according to it, are those that are in intellectual confirmation and not at the same time in voluntary confirmation. On the other hand, those who confirm falsity of doctrine and who live according to it are those that are in voluntary confirmation and at the same time in intellectual confirmation. This is because the understanding does not flow into the will, but the will flows into the understanding. Hence it is also evident what the falsity of evil is, and what the falsity which is not of evil. Falsity of which is not of evil can be conjoined with good, but falsity of evil cannot; because falsity which is not of evil is falsity in the understanding and not in the will, while falsity of evil is falsity in the understanding arising from evil in the will.

10. Fifth: The confirmation of evil that is both voluntary and intellectual causes man to believe that his own prudence is everything and the Divine Providence nothing, but not the confirmation that is only intellectual. There are many who confirm in themselves their own prudence from appearances in the world but yet do not deny the Divine Providence; and theirs is only intellectual confirmation. With others however, who at the same time deny the Divine Providence there

also exists voluntary confirmation; but this, together with persuasion, is chiefly to be found with those who are worshipers of nature and also worshipers of self.

11. Sixth: Everything confirmed by both the will and the understanding remains to eternity, but not what has been confirmed only by the understanding. For that which pertains to the understanding alone is not within the man but outside him: it is only in the thought. Moreover, nothing enters into man and is appropriated to him but what is received by the will, for it then comes to be of his life's love. It will now be shown that this remains to eternity.

Everything confirmed by both the will and the understanding remains to eternity because everyone is his own love, and love belongs to the will; also because every man is his own good or his own evil, for everything is called good, and likewise evil, that belongs to the love. Since a man is his own love he is also the form of his love, and may be called the organ of his life's love. I have stated before that the affections of a mans love and his consequent thoughts are changes and variations of the state and form of the organic substances of his mind, and what these changes and variations are and their nature will now be explained. Some idea of these may be obtained from the heart and lungs, where there are alternate expansions and compressions, or dilations and contractions, called in the heart systole and diastole, and in the lungs respirations; these are reciprocal extensions and retractions, or expansions and contractions of their lobes; such are the changes and variations of the state of the heart and lungs. There are similar changes and variations in the other viscera of the body and also in their parts, by which the blood and the animal juices are received and passed on.

(2) There are also similar changes and variations in the organic forms of the mind, which are the subjects of mans affections and thoughts, as was shown above; with this difference, that their expansions and compressions, or reciprocal actions, are respectively in such greater perfection that they cannot be expressed in words of natural language, but only in words of spiritual language which indicate by their sound that these changes and variations are vortex—like inward and outward gyrations, after the manner of perpetually circling spirals wonderfully combined into forms receptive of life.

(3) The nature of those purely organic substances and forms in the wicked and in the good will now be stated.

In the good those spiral forms are moved forward but in the wicked backward, and those that are moved forward are turned towards the Lord and receive influx from Him; while those that are moved backward are turned towards hell and receive influx from hell. It should be known that in the degree that they are turned backward, they are opened behind and closed in front; and, on the other hand, in the degree that they are turned forward, they are open in front and closed behind.

(4) Hence it may be evident what kind of a form or organ a wicked man is, and what kind of form or organ a good man is, and that they are turned in opposite directions; and as the turning once established cannot be reversed it is clear that such as a man is when he dies such he remains to eternity. It is the love of mans will that makes this turning, or which converts and inverts; for, as was said above, every man is his own love. Hence it is that after death everyone goes the way of his love: he who is in a good love goes to heaven, and he who is in an evil love goes to hell; nor does man rest but in that society where his ruling love is; and what is wonderful, everyone knows the way, as though he scented it with his nostrils.

IF MAN BELIEVED, AS IS THE TRUTH, THAT ALL GOOD AND TRUTH ORIGINATE FROM THE LORD, AND ALL EVIL AND FALSITY FROM HELL, HE WOULD NOT APPROPRIATE GOOD TO HIMSELF AND ACCOUNT IT MERITORIOUS, NOR WOULD HE APPROPRIATE EVIL TO HIMSELF AND ACCOUNT HIMSELF RESPONSIBLE FOR IT.

As this however, is contrary to the belief of those who have confirmed in themselves the appearance that wisdom and prudence originate from man, and do not flow in according to the state of the organization of men's minds, treated of above, it must now be demonstrated; and in order that this may be done clearly, the following order will be observed:

1. He who confirms in himself the appearance that wisdom and prudence originate from man and consequently are in him as his own must see that if this were not so he would not be a man, but either a beast or a statue; when yet the contrary is true.
2. To believe and think, as is the truth, that all good and truth originate from the Lord and all evil and falsity from hell, appears as if it were impossible, when yet it is truly human and consequently angelic.
3. To believe and think thus is impossible to those who do not acknowledge the Divinity of the Lord, and who do not acknowledge evils to be sins; but it is possible to those who acknowledge these two things.
4. Those who are in the acknowledgment of these two things reflect only upon the evils in themselves and, so far as they shun them as sins and turn away from them, they cast them out from themselves to the hell from which they come.
5. In this way the Divine Providence does not appropriate either evil or good to anyone, but ones own prudence appropriates both. These things will now be explained in the order proposed.

FIRST: He who confirms in himself the appearance that wisdom and prudence originate from man and are in man as his own must needs see that if this were not so he would not be a man, but either a beast or a statue, when yet the contrary is true.

It is in accordance with a law of the Divine Providence that man should think as of himself and should act prudently as of himself, but yet should acknowledge that he does so from the Lord. Hence it follows that he who thinks and acts prudently as of himself and at the same time acknowledges that he does so from the Lord is a man. On the other hand, he is not a man who confirms in himself the idea that all he thinks and does is from himself; neither is he a man who, because he knows that wisdom and prudence originate from God, still waits for influx; for the latter becomes like a statue, and the former like a beast. It is clear that he who waits for influx is like a statue; for he must stand or sit motionless, with hands hanging down and eyes either shut or open without winking, neither thinking nor breathing. What life then has he?

[2] It is also clear that he who believes that everything he thinks and does is from himself is not unlike a beast, for he thinks only from the natural mind which man has in common with the beasts, and not from the spiritual rational mind which is the truly human mind; for this mind acknowledges that God alone thinks from Himself, and that man thinks from God. Therefore, one who thinks only from the natural mind knows no difference between a man and a beast except that a man speaks and a beast makes sounds, and he believes that they both die in a similar manner.

[3] Of those who wait for influx this further may be said. They receive none, except the few from their heart desire it; and they occasionally receive some response by a vivid perception, or by tacit speech in the response, in their thought but rarely by any manifest speech. It is then to this effect that they should think and act as they wish and as they can, and that he who acts wisely is wise and he who acts foolishly is foolish. They are never instructed what to believe and what to do, and this in order that the human rational principle and human freedom may not perish; that is, that everyone may act from freedom according to reason, to all appearance as from himself. Those who are instructed by influx what to believe or what to do are not instructed by the Lord or by any angel of heaven but by some Enthusiast, Quaker, or Moravian spirit and are led astray. All influx from the Lord is effected by enlightenment of the understanding, and by the affection for truth, and through the latter passing into the former.

[4] SECOND: To believe and think, as is the truth, that all good and truth originate from the Lord and all evil and falsity from hell, appears as if it were impossible, when yet it is truly human and consequently angelic. To believe and think that all good and truth are from God appears possible, provided nothing further is said, because it is according to theological faith, and it is not allowable to think contrary to this. On the other hand, to believe and think that all evil and falsity are from hell appears to be impossible, because one would then believe that man could not think at all. Yet man does think as from himself even though from hell, because the Lord grants to everyone that his thought, whatever its origin, should appear in him as his own. Otherwise a man would not live as a man, nor

could he be led out of hell and introduced into heaven, that is, be reformed, as has been frequently shown in my works.

[5] Therefore also the Lord grants to man to know and consequently to think that he is in hell when he is in evil, and that he thinks from hell if he thinks from evil. He also grants to him to think of the means by which he may escape out of hell and not think from it, but may enter heaven and there think from the Lord; and he further grants to man freedom of choice. From these considerations it may be seen that man is able to think evil and falsity as if from himself, and also to think that this or that is evil or false; consequently that it is only an appearance that he does so of himself, for without this appearance he would not be a man. To think from truth is the human and consequently the angelic principle itself; as it is a truth that man does not think from himself, but that it is granted him by the Lord to think, to all appearance as from himself.

[6] THIRD: To believe and think thus is impossible to those who do not acknowledge the Divinity of the Lord, and who do not acknowledge evils to be sins, but it is impossible to those who acknowledge these two things. It is impossible to those who do not acknowledge the Divinity of the Lord because it is the Lord alone who grants to man to think and to will; and those who do not acknowledge the Divinity of the Lord, being separated from Him, believe that they think from themselves. It is impossible also to those who do not acknowledge evils to be sins, because they think from hell; and in hell everyone imagines that he thinks from himself. However, that it is possible to those who acknowledge these two things may be evident from what has been fully set forth above.

[7] FOURTH: Those who are in the acknowledgment of these two things reflect only upon the evils in themselves; and, so far as they shun them as sins and turn away from them, they cast them out from themselves to the hell from which they come. Everyone knows, or may know that evil originates from hell and that good is from heaven. Consequently, everyone may know that so far as man shuns evil and turns away from it, so far he shuns and turns away from hell. So, too, he may know that so far as anyone shuns evil and turns away from it so far he wills and loves good; and consequently so far is he brought out of hell by the Lord and led to heaven. These things every rational man may see, provided he knows that there is a heaven and a hell, and that evil and good are from their own respective sources. Now if a man reflects upon the evils in himself, which is the same thing as examining himself, and shuns them, he then frees himself from hell and casts it behind him, and introduces himself into heaven where he sees the Lord face to face. It is stated that man does this, but he does it as of himself, and then from the Lord. When a man from a good heart and a pious faith acknowledges this truth, it lies inwardly concealed in everything that he afterwards thinks and does as from himself. It is like the prolific principle in a seed, which inwardly remains with it even until the production of new seed; and like the pleasure in the appetite for food, which a man has once recognized

to be wholesome for him; in a word, it is like the heart and soul in everything that he thinks and does.

[8] FIFTH: In this way the Divine Providence does not appropriate either evil or good to anyone, but ones own prudence appropriates both. This follows from all that has now been said. The end in view of the Divine Providence is good; accordingly it purposes good in every operation. Therefore it does not appropriate good to anyone for such good would thereby become meritorious; nor does it appropriate evil to anyone for it would thereby make him answerable for the evil. Yet man does both from his proprium because this is nothing but evil. The proprium of his will is the love of self, and the proprium of his understanding is the pride of his own intelligence, and from this arises mans own prudence.

EVERY MAN MAY BE REFORMED, AND THERE IS NO SUCH THING AS PREDESTINATION.

It is a dictate of sound reason that all are predestined to heaven, and no one to hell; for all are born men, and consequently the image of God is in them. The image of God in them consists of this: that they are able to understand truth and to do good. To be able to understand truth is from the Divine Wisdom, and to be able to do good is from the Divine Love. This power constitutes the image of God, which remains with the man of sound mind, and is not eradicated. In consequence of this he can become a civil and a moral man; and he that becomes this can also become spiritual; for what is civil and moral is the receptacle of what is spiritual. He who knows the laws of the state of which he is a citizen and lives according to them is said to be a civil man; and he is said to be a moral man who makes those laws the standard of his morals and of his virtues, and from reason lives according to them.

2. I will now state how the civil and the moral life is the receptacle of the spiritual life:

Live these laws not only as civil and moral laws but also as Divine laws, and you will be a spiritual man. There scarcely exists a nation so barbarous that it has not by its laws prohibited murder, adultery with the wife of another, theft, false witness and the violation of another's property. The civil and the moral man observes these laws in order that he may be, or seem to be, a good citizen; but if he does not at the same time regard these laws as Divine he is only a civil and a moral natural man; and if he also regards them as Divine he becomes a civil and a moral spiritual man. The difference is, that the latter is a good citizen not only of an earthly kingdom but also of the heavenly kingdom, while the former is a good citizen of an earthly kingdom but not of the heavenly kingdom. They are distinguished by the good they do. The good which civil and moral natural men do is not good in itself, for man and the world are in it; while the good which civil and moral spiritual men do is good in itself because the Lord and heaven are in it.

3. Hence it may be evident that every man because he is born such that he can become a civil and moral natural man, is also born such that he can become a civil and moral spiritual man. The only condition is that he should acknowledge God and not do evil because it is against God, but should do good because it is in harmony with God. When this condition is observed a spirit enters into his civil and moral actions, and they live; but when it is not observed there is no spirit in them, and consequently they do not live. Therefore the natural man, however civil and moral his actions may be, is called dead, while the spiritual man is called alive.

4. It is of the Lords Divine Providence that every nation has some form of religion; and the primary essential of every religion is the acknowledgment that there is a God, otherwise it is not called a religion; and every nation that lives according to its religion, that is, which refrains from doing evil because it is contrary to its God, receives something spiritual in its natural. When one hears some Gentile say that he will not commit this or that evil because it is contrary to his God, does he not say to himself, "Is not this man saved?" It appears as if it could not be otherwise: sound reason declares this to him. On the other hand, when one hears a Christian say, "I regard this or that evil as of no moment;" what does it signify but that it is contrary to God? Does he not say to himself, "Surely this man cannot be saved?" It seems to be impossible that he should. This is also as sound reason would declare.

5. Should such a one say, I was born a Christian, I have been baptised, I have known the Lord, I have read the Word, and I have attended the sacrament of the supper, do these things avail when he does not regard as sins murder, or the revenge which inspires murder, adultery, secret theft, false testimony or lying, and various types of violence? Does such a man think of God or of any eternal life? Does he think that these exist? Does not sound reason declare that such a one cannot be saved? These things have been said of the Christian because the Gentile thinks more about God from religion related to life than the Christians do. More however, will be said on this subject in what follows in this order:

I.   The end of creation is a heaven from the human race.
II. Therefore it is from the Divine Providence that every man can be saved; and that those are saved who acknowledge God and live well.
III The man himself is at fault if he is not saved.
IV Thus all are predestined* to heaven, and no one to hell.

I. THE END OF CREATION IS A HEAVEN FROM THE HUMAN RACE.

That heaven consists solely of those who have been born men is shown in a work called "HEAVEN AND HELL," published in London in the year 1758, and also in my own works, which are made readily available to the public. And as heaven consists of no others it follows that the end of creation is a heaven from the human race. That this was the end of creation will be seen more clearly from an explanation of the following points:

1) Every man is created that he may live forever.
2) Every man is created that he may live forever in a state of happiness.
3) Thus every man is created that he may enter heaven.
4) The Divine Love cannot do otherwise than desire this, and the Divine Wisdom cannot do otherwise than provide for it.

Since from these considerations it may also be seen that the Divine Providence is none other than Predestination to heaven and cannot be changed into any other, it falls to be shown here in the order set forth that the end of creation is a heaven from the human race. If you are created, you will eventually become a heaven, and an angel.

FIRST: Every man is created that he may live forever. In a treatise called "The Divine Love and Wisdom," parts third and fifth, it is shown that in man there are three degrees of life, which I have many times spoken of, called the NATURAL, THE SPIRITUAL AND THE CELESTIAL, and that these degrees are actually in every man; while in

*Predestined—to destine, decree, determine, appoint, or settle before hand. Therefore it is settled that all men will go to heaven. beasts there is only one degree of life, which is similar to the lowest degree in man called the natural. From this it follows that man by the elevation of his life to the Lord is in such a state above the beasts that he is able to understand what pertains to the Divine Wisdom and to will what pertains to the Divine Love, and in this way to receive the Divine; and he who can receive the Divine so as to see and perceive it in himself cannot be otherwise than conjoined to the Lord, and through this conjunction cannot but live forever.

[2] Having surrounded Himself with the whole of the created universe, what would the Lord be had He not also created images and likenesses of Himself to whom He could impart His Divine. Otherwise what would He be but a creator causing something to be and not to be, or to exist and not to exist, and this for no other purpose than that He might contemplate from afar a mere shifting of scenes and continual changes as in some theatre? Why should the Divine be in these images and likenesses were it not that they might be of service to subjects that would receive the Divine more intimately, and see and feel it? Further, as the Divine is a being of inexhaustible glory, would He retain it to Himself alone, or indeed could He? For love desires to communicate its own to another, and even to give

from its own as much as it can. What then would the Divine Love, which is infinite, not give? Can that give and take away again? Would not this be giving what is about to perish? Inwardly in itself this is nothing, as when anything perishes it comes to naught, that which IS not being in it. But the Divine Love gives what IS, that is, which does not cease to be, and this is eternal.

[3] In order that every man may live forever, what is mortal with him is taken away. His mortal part is the material body that is taken away by his death. His immortal part, which is his mind, is thus unveiled and he then becomes a spirit, in human form, his mind being that spirit. The sages or wise men of old perceive that the mind of man cannot die; for they said, "How can spirit (animus) or mind die when it can exercise wisdom? Few men at the present day know what they interiorly understand by this: but there was an idea which descended from heaven into their general perception that God is wisdom itself which man shares; and God is immortal or eternal.

[4] As it has been granted me to speak with angels I will also say something from my own experience. I have talked with some who lived many ages ago, with some who lived before the flood and with some who lived after it, with some who lived in the time of the Lord, with one of His apostles, and with many who lived in later times. They all appeared like men of middle age, and they said they did not know what death is, but only that there is condemnation. Moreover, all who have lived well, when they enter heaven, come into the state of early manhood they reached in the world and continue in it to eternity, even those who had been old and decrepit men in the world. Women, too, although they had been shrunken and aged, return to their flowering period of their age and beauty.

[5] That man after death lives forever is manifest from the Word where life in heaven is called eternal life, as in Matthew 19:29, 25:46; Mark 10:17; Luke 10:25, 28:30; John 3:15,16,36, 5:24,25,39, 6:27,40,68,12:50.

Also heaven is called simply life in Matthew 18:8,9; John 5:40, 20:31.

The Lord also said to the disciples: Because I live, ye shall live also (John 14:19).

And concerning the resurrection, that God is a God of the living, and not a God of the dead. And that they cannot die anymore (Luke 20:38,36).

[6] Second: Every man is created that he may live forever in a state of happiness. This follows as a consequence; for He who wills that man should live forever also wills that he should live in a state of happiness. What would eternal life be without that? All love desires the good of another. The love of parents desires the good of their children; the love of the bridegroom and of the husband desires the good of the bride and of the wife; and friendships loves desires the good of friends. What then does the Divine Love not desire? What is good but delight? And what is Divine Good but eternal happiness? All good is called good from its delight or happiness. That which is given and possessed is indeed called good,

but unless it is also delightful it is a barren good, not good in itself. Hence it is clear that eternal life is also eternal happiness. This state of man is the end of creation; and it is not the Lords fault but mans that only those who enter heaven are in that state. That man is at fault will be seen in what follows.

[7] Third: Thus every man is created that he may enter heaven. This is the end of creation; but all do not enter heaven because they become imbued with the delights of hell which are opposite to the happiness of heaven; and those who are not in the happiness of heaven cannot enter heaven, for they cannot endure it. To no one who enters the spiritual world is it denied to ascend to heaven; but when one who is in the delight of hell enters heaven his heart palpitates, his breathing is laboured, his life begins to fail, he is in anguish, distress and torment, and he writhes like a serpent placed close to a fire. This is so because opposites act against each other.

[8] Nevertheless, they cannot die, as they were born men and thereby with the faculty of thinking and willing, and consequently of speaking and acting. However, as they can live only with those who are in a similar delight of life they are sent to them; thus those who are in the delights of evil and those who are in the delights of good are sent to their own appropriate companions. It is indeed granted everyone to experience the delight of his own evil provided he does not molest any who are in the delight of good; but as evil cannot do otherwise than molest good for there is an inherited hatred in evil against good, therefore lest the wicked should inflict injury they are removed and cast down to their own place in hell, where their delight is turned to what is the reverse of delightful.

[9] But this does not alter the fact that man by creation is such, and consequently is born such, that he may enter heaven; for everyone who dies in infancy goes to heaven, and is there brought up and instructed as a person is in the world; and through his affection for good and truth he is imbued with wisdom and becomes an angel. Such also might the man become who is brought up and instructed in the world, for there is inherent in him the same as in the infant. Concerning infants in the spiritual world see the work "HEAVEN AND HELL," Nos. 329-345.

[10] With many in the world this does not take place, because they love the first degree of their life, called the natural, and have no desire to withdraw from it and become spiritual. The natural degree of life regarded in itself loves only self and the world, for it clings to the bodily senses and these occupy a prominent place in the world; but the spiritual degree of life regarded in itself loves the Lord and heaven, and also itself and the world, but God and heaven as higher, principal and ruling, and itself and the world as lower, instrumental and serving.

[11] Fourth: The Divine Love cannot do otherwise than desire this, and the Divine Wisdom cannot do otherwise than provide for it. It is shown at length in the treatise, "THE DIVINE LOVE AND WISDOM," that the Divine Essence

is Divine Love and Divine Wisdom; and it is also demonstrated there (Nos. 358-370), that in every human embryo the Lord forms two receptacles, one for the Divine Love and the other for the Divine Wisdom, a receptacle for the Divine Love for the future will of the man, and a receptacle of the Divine Wisdom for his future understanding; and that in this way He has endowed every man with the faculty of willing good and the faculty of understanding truth.

[12] Now since man from his birth is endowed with these two faculties by the Lord, and consequently the Lord is in them as in His own with man, it is clear that His Divine Love cannot but will that man should go to heaven and there enjoy eternal happiness; and also that the Divine Wisdom cannot but provide for this. But since it is from the Lords Divine Love that man should feel heavenly blessedness in himself as his own, and this is impossible unless he is kept completely in the appearance that he thinks, wills, speaks, and acts of himself, therefore the Lord can lead man only according to the laws of His Divine Providence.

THEREFORE IT IS FROM THE DIVINE PROVIDENCE THAT EVERY MAN CAN BE SAVED AND THAT THOSE ARE SAVED WHO ACKNOWLEDGE GOD AND LIVE WELL.

It is clear from what has been shown above that every man can be saved. Some are of the opinion that the Church of the Lord is only in the Christian world, because there alone the Lord is known and there alone is the Word. Still however, many believe that the Church of the Lord is general, that is, spread and dispersed throughout the world, thus existing also with some who are ignorant of the Lord and who do not have the Word. They maintain that it is not the fault of those men that they cannot overcome their ignorance, and that it is contrary to the love and mercy of God that some should be born for hell when yet they also are equally men.

2.   Now since many if not all Christians believe that the Church is general, being called indeed a communion, it follows that there are fundamental principles of the Church, which enter into all religions and constitute that communion. That these fundamental general principles are the acknowledgment of God and the good of life will be seen in the following order:

    (1) The acknowledgment of God brings about the conjunction of God with man and of man with God, and the denial of God causes their separation.
    (2) Everyone acknowledges God and is conjoined to Him according to the good of his life.
    (3) The good of life, that is, living well, is shunning evils because they are contrary to religion, thus contrary to God.
    (4) These are the general principles of all religions by which everyone can be saved.

THESE PROPOSITIONS MUST NOW BE EXAMINED AND DEMONSTRATED ONE BY ONE:

First: The acknowledgment of God brings about the conjunction of God with man and of man with God, and the denial of God causes their separation. Some may think that those who do not acknowledge God can be saved just as well as those who do, provided they lead a moral life. They say, "What does acknowledgment accomplish? Is it not mere thought? Can I not easily acknowledge God when I know for certain that there is a God? I have heard of Him but I have not seen Him. Make me see Him and I will believe." Such is the language of many who deny God when they have an opportunity to reason freely with one who acknowledges God. However, that the acknowledgment of God conjoins and the denial of Him separates will be illustrated by some things made known to me in the spiritual world. In that world when anyone thinks about another and desires to converse with him, the other is immediately present. This is general there and never fails. The reason is that in the spiritual world there is no distance as in the natural world, but only an appearance of distance.

[2] Another fact is that as thought from some knowledge of another causes his presence so love from any affection for another causes conjunction with him. Thus it comes to pass that people go about and converse in a friendly way, live together in one house or one society, frequently meet and render mutual services. The opposite also happens; thus he who does not love another, and still more, he who hates another, does not see or meet him; and the distance they are apart is according to the degree that love is wanting or hate is present. Indeed, should he come into the others presence and remembers his hatred he becomes invisible to him.

[3] From these few particulars it may be evident how presence and conjunction are brought about in the spiritual world; namely, that presence arises from recalling another with a desire to see him and that conjunction arises from an affection, which springs from love. It is the same with all the things that are in the human mind. In it there are numeral things and the several particulars are there associated and conjoined according to affections, or as one thing is attracted to another.

[4] This is spiritual conjunction, which is the same in general things and in particular things. This spiritual conjunction has its origin from the conjunction of the Lord with the spiritual world and with the natural world, in general and in particular. From this it is clear that so far as one knows the Lord and from this knowledge thinks about Him, so far the Lord is present; and so far as anyone acknowledges Him from an affection of love, so far the Lord is conjoined to him: but on the other hand, so far as anyone does not know the Lord so far the Lord is absent; and so far as anyone denies Him, so far is He separated from him.

[5] The result of conjunction is that the Lord turns a mans face to himself and then leads him; while the result of separation is that hell turns a mans face to itself and leads him. Therefore all the angels of heaven turn their faces to the Lord as the sun, and all the spirits of hell turn their faces away from the Lord. Hence it is evident what results from the acknowledgement of God, and what from the denial of Him. Those who deny God in the world deny Him after death, and they become organisms according to the description given above; and the organization induced in the world remains forever.

[6] SECOND: Everyone acknowledges God and is conjoined to Him according to the good of his life. All can have a knowledge of God who know anything from religion. They can also speak of God from knowledge (scientia), that is, from what is in the memory, and some may also think about Him from the understanding. However, if one does not live well, this only brings about presence; for he can nevertheless turn himself away from God towards hell; and this happens if he lives wickedly. But only those can acknowledge God in their hearts who live well; and these according to the good of their life the Lord turns away from hell and towards Himself. The reason is that these alone love God, for they love Divine things, which are from Him, in doing them. The Divine things, which are from God, are the precepts of His Law. These are God because He is His own Divine going forth: this is to love God, and therefore the Lord says: He that keepeth my commandment, he it is that loveth me . . . . But he that keepeth not my commandments loveth me not (John 14:21,24.

[7] This is the reason why there are two tables of the Decalogue, one relating to God and the other relating to man. God works unceasingly that man may receive what is in his own table; but if man does not do the things that are in his table he does not receive with acknowledgment of heart the things that are in Gods table; and if he does not receive them he is not conjoined. Therefore those two tables were so joined together as to be one, and were called the tables of the covenant, for covenant signifies conjunction. Everyone acknowledges God and is conjoined to Him according to the good of his life because the good of life is like the good that is in the Lord, and consequently that originates from the Lord. Therefore when man is in the good of life conjunction is effected. The contrary is the case with evil of life; for this rejects the Lord.

[8] THIRD: The good of life, that is, living well, is shunning evils because they are contrary to religion, thus contrary to God. That this is the good of life, or living well, is fully shown in, "THE DOCTRINE OF LIFE," FROM BEGINNING TO END. To this I will merely add that if you do good to the fullest extent, for example, if you build churches, adorn them and fill them with votive offerings; if you expend money lavishly on hospitals and guest-houses for strangers, give alms daily, succour widows and orphans; if you diligently observe the holy things of worship, indeed, if you think about them, speak and preach about them as from the heart, and yet do not shun evils as sins against God, all those goods

are not good. They are either hypocritical or meritorious, for there is still evil interiorly within them, since the life of everyone is in all things that he does, in general and in particular. Goods only become good by the removal of evil from them. Hence it is clear that shunning evils because they are contrary to religion, thus contrary to God, is living well.

[9]   FOURTH: These are the general principles of all religions by which everyone can be saved. To acknowledge God and to refrain from doing evil because it is against God are the two things, which make religion to be religion. If one of them is wanting it cannot be called religion, since to acknowledge God and to do evil is a contradiction; so also is to do good and yet not acknowledge God, for one is not possible without the other. It has been provided by the Lord that almost everywhere there should be some form of religion, and that in every religion there should be these two principles; and it has also been provided by the Lord that everyone who acknowledges God and refrains from doing evil because it is against God should have a place in heaven. For heaven in the complex resembles one Man whose life or soul is the Lord. In that heavenly Man there are all things that are in a natural man with that difference which exists between things heavenly and things natural.

[10] It is well known that in man there are not only forms, organized from blood vessels and nerve fibres, called viscera, but also skins, membranes, tendons, cartilages, bones, nails and teeth, which have life in a less degree than the organized forms themselves which they serve as ligaments, coverings and supports. The heavenly Man, which is heaven, in order that all these things may be in it, cannot be composed of men all of one religion but of men of many religions. Therefore, all who make these two universal principles of the Church part of their life have a place in that heavenly Man, that is, heaven, and there enjoy happiness in their own degree.

[11] That these two are the primary principles in every religion may be evident from the fact that they are the two, which the Decalogue teaches. The Decalogue was the principal constituent of the Word, and, promulgated by Jehovah by a living voice from Mount Sinai, was written upon two tables of stone by the finger of God. It was then placed in the Ark and was called Jehovah, and constituted the Holy of Holies in the tabernacle, and formed the shrine in the temple at Jerusalem, and all the things there derived their sanctity from it alone. There are many more details from the Word concerning the Decalogue in the Ark set forth in "THE DOCTRINE OF LIFE," which was included in my last book, "Wisdom of God;" and to these I will add the following:

It is well known from the Word that the Ark containing the two tables on which the Decalogue was written was taken by the Philistines and placed in the temple of Dagon in Ashdod; and that Dagon fell to the earth before it, and afterwards his head with the palms of his hands torn from his body lay upon the threshold of the temple; and that the people of Ashdod and Ekron, to the number of many thousands, were smitten with emerods on account of the Ark, and their land was ravished by mice; also that the Philistines, on the advice of the chiefs of their nation, made five golden emerods and five golden mice, and a new cart on which they placed the Ark with the golden emerods and mice beside it; and, drawn by two cows they lowed on the way before the cart, they sent the Ark back to the Children of Israel; and by them the cows and the cart were offered up in sacrifice (see 1Samuel V and VI).

THE MAN HIMSELF IS AT FAULT IF HE IS NOT SAVED.

Every rational man, as soon as he hears it, acknowledges the truth that evil cannot flow from good nor good from evil, because they are opposites; consequently, that from good there flows nothing but good, and from evil nothing but evil. When this truth is acknowledged it is also acknowledged that good can be turned into evil not by a good but by an evil recipient; for every form converts into its own quality what flows into it. Now since the Lord is good in its very essence, or Good itself, it is evident that evil cannot flow from Him or be produced by Him; but that good can be turned into evil by the recipient subject whose form is a form of evil. Such a subject is man as to his proprium, which continually receives good from the Lord and continually turns it into the nature of its own form, which is a form of evil. Hence it follows that man is in fault if he is not saved. Evil is indeed from hell; but as man receives it from hell as his own, and thereby appropriates it to himself, therefore it is the same whether it is said that evil is from man or from hell. But how there comes to be such an appropriation of evil that at length religion perishes will be explained in the following order:

(1) Every religion in process of time declines and is consummated.
(2) Every religion declines and is consummated by the inversion of the image of God in man.
(3) This takes place from the continual increase of hereditary evil in successive generations.
(4) Nevertheless it is provided by the Lord that everyone may be saved.
(5) It is also provided that a New Church should succeed in place of the former devastated Church.

These propositions are now to be demonstrated in their order:

FIRST: Every religion in process of time declines and is consummated. On this earth there have been several Churches, as I have before mentioned, one after another; as wherever the human race exists there a Church exists; for, as was shown above, heaven—which is the end of creation is from the human race; and no one can enter heaven unless he is in the two universals of the Church which, as was shown above, are the acknowledgment of God and the leading of a good life. Hence it follows that there have been Churches on this earth from the most ancient times down to the present. These Churches are described in the Word, but not historically with the exception of the Israelitish and the Jewish Church. Before that, however, there were several that are only described in the Word under the names of nations and of persons, and by certain particulars concerning them.

2. The Most Ancient Church, which was the first, is described under the name of Adam and his wife Eve. The Church that followed, called the Ancient Church, is described under the name of Noah, his three sons and their posterity. This was a wide spread Church, extending over many of the kingdoms of Asia, namely, the land of Canaan on both sides of the Jordan, Syria, Assyria and Chaldea, Mesopotamia, Egypt, Arabia, Tyre and Sidon. These had the ancient Word referred to in, "THE DOCTRINE OF THE NEW JERUSALEM CONCERNING THE SACRED SCRIPTURE (n. 101-103), better known simply as the "DOCTRINE OF SACRED SCRIPTURE". That such a Church existed in those kingdoms is evident from various particulars recorded concerning them in the prophetical parts of the Word. This Church however, was notably changed by Eber, from whom arose the Hebrew Church, in which worship by sacrifices was first instituted. From the Hebrew Church sprang the Israelitish and the Jewish Churches, established with due solemnity for the sake of the Word which was there to be written.

3. These four Churches are meant by the image seen by Nebuchadnezzar in a dream, the head of which was of pure gold, the breast and arms of silver, the belly and thighs of brass, and the legs and feet of iron and clay (Daniel 2:32,33). The same is meant by the golden, the silver, the copper and the iron ages, mentioned by ancient writers. It is well known that the Christian Church succeeded the Jewish Church; and it may be seen from the Word that all these Churches in process of time declined until they reached their end, which is called their consummation.

4. The consummation of the Most Ancient Church, brought about by the eating of the tree of knowledge, by which is signified the pride of ones own intelligence, is described by the flood. The consummation of the Ancient Church is described by various devastations of nations treated of both in the historical and in the prophetical parts of the Word, especially by the driving out of the nations from the land of Canaan by the Children of Israel. The consummation of the Church of Israel and Judah is understood by the destruction of the temple at Jerusalem, and by the carrying away of the people of Israel into perpetual captivity, and of the Jewish nation to Babylon, and finally by the second destruction of the temple and of Jerusalem at the same time and the dispersion of that nation. This consummation is foretold in many places in the Prophets and in Daniel 9:24-27; while the gradual devastation

of the Christian Church until its end is described by the Lord in Matthew 24, in Mark 13, and in Luke 21, but the consummation itself in the Apocalypse. From these considerations it may be evident that a Church in process of time declines and is consummated; and so also does a religion. But let it be known that the four main Churches to have been in the world since the beginning are The Most Ancient Church; The Ancient Church, The Jewish Church, and the Christian Church. There have been many other satellite Churches, or representative Churches, including the Israelitish Church, but for future references keep in mind the main four.

5. SECOND: Every religion declines and is consummated by the inversion of the image of God in man. It is well known that man was created in the image of God, according to the likeness of God (Genesis 1:26). It will now be explained what the image and what the likeness of God is.

God alone is Love and Wisdom; and man was created to be a receptacle of both, that his will might be a receptacle of the Divine Love and his understanding the receptacle of the Divine Wisdom. It was shown above that these two receptacles are in man from creation, that they constitute man and that they are formed in everyone in the womb. Thus mans being an image of God means that he is a recipient of the Divine Wisdom, and his being a likeness of God means that he is a recipient of the Divine Love. Therefore the receptacle called the understanding is an image of God, and the receptacle called the will is a likeness of God. Since man then was created and formed to be a receptacle, it follows that he was created and formed that his will might receive love from God and that his understanding might receive wisdom from God. These man receives when he acknowledges God and lives according to His commandments, but in a lesser or a greater degree as he has from religion a knowledge of God and of His commandments; and consequently as he has a knowledge of truths; for truths teach what God is and how He is to be acknowledged, also what His commandments are and how man is to live according to them.

6. The image and likeness of God are not destroyed in man though they may be seemingly destroyed; for they remain inherent in his two faculties called liberty and rationality, which have been treated of above in many places. They have become seemingly destroyed when has made the receptacle of Divine Love, that is, his will, a receptacle of self-love, and the receptacle of Divine Wisdom, that is, his understanding, a receptacle of his own intelligence. By doing this he has inverted the image and likeness of God, for he has turned these receptacles away from God and has turned them towards himself. Consequently they have become closed above and opened below, or closed in front and opened behind, although by creation they were opened in front and closed behind. When they have thus been inversely opened and closed, the receptacle of love, that is, the will, receives influx from hell or from ones own proprium; and so also does the receptacle of wisdom, that is, the understanding. Hence arose in the Churches the

worship of men in place of the worship of God, and worship based on doctrines of falsity in place of worship based on doctrines of truth, the latter from ones own intelligence and the former from the love of self. From this it is clear that religion in process of time declines and is consummated by the inversion of the image of God in man.

7. THIRD: This takes place from the continual increase of hereditary evil in successive generations. It was stated and explained above that hereditary evil is not what has come down from Adam and his wife Eve by their eating of the Tree of Knowledge, but that it is successively derived and transmitted from parents to their offspring, and thus by continual increase grows from generation to generation. When evil thus increases among many, it spreads evil amongst many more; for in all evil there is the lust of leading astray, and in some this burns with anger against what is good, giving rise to contagion of evil. When this has permeated the leaders, and the rulers, and those prominent in the Church, religion becomes perverted, and the means of restoring it to health, which are truths, become corrupted by falsification. Hence there now proceeds a gradual vastation of good and desolation of truth in the Church until its consummation is reached.

8. FOURTH: Nevertheless it is provided by the Lord that everyone may be saved. It is provided by the Lord that there should be a religion everywhere; and that in every religion there should be two essentials of salvation, namely, to acknowledge God and to refrain from evil because it is against God. All other things pertaining to the understanding and thence to thought, which are called matters of faith, are provided to everyone according to his life, for they are accessories of the life; and if these are given precedence (over the essentials) still they do not receive life. It is also provided that all who have lived well and have acknowledged God are instructed after death by angels; and then those who have observed these two essentials of religion while in the world accept the truths of the Church as they are in the Word, and acknowledge the Lord as the God of heaven and of the Church. This teaching they receive more readily than Christians who have brought with them from the world an idea of the Lords Human separated from His Divine. It is moreover provided by the Lord that all are saved who die in infancy, no matter where they have been born.

9. Further, there is granted to everyone after death the opportunity of amending his life, if that is at all possible. All are instructed and led by the Lord by means of angels; and as they now know that they live after death, and that there is a heaven and a hell, they at first receive truths. Those however, who have not acknowledged God and who have not shunned evils as sins when in the world soon show a distaste for truths and withdraw; while those who acknowledge truths with the lips but not with the heart are like the foolish virgins who had lamps but no oil, and who begged oil of others and also went away and bought it, and yet were not admitted to the wedding. Lamps signify truths of faith

and oil signifies the good of charity. Hence it may be evident that the Divine Providence designs that everyone can be saved, and that man himself is in fault if he is not saved.

10. FIFTH: It is also provided that a New Church should succeed in place of the former devastated Church. This has been the case from the Most Ancient times, namely, that when a former Church was devastated a new Church has taken its place. The Ancient Church succeeded the Most Ancient; after the Ancient Church the Israelitish or Jewish Church followed; and after this the Christian Church, as was stated above. Moreover, it is foretold in the Apocalypse that this will be followed by a new Church, which is there meant by the New Jerusalem descending from heaven. The reason why a new Church is being provided by the Lord to succeed in place of the former devastated Church may be seen in "THE DOCTRINE OF SACRED SCRIPTURE" [Nos. 104-113].

THUS ALL ARE PREDESTINED TO HEAVEN AND NO ONE TO HELL.

That the Lord casts no one down to hell, but that the spirit casts himself, is shown in the work "HEAVEN AND HELL" [Nos. 545-550]. This happens with every wicked and impious person after death; and it is the same with the wicked and impious person in the world with this difference, that while in the world he is capable of being reformed, and may acquire and use to his advantage the means of salvation, but not after his departure from the world. The means of salvation relate to these two essentials, that evils must be shunned because they are contrary to the Divine laws in the Decalogue, and there must be the acknowledgment that there is a God. This everyone can do provided he does not love evils; for the Lord is continually flowing into his will with power that he may be able to shun evils, and into his understanding with power that he may be able to think that there is a God. Nevertheless, no one can do the one without at the same time doing the other, for these two things are joined together like the two tables of the Decalogue, one of which relates to God and the other to man. The Lord in accordance with what is in His table enlightens everyone and gives him power; but man receives power and enlightenment only so far as he carries out what is laid down in his table: before this, the two appear as id lying one upon the other and fastened with a seal; but as man carries out what is in his table they are unsealed and opened.

[2] What is the Decalogue at the present day but like a little closed book or religious primer, opened only in the hands of infants and children? Say to anyone of mature age, Do not do this because it is contrary to the Decalogue, and who pays any attention? But if you say, Do not do this because it is contrary to the Divine Laws, he may give this his attention; and yet the commandments of the Decalogue are the Divine Laws themselves.

An experiment was made with several spirits in the spiritual world, and when the Decalogue or Catechism was mentioned they rejected it with contempt. The reason for this is that the Decalogue in its second table, which is mans table, teaches that evils are to be shunned; and he who does not shun them, whether from impiety or from religious belief that works avail nothing, but only faith, hears with some contempt the Decalogue or Catechism being mentioned as though he heard mention made of a book for children, in which is no longer of any use to him.

[3] These things have been stated in order that it may be known that a knowledge of the means by which he may be saved, or the power, is not wanting to anyone if he desires to be saved. From this it follows that all are predestined to heaven, and no one to hell. As, however, there has prevailed among some belief in predestination to the opposite of salvation, that is, to condemnation, and as this belief is harmful and cannot be dispelled unless the reason sees the folly and the cruelty of it, it must therefore be considered in the following order:

1. Any predestination except to heaven is contrary to the Divine Love and its infinity.
2. Any predestination except to heaven is contrary to the Divine Wisdom and its infinity.
3. It is foolish heresies that only those are saved who are born within the Church.
4. It is a cruel heresy that any of the human race are condemned by predestination.

In order that it may be apparent how harmful is the belief in predestination as generally understood, these four propositions must be taken up and established.

FIRST: Any predestination except to heaven is contrary to the Divine Love, which is infinite. It has been shown in the treatise, "THE DIVINE LOVE AND WISDOM," THAT Jehovah or the Lord is Divine Love, and that the Divine Love is infinite and the being (ESSE) of all life, and also that man was created in the image according to the likeness of God. Since also everyone is formed in the womb in that image according to that likeness by the Lord, as has also been shown, it follows that the Lord is the heavenly Father of all men, and that men are His spiritual children. So is Jehovah or the Lord called in the Word, and so also are men; and therefore He says: Call no father (A.V. man) your father upon the earth: for one is your Father, who is in the heavens (A.V. heaven), Matthew 23:9. By this is meant that He alone is the Father as to life, and that the earthly father is father only as to the covering of life, which is the body. Therefore in heaven no other than the Lord is called Father. That men who do not pervert that life are said to be His sons and to be born of Him is also clear from many passages in the Word.

(2) Hence it may be evident that the Divine Love is in every man, both the wicked and the good; consequently that the Lord who is Divine Love cannot act otherwise than as a father on earth acts towards his children, and infinitely more so, because the Divine Love is infinite; and also that He cannot withdraw from anyone because the life of everyone is derived from Him. He appears to withdraw from the wicked; but it is the wicked who withdraw, while He from love still leads them. Therefore the Lord says: Ask, and it shall be given you; seek, and ye shall find; knock, and it shall be opened unto you. What man is there of you, who if his son ask bread will give him a stone? . . . If ye then, being evil, know how to give good gifts unto your children, how much more shall your Father who is in the heavens give good things to them that ask Him (Matthew 7:7-11)? And elsewhere: He maketh His sun to rise on the evil and on the good, and sendeth rain on the just and on the unjust (Matthew 5:45). Moreover, it is well known in the Church that the Lord desires the salvation of all, and the death of no one. Hence it may be seen that any predestination except to heaven is contrary to the Divine Love.

(3) SECOND: Any predestination except to heaven is contrary to the Divine Wisdom, which is infinite. The Divine Love through its Divine Wisdom provides the means by which every man may be saved; and therefore to say that there is any predestination except to heaven is to say that the Divine Love cannot provide the means by which salvation may be effected. Nevertheless, as has been shown above, all have the means, and these are from the Divine Providence, which is infinite. However, there are some who are not saved, because the Divine Love desires that man should feel in himself the happiness and the blessedness of heaven, for otherwise it would not be heaven to him, and this cannot take place unless it appears to man that he thinks and wills from himself. For without this appearance nothing would be appropriated to him nor would he be a man. For this reason there is the Divine Providence, which is of the Divine Wisdom from the Divine Love.

(4) This however, does not deny the truth that all are predestined to heaven and no one to hell; but it would deny it if the means of salvation were wanting. And if man can do nothing on his own, he cannot even cause himself to spend eternity in hell. And so it has been shown above that the means of salvation have been provided for everyone, and that heaven is such that all who live well, of whatever religion they may be, have a place there. If you don't live well in this lifetime, you will eventually. Man is like the earth, which produces fruits of every kind, and it is by virtue of this power that the earth is the earth. The fact that it produces evil fruits does not deny its power to produce good fruits also, but it would if it only had the power to produce evil fruits. Again, man is like an object, which variegates in itself the rays of light. If the object only presents colours that are not pleasing, the light is not the cause of this, for its rays may be variegated to produce pleasing colours.

(5) THIRD: It is a foolish heresy that only those are saved who are born within the Church. Those who are born outside the Church are men as well as those born within it, being of the SAME HEAVENLY ORIGIN, and are equally living and immortal souls. They also have a form of religion from which they acknowledge that there is a God, and that they ought to live well; and he who acknowledges God and lives well becomes spiritual in his own degree and is saved, as was shown above. It is urged that these have not been baptised; BUT BAPTISM DOES NOT SAVE ANY EXCEPT THOSE WHO ARE SPIRITUALLY WASHED, THAT IS, REGENERATED, FOR BAPTISM IS A SIGN AND A MEMORIAL OF THIS.

(6) It is also urged that the Lord is not known to them, and that without the Lord there is no salvation. Salvation however, does not come to anyone because the Lord is known to him, but because he lives according to the Lords commandments; and the Lord is known to everyone who acknowledges God, for the Lord is the God of heaven and earth, as He Himself teaches (Matthew 28:18 and elsewhere). Moreover, those who are outside the Church have a clearer idea of God as a man than Christians have; and those who have the idea of God as a man and live well are accepted by the Lord. They also acknowledge God as one in Person and in Essence, which Christians do not. They also think of God in their life; for they regard evils as sins against God, and those who do this think of God in their life. Christians derive their precepts of religion from the Word, but few of them draw any precepts of life from it.

(7) Roman Catholics do not read the Word; and protestants who are in faith separated from charity pay no attention to those things in the Word which relate to life, but only to those which relate to faith: And yet the whole Word is nothing else than the doctrine of life. Christianity prevails only in Europe; Mohammedanism and Gentilism prevail in Asia, the Indies, Africa and America, and the population in these parts of the Globe is ten times more numerous than in the Christian part; and in the Christian part there are but few who place religion in the life. What then is more foolish than to believe that only these latter are saved and the former are condemned, and that a man gains heaven by his birth and not by his life? Therefore the Lord says:

I say unto you, That many shall come from the East and West, and shall sit down with Abraham, Isaac, and Jacob in the kingdom of heaven:

But the children of the kingdom shall be cast out (Matthew 8:11,12).

(8) FOURTH: It is a cruel heresy that any of the human race are condemned by predestination. For it is cruel to believe that the Lord, who is Love itself and Mercy itself, suffers so great a multitude of men to be born for hell, or so many myriads of myriads will be born condemned and doomed, that is, to be born devils and satans; and that He does not from His Divine Wisdom provide that

those who live well and acknowledge God should not be cast into everlasting fire and torment. The Lord is ever Creator and Savior of all; and He alone leads all and desires the death of no one. It is therefore cruel to believe and think that so great a multitude of nations and peoples under His auspices and oversight should be handed over as prey to the devil by predestination.

THE LORD CANNOT ACT CONTRARY TO THE LAWS OF THE DIVINE PROVIDENCE, BECAUSE TO ACT CONTRARY TO THEM WOULD BE TO ACT CONTRARY TO HIS DIVINE LOVE AND HIS DIVINE WISDOM, THUS CONTRARY TO HIMSELF.

It has been shown in "THE DIVINE LOVE AND WISDOM," that the Lord is Divine Love and Divine Wisdom, and that these two are being (ESSE) itself and life itself, from which everything is and lives. It is shown also that there is a like proceeding from Him, and that the Divine proceeding is Himself. Among the things which proceed the Divine Providence is primary, for this is continually in the end for which the universe was created. The operation and the progression of the end through means is what is called the Divine Providence.

[2] Now since the Divine proceeding is Himself and the Divine Providence is the primary thing that proceeds, it follows that to act contrary to the laws of His Divine Providence is to act contrary to Himself. It may also be said that the Lord is Providence, as it is said that God is order, for the Divine Providence is the Divine Order primarily with regard to the salvation of men; and as there is no order without laws, for laws constitute order and every law derives from order that it also is order, it follows that as God is Order He is also the law of His own Order. Similarly, it may be said of the Divine Providence that as the Lord is His own Providence He is also the law of His own Providence. Hence it is clear that the Lord cannot act contrary to the laws of His Divine Providence, because to act contrary to them would be to act contrary to Himself.

[3] Further, there can be no operation except upon a subject and upon it through means; for operation is impossible except upon a subject and upon it through means. The subject of the Divine Providence is man; the means are Divine Truths by which man acquires wisdom, and Divine Goods by which he acquires love. The Divine Providence through these means works out its end, which is mans salvation; for he who wills an end wills also the means; and therefore when he, who thus wills, works out an end he works it out through means.

    This concludes this section; and now for the explanation of the Parable of the Shrewd Manager. I know you thought you were just reading the explanation, but actually I was laying some groundwork.

Explanation of the shrewd Manager

Now the parable makes it look as though the Rich man is just some man with a lot of money and possessions. This is only representative however, for the Word speaks of things of the spiritual world alone, but written so those in this world can understand by correspondences. So we have as representatives the Rich Man, the Shrewd Manager, and the rich mans Debtors. The Rich man represents those in the Church, who have the truths of the Word, but they keep them from the Gentiles, or those outside the Church. For the Church takes the Word and twists it around to fit their doctrines, in which case the Gentiles never actually receive the truths. The Shrewd Manager represents the Preachers of the churches who mismanage the Word in the Church, and they will be removed from their positions when God is finished using them for his intended purpose. And because they know that they are teaching false doctrine, they also know they will one day have to give an account for their actions. Because of this they attempt to make many friends within the Church, building up their reputation, and helping those within the Church walls who are their followers, and who represent their debtors, believe they do not have to give a full account of their debt (Which represents the false belief that they are saved), because the falsities in the worldly Church have drowned out all truth. This is also the spiritual representative of the tithes and offerings that are required of those in the Church, who believe they can receive salvation by their offerings and sacrifices, as well as works. They believe they should give more, because the preachers lay this guilt trip on the people, so as to line their pockets with riches from the Church members, saying it is only to build a bigger Church, or to pay Church overhead. In this case the Rich man is God, the shrewd Manager is the Preacher, and the Lords Church is what the Manager is miss-managing. The preachers are seeking friends in the Church because they know one day they will be held accountable for the intended false doctrines they teach, and are afraid of losing their church. They are lazy and cant dig; and they are surely too proud to beg. They also know that God knows that they are aware that they teach certain lies, and that they know they are lies. But the preacher pretends to know how to be saved, and earns his friends in the Church by tickling their ears, telling them what they want to hear. The preacher hopes some will actually be saved, and they will one day pray for his salvation as well, in which case he will be welcomed into eternal dwellings. And now the natural explanation: If you are truly living for God and you have needs, or wish to help your neighbor all the time, you will have to act as the world acts. Will you steal to help the needy? For those who are of the kingdom are not shrewd, and are as gentle as a dove. If you risk your own self for your neighbor, you will receive admittance into eternal dwellings. If you cannot manage what is given to you in this world, which is considered little compared to what you will receive in the heavens, who will trust you with true riches? If you are dishonest with little you will be dishonest with much. These latter were represented by the Pharisees of course in the literal sense. But what else do we read from this parable? Render unto Caesar what is Caesars, and render unto God what is Gods. I thought I would throw that in. Christians believe that the things we receive in this world are Caesars, or the worlds, but they are Gods, and He expects his chosen children to manage their possessions well. And their possessions are whatever they can get, without harming anyone, offending anyone, or taking from the needy. For all is truly the Lords and his children's, when we realize we are truly His children. But if we live for our flesh, and the world, all that we have belongs to the world, or Caesar. For His children cannot steal what is already theirs. But Gods true Children, who are of the New Church, live to please and help their neighbor and not themselves. They do not take, unless it is to help another; and when they take, they take from what is already their own. The world is bent on greed and dishonest dealings, but Gods chosen are not hindered by these things. Take from the rich, so as to feed, and help the poor. FOR YOU ARE TAKING WHAT IS YOURS ALREADY. The Shrewd Manager is the Pharisees; the Shrewd Manager is Preachers in the world, who use Gods Church for his own gain. The Shrewd Manager is all those who live for themselves and the world. As you can see, and as we have all read in the Word, "Thou shalt not steal, and thou shalt not covet what is thy neighbors. But when you become regenerated by God, and realize that all is yours, you will truly see things as they are. As we read in 1 Corinthians: Therefore let no man glory in men. For all things are yours; whether Paul, or Apollos, or Cephas, or the world, or life, or death, or things present, or things to come; all are yours; and ye are Christ's; and Christ is Gods (1Corinthians 3:21-23). Man looks at these verses and does not know what to think of them, but they are true. If you are in a Godly life, all things are truly yours, but permit yourself to be led by God. For when you are led by self, all things are not yours, but belong to the world, and anything you take would be stealing. So be shrewd in the world, if you are truly of the New Church, but be careful, and do not live for your flesh, or the world. If you truly seek the kingdom of heaven all these things will be given unto you.

THE KNOWLEDGE OF THE SECRETS OF THE KINGDOM OF HEAVEN HAS BEEN GIVEN TO YOU, BUT NOT TO THEM. Whoever has will be given more, and he will have an abundance. Whoever does not have, even what he has will be taken from him (Matthew 13:11). Believe in God and shun evil!

(CONTINUATION OF THE DOCTRINE OF SACRED SCRIPTURE)

[76] VIII

The Church exists from the Word, and it is such as is its understanding of the Word. There is no doubt that the Church exists from the Word; for the Word is Divine Truth itself Nos. 1-4; the doctrine of the Church is from the Word, Nos. 50-61; and conjunction with the Lord is effected by means of the Word. It may, however, be doubted that it is the understanding of the Word which constitutes the Church, as there are some who believe that they belong to the Church because they have the Word, read it or hear it read by a preacher and know something of the sense of the letter, although they do not know how certain passages in it are to be understood; while some regard this of no importance. It will be necessary, then, to prove that it is not the Word, but the understanding of it, which constitutes the Church, and that the quality of the Church is according to the understanding of the Word with those who are in the Church. This is provided by the following considerations.

[77] The Word is the Word according to the understanding of it with man, that is, as it is understood. If it is not understood, the Word is indeed called the Word, but with man it does not exist. The Word is truth according to the understanding of it; for the Word may not be truth, as it can be falsified. The Word is spirit and life according to the understanding of it; for the letter without the understanding of it is dead. Since man has truth and life according to his understanding of the Word, according to that also he has faith and love, for truth is of faith and love is of life. Now, since the Church exists through faith and love and according to these, it follows that through the understanding of the Word and according to it, the Church is a Church—a noble Church if it is in genuine truths, an ignoble Church if it is not in genuine truths, and a Church destroyed if it is in falsified truths.

[78] Moreover, the Lord is present and conjoined with man through the Word because the Lord is the Word, and He, as it were, converses in it with man; and further, because the Lord is Divine Truth itself, and the Word also is Divine Truth. From this it is evident that the Lord is present with man, and at the same time conjoined with Him, according to his understanding of the Word; for, according to that, man has truth and consequently faith, and also love and consequently life. The Lord, however, is present with man through the reading of the Word; but He is conjoined with him through his understanding of truth from the Word and according to it; and in the degree that the Lord is conjoined with man, the Church is in him. The Church is within man. The Church that is outside of him is the Church among the many within whom the Church exists. This is meant by the Lords words to the Pharisees who asked when the kingdom of God should come:

The kingdom of God is within you (Luke 17:21).

By the kingdom of God is here meant the Lord, and the Church from Him.

[79] The Prophets in many passages treat of the understanding of the Word where the subject is the Church; and they teach that the Church exists only where the Word is rightly understood; and that the nature of the Church is according to the understanding of the Word with those who are in the Church. The Prophets also in many passages describe the Church among the Israelitish and Jewish nation as totally destroyed and brought to naught because they falsified the meaning or understanding of the Word; for nothing else destroys the Church.

2. The understanding of the Word, both true and false, is described in the Prophets, particularly in Hosea, by Ephraim; for the understanding of the Word is signified in the Word by Ephraim. Since the understanding of the Word constitutes the Church, therefore Ephraim is called:

> A dear son, and a pleasant child (Jeremiah 31:20).
> The first born (Jeremiah 31:9).
> The strength of the head of Jehovah (Psalms 60:7; 108:8).
> A mighty man (Zechariah 10:7); Filled with the bow (Zechariah 9:13).
> And the sons of Ephraim are called
> Armed, and shooters with the bow (Psalms78:9).

For a bow signifies doctrine from the Word fighting against falsities. For the same reason also;

Ephraim was transferred to Israelis right hand and blessed; and accepted in place of Reuben (Genesis 48:5,11-15).

For the same reason also:

Ephraim with his brother Manasseh, under the name of their father Joseph, was exalted above all the rest by Moses in his blessing of the sons of Israel (Deuteronomy33: 13-17).

3. The nature of the Church when the understanding of the Word is destroyed is also described in the Prophets by Ephraim, particularly in Hosea; as is clear from the following passages:

> Israel and Ephraim shall fall together . . . Ephraim shall be desolate . . . Ephraim is oppressed and broken in judgment. I will be unto Ephraim as a lion . . . I will tear and go away; I will take away, and none shall rescue him (Hosea 5:5,9,11-14).

> O Ephraim, what shall I do unto thee? For your holiness (A.V. goodness) is as a morning cloud, and as the early dew it goeth away (Hosea 6:4).

> They shall not dwell in the land of Jehovah; but Ephraim shall return to Egypt, and shall eat an unclean thing in Assyria (Hosea 9:3).

4. The land of Jehovah is the Church; Egypt is the scientific principle of the natural man, and Assyria is reasoning there from; by these two the Word as to the understanding of it is falsified; and therefore it is said that Ephraim shall return to Egypt, and shall eat an unclean in Assyria.

5. Ephraim feedeth on wind, and followeth after the east wind: he daily increaseth lies and desolation; and he maketh (A.V. They do make) a covenant with the Assyrians, and oil is carried into Egypt (Hosea 12:1).

> To feed on wind, to follow after the east wind and to increase lies and desolation, is to falsify truths and so to destroy the Church.

6. The same is also signified by the whoredom of Ephraim; for whoredom signifies the falsification of the understanding of the Word, that is, of its genuine truth, as in these passages:

I know Ephraim . . . he has altogether committed whoredom, and Israel is defiled (Hosea 5:3).

I have seen an horrible thing in the house of Israel: there is the whoredom of Ephraim, and Israel is defiled (Hosea 6: 10).

Israel is the Church itself, and Ephraim, the understanding of the Word from which and according to which the Church exists; therefore it is said that Ephraim commits whoredom and Israel is defiled.

7. As the Church among the Jews was totally destroyed by falsifications of the Word, therefore it is thus said of Ephraim:

I will give thee up, Ephraim will deliver thee up, Israel, I will make thee as Admah, I will set thee as Zeboim (Hosea 11:8).

Now since the Prophet Hosea, from the first chapter to the last, treats of the falsification of the Word and the consequent destruction of the Church, and since by whoredom is signified the falsification of truth in the Word, therefore he was commanded to represent this state in the Church.

By taking a harlot for his wife, and begetting children by her Hosea 1; and again, by taking a woman who was an adulteress Hosea 3.

8. These passages are quoted that it may be known and proved from the Word that the nature of the Church is according to its understanding of the Word-excellent and precious if its understanding is founded on genuine truths from the Word, but ruined and indeed defiled if founded on truths falsified. In confirmation that by Ephraim is signified the understanding of the Word, and in the opposite sense that understanding falsified from which results the destruction of the Church, the other passages where Ephraim is treated of may be consulted: As Hosea 4:17,18; 7:1,11; 8:9,11; 9:11-13,16; 10:11; 11:3; 12:1,8,14; 13:1,12; Isaiah 17:3; 28:1; Jeremiah 4: 15; 31:6,18; Ezekiel 37:16; 48:5; Obadiah 19; Zechariah 9:10.

[80] IX

In every detail of the Word there is the marriage of the Lord and the Church, and consequently the marriage of good and truth. Hitherto it has not been recognized that there is in every detail of the Word the marriage of the Lord and the Church, and consequently the marriage of good and truth; nor could it be seen, because the spiritual sense of the Word had not been revealed until now, and this sense alone can make this marriage evident. For there are two senses in the Word, called the spiritual and the celestial, concealed within the sense of the letter; what belongs to the spiritual sense has special reference to the Church, and what belongs to the celestial sense to the Lord. The content also of the spiritual sense has reference to Divine Truth, and the content of the celestial sense to Divine Good; and consequently there is in the sense of the letter of the Word this marriage. However, this is apparent only to those who, from the spiritual and celestial senses of the Word, know the signification of words and names, some words and names being predicated of good, some of truth, and some including both references. Therefore without a knowledge of this signification, this marriage in every detail of the Word cannot be seen, and consequently this Arcanum has not hitherto been discovered.

[81] Since there exists such a marriage in every detail of the Word, therefore double expressions frequently occur in it, which seem like repetitions of the same thing. They are, however, not repetitions; but one relates to good and the other to truth, and when both are taken together they effect the conjunction of good and truth, and so combine them into one. This also is the ground of the Divinity and sanctity of the Word; for in every Divine work there is a conjunction of good with truth, and of truth with good.

[82] It is said that in every detail of the Word there is the marriage of the Lord and the Church, and consequently the marriage of good and truth; because where there is the marriage of the Lord and the Church, there is also the marriage of good and truth, the latter resulting from the former. For when the Church, or a man of the Church, is principled in truths, the Lord then enters into those truths with good, and makes them live; or what is the same, when the Church, or a man of the Church, is in intelligence by means of truths, the Lord then enters his intelligence through the good of love and charity, and thus infuses life into it.

[83] There are two faculties of life in every man, the understanding and the will, the understanding being the receptacle of truth, and thence of wisdom, the will being the receptacle of good, and thence of love. These two faculties aught to make one, that a man may be a member of the Church; and they are united when a man forms his understanding from genuine truths, apparently of himself, and when his will is filled with the good of love, which is done by the Lord. In this way a man has the life of truth and the life of good, the life of truth in his understanding from the will, and the life of good in his will through the understanding. This is the marriage of truth and good with man, and also the marriage of the Lord and the Church in him. But concerning this reciprocal conjunction, here called a marriage, more will be seen in Divine Providence; Divine Love and Wisdom; and the Doctrine of Life; all works of Emanuel Swedenborg, and readily available to the public.

[84] Those who read the Word attentively cannot help noticing the use of double expressions which seem like repetitions of the same thing; as for instance brother [and companion, poor] and needy, wilderness and desert, void and emptiness, foe and enemy, sin and iniquity, anger and wrath, nation and people, joy and gladness, mourning and weeping, justice* (or righteousness) and judgment, and so on. These appear to be synonymous expressions, when in fact they are

not. For the words brother, poor, wilderness, [void], foe, sin, anger, nation, joy, mourning and justice are used with reference to good, and in the opposite sense, to evil; while the words companion, needy,

*   Justice, righteousness: Both these words are used, as in the A.V; both these words are used, as in the A.V., to render the Latin word Justitia. desert, emptiness, enemy, iniquity, wrath, people, gladness, weeping and judgment are used with reference to truth, and in the opposite sense, to falsity. Yet it seems to the reader who is ignorant of the truth involved that poor and needy, wilderness and desert, void and emptiness, foe and enemy, are one and the same thing; likewise sin and iniquity, anger and wrath, nation and people, joy and gladness, mourning and weeping, justice and judgment, whereas they are not one, but become one by conjunction. In the Word also many other things are closely associated, as fire and flame, gold and silver, brass and iron, wood and stone, bread and water, bread and wine, purple and fine linen, and so on. This is because fire, gold, brass, wood, bread and purple signify good, while flame, silver, iron, stone, water, wine and fine linen signify truth. In like manner it is said that men should love God with all the heart and with all the soul; and also that God will create in man a new heart and a new spirit, for heart is used with reference to the good of love, and soul, of truth from that good. There are moreover some expressions, which, because they partake of both good and truth, are used by themselves without the addition of others; but these and many other things are evident only to the angels, and to those who, while they perceive the natural sense, understand also the spiritual sense.

[85] It would be tedious to show from the Word that such double expressions occur there, apparently repetitions of the same thing, for this would fill pages. But in order to remove all doubt, I will quote some passages where judgment and justice (or righteousness) are used together, than also nation and people, and also joy and gladness. The following are passages where judgment and justice are named together:

The city . . . was full of judgment, and righteousness lodged in her (Isaiah 1:21).

Zion shall be redeemed in righteousness, and they that return of her in judgment (Isaiah 1:27).

Jehovah of hosts shall be exulted in judgment, and the holy God shall be sanctified in righteousness (Isaiah 5:16).

He shall sit upon the throne of David, and upon his kingdom . . . to establish it in judgment and in righteousness (Isaiah 9:7).

Jehovah shall be exalted; for He dwelleth on high: He hath filled the earth (AN. Zion) with judgment and righteousness (Isaiah 33:5).

Thus saith Jehovah, keep ye judgment, and do justice: for my salvation is near, that my righteousness may be revealed (Isaiah 56:1).

As a nation that did righteousness and forsook not the judgment of their God: they ask . . . the judgments of justice (Isaiah 58:2).

Swear by the living Jehovah . . . in judgment and in righteousness (Jeremiah 4:2).

Let him that glorieth glory in this . . . that Jehovah doeth judgment and righteousness in the earth (Jeremiah 9:24).

Judgment and justice are so often mentioned because judgment is predicated of truths, and justice of good. Therefore by executing judgment and justice is also meant to act from truth and from good. The reason why judgment is predicated of truth and justice of good is, that the Lords government in the spiritual kingdom is called judgment, and the Lords government in the celestial kingdom is called justice. On this subject see the work HEAVEN AND HELL, Nos. 214,215. As judgment is predicated of truth, therefore in certain passages we read, Truth (veritas) and righteousness (justitia). Isaiah 11:5; Psalms 85:11; and elsewhere.

[86] That repetitions apparently of the same thing occur in the Word on account of the marriage of good and truth may be seen quite clearly from the following passages where nations and peoples are mentioned:

Woe to the sinful nation, a people laden with iniquity (Isaiah 1:4)!

The people that walked in darkness have seen a great light . . . thou hast multiplied the nation (Isaiah 9:2,3).

O Assyrian, the rod of mine anger . . . I will send him against an hypocritical nation and against the people of my wrath will I give him a charge (Isaiah 10:5,6).

And in that day there shall be a root of Jesse, which shall stand for an ensign of the people; to it shall the nations (A.V. Gentiles) seek (Isaiah 11:10).

Jehovah smote the people . . . with a continual stroke, He that ruled the nations in anger (Isaiah 14:6).

In that time shall the present be brought unto Jehovah Zebaoth of a people scattered and peeled . . . a nation meted out and trodden under foot (Isaiah 18:7).

Therefore shall the strong people glorify thee; the city of the terrible nations shall fear thee (Isaiah 25:3).

Jehovah will destroy . . . the face of the covering over all people, and the veil that is spread over all nations (Isaiah 25:7). Come near . . . ye nations: and hearken, ye people (Isaiah34: 1).

I . . . have called thee . . . for a covenant to the people, for a light of the nations (A.V. Gentiles). Isaiah 42:6

Let all the nations be gathered together, and let the people be assembled (Isaiah 43:9).

Behold, I will lift up mine hand to the nations, and set up my standard to the people (Isaiah 49:22).

Behold, I have given him for a witness to the people, a leader and lawgiver to the nations (Isaiah 55:4).

Behold, a people cometh from the north country, and a great nation . . . from the sides of the earth (Jeremiah 6:22).

Nations and peoples are mentioned together, because by nations are meant those who are in good, and in the opposite sense, those who are in evil; and by peoples those who are in truths, and in the opposite sense, those who are in falsities. For this reason those who belong to the Lords spiritual kingdom are called peoples, and those who belong to His celestial kingdom are called nations; for all in the spiritual kingdom are in truths and consequently in wisdom, while all in the celestial kingdom are in good, and consequently in love.

[87] Other expressions are used in this way like joy and gladness, as in the following passages:

Behold joy and gladness, slaying the ox (Isaiah 22:13).

They shall obtain joy and gladness, and sorrow and sighing shall flee away (Isaiah 35:10; 51:11).

Is not . . . gladness and joy cut off from the house of our God (Joel 1:16)?

The voice of joy shall cease and the voice of gladness (Jeremiah 7:34; 25:10).

The fast of the tenth month shall be to the house of Judah joy and gladness (Zechariah 8:19).

That we may rejoice . . . all our days. Make us glad (Psalms 90:14,15).

Be glad in Jerusalem, and rejoice in her (Isaiah 66:10).

Rejoice and be glad, o daughter of Edom (Lamentations 4:21).

Let the heavens be glad (A.V. rejoice) and let the earth rejoice (A.V. be glad) (Psalms 96:11).

Make me to hear joy and gladness (Psalms 51:8).

Joy and gladness shall be found in Zion, confession (A.V. thanksgiving) and the voice of melody (Isaiah 51:3).

There shall be gladness, and many shall rejoice at His birth (Luke 1:14).

I will cause to cease . . . the voice of joy (A.V. mirth), and the voice of gladness, the voice of bridegroom, and the voice of the bride (Jeremiah 7:34; 16:9; 25:10).

Again there shall be heard in this place . . . the voice of joy, and the voice of gladness; the voice of the bridegroom and the voice of the bride (Jeremiah 33:10,11). And elsewhere.

2. Both joy and gladness are mentioned in these passages because joy relates to good and gladness to truth; or, joy relates to love and gladness to wisdom. For joy pertains to the heart and gladness to the soul; that is, joy pertains to the will and gladness to the understanding. It is evident that the marriage of the Lord and the Church is also involved in these dual expressions, as mention is made of:

The voice of joy and the voice of gladness, the voice of the bridegroom and the voice of the bride (Jeremiah 7:34; 16:9; 25:10; 33:10,11).

For the Lord is the bridegroom and the Church is the bride.

That the Lord is the bridegroom may be seen in (Matthew 9:15; Mark 2:19,20;Luke 5:35).

And that the Church is the bride may be seen in (Revelation 21:2,9; 22:17).

Therefore John the Baptist says of Jesus: He that hath the bride is the bridegroom (John 3:29).

[88] On account of the marriage of the Lord with the Church, or what is the same, the marriage of Divine Good and Divine Truth, in every part of the Word, Jehovah and God, and also Jehovah and the Holy One of Israel, so frequently occur, as if they were two when yet they are one. For by Jehovah is meant the Lord as to Divine Good, and by God the Lord as to Divine Truth. Although Jehovah and God, and Jehovah and the Holy One of Israel, are spoken of in many passages in the Word, still one only is meant, and He is the Lord, as may be seen in "THE DOCTRINE OF THE LORD."

[89] Since in the whole Word and in every part of it there is the marriage of the Lord and the Church, it may be evident that all things of the Word, in general and in particular, treat of the Lord, as is shown in "THE DOCTRINE OF THE LORD," Nos. 1-7. The Church, which is likewise treated of, is also the Lord; for the Lord teaches that the man of the Church is in Him, and He in him (John 6:56; 14:20,21; 15:5,7).

[90] As the Divinity and Sanctity of the Word are here treated of, there may be added an experience worthy of note to what has already been said. There was once sent down to me from heaven a piece of paper covered with Hebrew characters, but written as they used to be among the Ancients, with whom those letters, which today are partly linear were curved with little flourishes turning upwards. The angels who were then with me said that they understood a complete sense from the letters themselves, but a special sense from the curves and the upturned flourishes over any letter. They explained what the letters and the inflections signified, both separately and conjointly; and they said that the letter H, which was added to the names Abram and Sarai, signified the infinite and the eternal. They also explained to me the meaning of the Word in Psalm 32:2 from the letters or syllables alone; adding that the meaning of the letters with all the inflections included was, that the Lord is merciful even to those who do evil.

2.   They informed me that writing in the third heaven consisted of letters inflected and variously curved each of which contained a certain meaning; that the vowels there indicated sound, which corresponds to affection; that in that heaven they cannot pronounce the vowels i and e, but employ instead of them y and eu ; and that the vowels a, o and u are in use among them, because these have a full sound. They also said that they did not sound any consonants hard, but soft;

and for this reason certain Hebrew letters had dots with them, as a sign that they should have a soft pronunciation. They added that a hardness in sounding letters was in use in the spiritual heaven, because there the angels are in truths, and truth admits of hardness; but good does not, in which are the angels of the celestial or third heaven. They said, moreover, that they had the Word among them written in letters inflected with the upturned flourishes (tittles), which have a meaning of their own. From this it was plain what is signified by these words of the Lord: One jot or one tittle shall in no wise pass from the law, till all be fulfilled (Matthew 5:18).

And also: It is easier for heaven and earth to pass, than one tittle of the Law to fail (Luke 16:17).

[91] X

Heresies may be formulated from the sense of the letter of the Word, but it is harmful to confirm them. It was shown above that the Word cannot be understood without doctrine, and that doctrine is like a lamp to make genuine truths visible. This is because the Word is written by pure correspondences; and consequently many things in it are appearances of truth, and not unveiled truths. Many of these are adapted to the comprehension of the natural, and indeed of the sensual man, yet in such a way that the simple can understand it in simplicity, the intelligent intelligently, and the wise in wisdom. Now since the Word is of this nature, appearances of truth, which are truths veiled, may be taken for unveiled truths; and when these are confirmed, they become falsities. This is done, however, by those who consider themselves to be wise above others, when yet they are not wise; for being wise consists in seeing whether a thing is true before it is confirmed, but not in confirming whatever one pleases. The latter is the practice with those who are by nature strongly inclined to confirming, and who take pride in their own intelligence; but the former obtains with those who love truths and are affected by them because they are truths, and who apply them to the uses of life; for they are enlightened by the Lord and see truths from the light of truth, whereas the others are enlightened by themselves and see falsities from the light of falsities.

[92] Appearances of truth, that is, veiled truths, may be taken from the Word for unveiled truths, and when confirmed, they become falsities. This may be evident from the many heresies, which have been and still are prevalent in Christendom. Heresies themselves do not condemn men, but an evil life; and men are also condemned by confirming from the Word falsities, which are inherent in heresy, and by reasoning from the natural man. For everyone is born into the religion of his parents, and is initiated into it from infancy. He later adheres to it, nor can he of himself get rid of its falsities because of his business connections in the world. What does condemn is living an evil life, together with the confirmation of falsities to the utter destruction of genuine truth. That man is not sworn to falsity who adheres to his own form of religion and believes in God; and,

if a Christian, who believes on the Lord, regards the Word as holy and from religious principles lives according to the commandments of the Decalogue. Therefore when he hears the truth and perceives it according to his capacity, he can accept it, and thus be rid of his falsity. It is otherwise with the man who has confirmed the falsities of his religion, as a falsity confirmed remains, and cannot be eradicated. For after confirmation, a falsity is as though a man has sworn to it, especially if it agrees with his self-love, and consequently with the pride of his own wisdom.

[93] I have conversed in the spiritual world with some who lived many years ago, and who had confirmed themselves in the falsities of their religion; and I found that they still firmly adhered to them. I have also conversed with some in that world who had been of the same religion and had entertained the same ideas as the others, but had not confirmed themselves in its falsities; and I learned that they, after being instructed by angels had rejected the falsities and had acquired truths. These had been saved, but the others were not. Every man after death is instructed by angels, and those are received [into heaven] who perceive truths and, from truths, falsities; for everyone after death is granted to see truths spiritually. They see truths who have not confirmed themselves in falsities; but those who have so confirmed themselves do not wish to see truths; and if they are presented to them, they turn themselves away, and then either ridicule or falsify them.

[94] This may be illustrated by an example:

In many passages in the Word anger, wrath and revenge are attributed to the Lord: and it is said that He punishes, casts into hell, tempts and does many other things of a similar nature. He who believes this in simplicity, and therefore fears God, and takes care not to sin against Him, is not condemned for this simple faith. He, however, is condemned whose confirmed belief is that anger, wrath, revenge, thus such things as originate in evil, exist in the Lord; and that He punishes men and casts them into hell from anger, wrath and revenge. Such a man is condemned because he has destroyed the genuine truth, which is, that the Lord is Love itself, Mercy itself and Goodness itself; and being these, that He cannot be angry, wrathful and revengeful. These things are attributed to the Lord according to the appearance; and so in many other cases.

[95] Many other things in the sense of the letter are apparent truths, within which genuine truths lie concealed. It is not hurtful to think and to speak according to such apparent truths; but it is harmful to confirm them so as to destroy the genuine truth concealed within them. This may be illustrated by an example from nature, adduced because what is natural instructs and convinces more clearly than what is spiritual.

2. To the eye, the sun appears to make a daily and also an annual revolution around the earth. Accordingly it is said in the Word that the sun rises and

sets; that it causes morning, noon, evening and night; and also the seasons of spring, summer, autumn, and winter, and consequently, days and years. But in reality the sun is stationary, being an ocean of fire round which the earth, revolving daily, is carried annually. The man, who in simplicity and ignorance, supposes that the sun revolves, does not destroy the natural truth that the earth rotates daily on her axis and makes an annual revolution in the ecliptic. But he, who confirms the suns apparent motion and course by the Word and by reasoning's from the natural man, invalidates and even destroys the truth.

3. That the sun moves, is an apparent truth; that it does not move, is a genuine truth. Everyone may speak according to the apparent truth, and indeed does so speak; but to think according to it from confirmation (that it is true) blunts and obscures the rational understanding. It is similar with the stars of the starry heaven. The apparent truth is that they also, like the sun, make a daily revolution; and therefore it is said also of the stars that they rise and set. But the genuine truth is that the stars are fixed, and that their firmament is immovable. Nevertheless everyone may speak according to the appearance.

[96] It is hurtful to confirm the apparent truth of the Word so as to destroy the genuine truth concealed within; because all things in the sense of the letter of the Word, both in general and in particular, communicate with heaven and open it, according to what was said above in Nos. 62-69. When therefore a man applies that sense to confirm the loves of the world, which are contrary to heavenly loves, then the internal of the Word is rendered false. Therefore, when its external, or sense of the letter whose internal is rendered false, communicates with heaven, then heaven is closed; for the angels who are in the internal of the Word, reject it. From this it is evident that a false internal, or truth falsified, destroys communication with heaven and closes it. This is why it is hurtful to confirm any heretical falsity.

[96a] The Word is like a garden, a heavenly paradise, in which are delicacies and delights of every kind, delicacies in its fruits and delights in its flowers. In the midst of it there are trees of life, and near by, fountains of living water with forest trees round about the garden. The man who is principled in Divine Truths from doctrine abides in the center of the garden where are the trees of life, and is in the actual enjoyment of its delicacies and delights. He, however, who is principled in truths, not from doctrine but only from the sense of the letter, lives in the outskirts of the garden, and sees only the forest; but he who is in the doctrine of a false religion and has confirmed its falsity in his own mind, dwells not even in the forest, but in a sandy plain beyond it, where there is not even grass. That such are the respective states of those men after death will be confirmed in its proper place.

[97] Moreover, it should be known that the sense of the letter of the Word is a guard for the genuine truths lying within it. It is a guard in this respect that it may be turned this way and that, and interpreted to ones own apprehension, without its interior content being injured or violated. It does no harm that the sense of the letter of the Word is understood differently by different persons: but harm results when Divine Truths, lying concealed within, are perverted, for in this way violence is inflicted on the Word. To prevent this, the sense of the letter is a guard; and it acts, as a guard with those who are in falsities from their religion, but who do not confirm these falsities, for such men do no violence to the Word.

2. This guard is signified by the Cherubim, and is also described by them in the Word. This is signified by the cherubim, which after the expulsion of Adam and his wife from the Garden of Eden, were placed at the entrance. Of these we read:

    When Jehovah God drove out the man, He placed at (ab) the east of the Garden of Eden cherubim and a flaming sword that turned every way, to keep the way of the tree of life (Genesis 3:23,24).

    By the cherubim is signified a guard; by the way of the tree of life, is signified access to the Lord, which men obtain through the Word; and by the flaming sword turning every way is signified Divine Truth in ultimates which, like the Word in the sense of the letter, can be so turned.

3. The same is meant by:

    The cherubim of gold placed over the extremities of the mercy-seat, which was above the Ark in the tabernacle (Exodus 25:18-21).

    Because this was signified by the cherubim therefore

    The Lord talked with Moses between the cherubim (Exodus 25:22; 37:9; Numbers 7:89).

    It may be seen above in Nos. 37-49 that the Lord does not speak with men except in fullness, and the Word in the sense of the letter is Divine Truth in fullness; and consequently the Lord talked with Moses between the cherubim. Nothing else was signified by:

    The cherubim upon the curtains of the tabernacle and upon the veils there (Exodus 26:1,31).

    For the curtains and the veils of the tabernacle signified the ultimates of heaven and the Church, and consequently of the Word, as may be seen above No. 46.

    Nothing else was signified by:

    The cherubim in the midst of the temple at Jerusalem (1Kings 6:23,28).

    Also by the cherubim carved on the walls and the doors of the temple (1Kings 6:29,32,35).

    And also by the cherubim in the new temple (Ezekiel 41:18-20).

    See also above No. 47.

4. Since cherubim signified a guard lest the Lord, heaven and Divine Truth as it is interiorly within the Word, should be approached immediately instead of mediately through ultimates, therefore it is said of the king of Tyre:

Thou sealest up the sum, full of wisdom, and perfect in beauty. Thou hast been in Eden, the Garden of God; every precious stone was thy covering . . . Thou, o cherub, art the spreading forth of the covering (A.V. art the anointed cherub that covereth) . . . I have destroyed thee o covering cherub, from the midst of the stones of fire (Ezekiel 28: 12,13,14,16).

Tyre signifies the Church as to the cognitions of truth and good; and hence its king signifies the Word, which is the source of cognitions. It is evident that the king here signifies the Word in its ultimate, that is, the sense of the letter, and the cherubim a guard, for it is said: "Thou sealest up the sum, every precious stone was thy covering; thou, O cherub, art the spreading forth of the covering;" and "O covering cherub." By the precious stones also mentioned here are signified the truths of the sense of the letter of the Word, as may be seen above at No. 45. Since by the cherubim is signified the ultimate of Divine Truth, and also a guard, therefore it is said in the Psalms:

Jehovah bowed the heavens, and came down . . . And He rode upon a cherub (Psalms18: 9,10).

O Shepherd of Israel . . . thou that dwellest upon the cherubim, shine forth (Psalms 81:1).

Jehovah sitteth upon the cherubim (Psalms 49:1).

To ride upon the cherubim, to dwell upon them and to sit on them, means on the ultimate sense of the Word.

5. Divine Truth in the Word and the nature of that Truth are described by the cherubim in Ezekiel 1,9,and 10. But as no one can know what is signified by the particulars of their description except one to whom the spiritual sense has been opened, therefore it has been revealed to me what is signified in brief by all those things which are said of the cherubim in the first chapter of Ezekiel, as:

The external Divine sphere of the Word is described in verse 4. This is represented as a man in verse 5. As conjoined with spiritual and celestial things in verse 6. The nature of the natural of the Word in verse 7. The nature of the spiritual and celestial of the Word conjoined with its natural, verse 8 and 9. The Divine Love of celestial, spiritual and natural good and truth therein, separately and together, verses 10 and 11. They look to one end, verse 12. The sphere of the Word from the Lords Divine Good and Divine Truth, from which the Word lives, verse 13 and 14. The doctrine of good and truth in the Word and from the Word, verses 15-21. The Divine of the Lord above it and in it, verses 22 and 23. And from it, verses 24 and 25. The Lord is above the heavens, verse 26. And to Him belong Divine Love and Divine Wisdom, verses 27 and 28.

These summaries have been compared with the Word in heaven, and are in conformity with it.

[98] XI

The Lord came into the world that He might fulfill all things of the Word, and thereby become Divine Truth, or the Word, even in ultimates. The Lord came into the world that He might fulfill all things of the Word. This may be seen in "THE DOCTRINE OF THE LORD," Nos. 8-11. That He thus became Divine Truth, or the Word, even in ultimates, is meant by the following passages in John:

The Word was made flesh and dwelt among us, and we beheld His glory, the glory as of the only begotten of the Father, full of grace and truth (John 1:14).

TO BE MADE FLESH IS TO BECOME THE WORD IN ULTIMATES; and what the Lord was, as the Word in ultimates, He showed to His disciples when He was transfigured (Matthew 17:2-9; Mark9: 2-9; and Luke 9:28-36).

It is there said that Moses and Elias appeared in glory; and by Moses and Elias is meant the Word, as may be seen above in No. 48. The Lord as the Word in ultimates is also described by John in the Revelation 1:13-16, where all the details in the description of Him signify the ultimates of Divine Truth, or of the Word. Before this the Lord was indeed the Word, but in first principles; for it is said:

In the beginning was the Word, and the Word was with God, and the Word was God. This was in the beginning with God (John 1:1,2).

When, however, the Word was made flesh, then the Lord became the Word in ultimates also; and from this fact He is called, "The First and The Last (Revelation 1:8,11,17; 2:8; 21:6; 22:12,13).

[99] By reason of the fact that the Lord also became the Word in ultimates, the state of the Church was entirely changed. ALL THE CHURCHES BEFORE HIS COMING WERE REPRESENTATIVE CHURCHES, and these were not able to see Divine Truth, except in the shade. But after the Lords coming into the world a Church was instituted by Him, which saw Divine Truth in the light. The difference is as between evening and morning. The state of the Church before His coming is also called evening, and the state of the Church after His coming is called morning. Before His coming into the World the Lord was indeed present with men of the Church, but mediately through heaven; whereas after His coming into the world He is present with men of the Church immediately. For in the world He put on the Divine Natural also, in which He is present with men. The glorification of the Lord is the glorification of His Human, which He assumed in the world; and the glorified Human of the Lord is the Divine Natural.

[100] Few understand how the Lord is the Word, for it is generally supposed that the Lord, by means of the Word, can enlighten and teach men, and yet He cannot, on this account, be called the Word. It should be known, however, that every man is his own love, and consequently his own good and his own truth. A man is a man for no other reason than this, and there is nothing else in him that is man. For the same reason that man is his own good and his own truth, angels and spirits are also men; and for all good and truth proceeding from the Lord,

is in its own form, man. But the Lord is Divine Good itself and Divine Truth itself; thus He is man Himself, from whom every man is man. That all Divine Good and Divine Truth is, in its own form, man, may be seen in the work on, "HEAVEN AND HELL, No.460; and will appear more clearly in the works that are to follow, which will treat of Angelic Wisdom.

[101] XII

Previous to the Word, which is now in the world, there was a Word, which is lost. Previous to the Word which was given by Moses and the Prophets to the Israelitish nation worship by sacrifices was known, and men prophesied from the mouth of Jehovah. This is evident from what is recorded in the books of Moses. That worship by sacrifices was known may be seen from the following references:

The Children of Israel were commanded to destroy the alters of the nations, break their images and cut down their groves (Exodus 34:13; Deuteronomy 7:5; 12:3).

Israel in Shittim began to commit whoredom with the daughters of Moab; and they called the people unto the sacrifices of their gods, and the people ate with them, and bowed themselves down to their gods. And especially joined themselves to Baal-peor; and on that account the anger of Jehovah was kindled against Israel (Numbers 25:1-3).

And Balaam, who was from Syria, caused alters to be built, and sacrificed oxen and sheep (Numbers 22:40; 23:1,2,14,29,30).

2. That men also prophesied from the mouth of Jehovah is evident from the prophesies of Balaam (Numbers 23:7-10, 18-24,24:3-9,16-24).

He also prophesied concerning the Lord, that a star should rise out of Jacob, and a Sceptre out of Israel (Numbers 24:17).

And he prophesied from the mouth of Jehovah (Numbers 22:13,18; 23:3,5,8,16,26; 24:1,13).

From these passages it is clear that among the nations there was Divine Worship similar to that instituted by Moses among the Israelitish nation.

3. That such worship existed before the time of Abram is in some measure evident from the words of Moses in Deuteronomy 32:7,8; but it is more evident from what is said of Melchizedek, king of Salem:

He brought out bread and wine, and blessed Abram; and Abram gave him tithes of all (Genesis 14:18-20).

And from the fact that Melchizedek represented the Lord, for he is called: The Priest of the most high God (Genesis 14:18).

And it is said of the Lord in the Psalms: Thou art a priest forever after the order of Melchizedek (Psalms 110:4).

This was why Melchizedek brought forth bread and wine, as holy things of the Church, even as they are holy in the sacrament of the Holy Supper; and why he was able to bless Abram, and why Abram gave him tithes of all.

[102] It was related to me by angels of heaven that there was a Word among the Ancients written by pure correspondences, but that it was lost; and I was told that it is still preserved among them, and is in use among the Ancients in their heaven who had that Word when they were in the world. Those Ancients, among whom that Word is still in use in heaven, were in part from the land of Canaan and from its neighboring countries, as Syria, Mesopotamia, Arabia, Chaldea, Assyria, Egypt, Sidon, Tyre and Nineveh. The inhabitants of all these kingdoms were in representative worship, and consequently were versed in the science of correspondences. The wisdom of that time was derived from that science, and by its means they had interior perception and communication with the heavens. Those who had an interior knowledge of the correspondences of that Word were called wise and intelligent, but in later times, diviners and magi.

2.   But because that Word was full of such correspondences as remotely signified celestial and spiritual things and consequently began to be falsified by many, therefore of the Lords Divine Providence it gradually disappeared in course of time, and at length was lost; and another Word was given, written by correspondences not so remote; and this was given through the prophets among the Children of Israel. In this Word, however, there were retained many names of places in the land of Canaan and in parts of Asia round about; and in this Word they signify the same things as in the Ancient world. It was for this reason that Abram was commanded to go to that land, and that his posterity from Jacob were introduced into it.

[103] That a Word existed among the Ancients is evident from the writings of Moses in which he mentions it, and gives quotations from it (Numbers 21:14,15,27-30).

Its historical parts were called "THE WARS OF JEJOVAH," and the Prophetical parts ENUNCIATIONS. From the historical parts of that Word Moses quotes the following:

Wherefore it is said in the book of THE WARS OF JEHOVAH, Vaheb in Supha, to the brooks of Arnon, and to the watercourse of brooks which turned away where Ar is inhabited, and which halted at the border of Moab. (A.V. What he did in the Red Sea-margin, Vaheb in Suphahand in the brooks of Arnon, and at the stream of the brooks that goeth down to the dwelling of Ar, and lieth upon the border of Moab.) (Numbers 21:14,15).

By the Wars of Jehovah mentioned in that Word, as in ours, are meant and described the Lords combats with hell and His victories over it, when He should come into the world. The same combats are also understood and described in many passages in the historical parts of our Word, as in the wars of Joshua with the nations of the land of Canaan, and in the wars of the Judges and kings of Israel.

2. From the prophetical parts of that Word Moses has quoted the following:

Wherefore the enunciators say (A.V. they that speak in proverbs), Come into Heshbon, let the city of Sihon be built and prepared:

For there is a fire gone out of Heshbon, a flame from the city of Sihon; it hath consumed Ar of Moab, and the lords of the high places of Arnon. Woe to thee, Moab! Thou art undone. O people of Chemosh! He hath given his sons that escaped, and his daughters, into captivity unto Sihon, king of the Amorites. We have slain them with darts (A.V. We have shot at them): Heshbon is perished even unto Dibon, and we have laid them waste even unto Nophah, which reacheth unto Medeba (Numbers 21:27-30).

The translators render Enunciatores "composers of proverbs," but they should be called Enunciators, and their compositions "Prophetical Enunciations," as is evident from the signification of the word Moshalim in the Hebrew tongue, which means not only proverbs, but also prophetical enunciations; as in Numbers 23:7,18; and 24:3,15. It is there said that Balaam uttered "his enunciation" (A.V. parable), which was also prophetical, concerning the Lord. His enunciation is called Mashal in the singular; moreover, what Moses quotes are not proverbs, but prophecies.

That Word like ours, was Divinely inspired, as is evident from a passage in Jeremiah, where almost the same language is used:

A fire has gone (A.V. shall come) forth out of Heshbon . . . and a flame from the midst of Sihon, and has devoured the corner of Moab, and the crown of the head of the sons of uproar. Woe be unto thee, O Moab! The people of Chemosh hath perished: for thy sons are taken away into captivity, and thy daughters into captivity (Jeremiah 48:45-46).

In addition to these books, mention is made by David and by Joshua of the prophetical book of the Ancient world, called the BOOK OF JASHER, or the BOOK OF THE UPRIGHT. David refers to it in the following passage:

David lamented . . . over Saul and over Jonathan . . . Also he bade them to teach the children of Judah the use of the bow: behold, it is written in the Book of Jasher (2 Samuel 1:17,18).

In Joshua it is mentioned in this passage:

Joshua said, Sun, stand thou still upon Gibeon: and thou, Moon, in the valley of Ajalon! Is not this written in the Book of Jasher (Joshua 10:12,13)?

Moreover, I was informed that the first seven chapters of Genesis are extant in that Ancient Word, and that not the least word is wanting.

[104] XIII

By means of the Word those also have light who are outside the Church, and do not possess the Word. There cannot be conjunction with heaven unless there exists somewhere on the earth a Church in possession of the Word by means of which the Lord is known; for the Lord is the God of heaven and earth, and without Him there is no salvation. It is enough that there is a Church in possession of the Word, even though it should consist of comparatively few persons; nevertheless, by means of the Word the Lord is present throughout the whole world, for it is the means by which conjunction is effected between heaven and the human race. Conjunction is by means of the Word, as may be seen above in Nos.62-69.

[105] It will now be shown how the Lord and heaven are present, and how conjunction with them is effected throughout the whole earth by means of the Word. The whole heaven is, in sight of the Lord, as one man. So also is the Church; and that they actually assume the appearance of a man may be seen in the work HEAVEN AND HELL Nos. 59-86. In this man the Church, where the Word is read and by means of which the Lord is known, is like the heart and lungs; the celestial kingdom is like the heart, and the spiritual kingdom like the lungs.

As from these two fountains of life in the human body all the other members and viscera subsist and live, so also do all those throughout the world who have a religion, worship one God and live good lives, thereby forming part of this man. They represent the members and viscera outside the chest in which are the heart and lungs and they subsist and live from the union of the Lord and heaven with the Church by means of the Word. For the Word in the Church, although it is with comparatively few, is life to the rest of the world from the Lord through heaven just as the members and viscera of the whole body receive life from the heart and lungs. The manner of communication between them is also similar; and for this reason Christians among whom the Word is read constitute the breast of this man. They are in the center of all, and round about them are the ROMAN CATHOLICS; around these again are the Mohammedans, who acknowledge the Lord to be the supreme Prophet and the Son of God. After these come the Africans, while the nations and peoples of Asia and the Indies form the outermost circumference. Some particulars of this arrangement of people may be seen in the little work entitled "THE LAST JUDGMENT" No. 48. All who are in this man also look toward the center where the Christians are.

[106] There is the greatest light in the center where are the Christians who have the Word; for light in the heavens is Divine Truth proceeding from the Lord as the sun there; and because the Word is that Truth, the greatest light is where those are who have the Word. Light thence as from its center spreads around to all the boundaries, even to the outermost; and consequently nations and peoples outside the Church also receive enlightenment through the Word. It may be seen in the work HEAVEN AND HELL Nos. 126-140, that light in the heavens is Divine Truth proceeding from the Lord, and that this light gives intelligence not only to angels but also to men.

[107] That this is true of heaven as a whole may be concluded from the fact that a like state prevails in every society there; for every society is a heaven on a small scale, and is also in the human form. This may be seen in HEAVEN AND HELL,

Nos. 41-87. In every society of heaven those who are in the center in like manner represent the heart and lungs; and they enjoy the greatest light. This light, with the consequent perception of truth, diffuses itself from center to circumference in every direction, thus reaching all in the society and giving rise to their spiritual life. It was shown me that when those in the center, who constitute the province of the heart and lungs and with whom light was greatest, were removed, those round about them experienced obscurity, and their perception of truth became so feeble, as to be hardly appreciable. As soon, however, as the others returned, light reappeared and their former perception of truth was restored.

[108] The same may also be illustrated by the following experience. There were with me African spirits from Abyssinia. On a certain occasion their ears were opened that they might hear singing in a temple in the world from a Psalm of David. They were moved by this with such delight that they joined in the singing. However, soon their ears were closed so that they no longer heard anything from the temple. But they were then moved with a delight still greater because spiritual; and they were at the same time filled with intelligence, because the Psalm treated of the Lord and of redemption. The reason for their increased delight was that communication was given them with that society in heaven which was in conjunction with those who were singing that Psalm in the world. From this experience and many others it was made evident to me that communication with the whole of heaven is effected through the Word. For this reason, by the Lords Divine Providence, there is universal intercourse of the kingdoms of Europe, chiefly of those where the Word is read, with nations outside the Church.

[109] This may be illustrated by comparison with the heat and light from the sun of this world which causes vegetation in trees and plants, even in those located towards the poles and in cloudy regions, provided the sun rises above the horizon and shows itself in the world. So it is with the light and heat of heaven proceeding from the Lord as the sun there; for that light is Divine Truth from which angels and men derive all their intelligence and wisdom. It is said therefore of the Word:

That it was with God, and was God;

That it lighteth every man that cometh into the world (John 1:1,9).

And that this light shineth also in darkness (John 1:5).

[110] From these considerations it may be evident that the Word as it is in the Church of the reformed, enlightens all nations and peoples by spiritual communication; and further, that the Lord provides that there should always be on earth a Church where the Word is read, and the Lord thereby made known. When therefore the Word was almost totally rejected by the Roman Catholic Church, through the Divine Providence of the Lord the Reformation took place, in consequence of which the Word was again received. It was also provided that the Word should be regarded as holy by an eminent nation among the Roman Catholics.

[111] As without the Word there is no rational conception of the Lord and thus no salvation, and when the Word with the Jewish nation was entirely falsified and defiled, and made as of none effect, it therefore pleased the Lord to descend from heaven; and, coming into the world, to fulfill the Word, and thus to renew and restore it, giving light again to the inhabitants of the earth, according to His own words:

The people, which sat in darkness, saw a great light (lumen); and to them which sat in the region and shadow of death light (lux) is sprung up (Matthew 4:16; Isaiah 9:2).

[112] It was foretold that, at the end of the present Church, darkness would arise from want of a rational conception and acknowledgment of the Lord as the God of heaven and earth, and from the separation of faith from charity. Lest therefore the genuine understanding of the Word should perish, it has pleased the Lord now to reveal the spiritual sense of the Word, and to show that the Word in that sense and from that in the natural sense, treats of the Lord and of the Church, and indeed of these alone; and to make many other revelations by means of which the almost extinct light of truth from the Word may be restored. That the light of truth would be almost extinguished at the end of the present Church is foretold in many passages of the Revelation, and is also meant by these words of the Lord in Matthew:

Immediately after the tribulation of those days shall the sun be darkened, and the moon shall not give her light, and the stars shall fall from heaven, and the powers of the heavens shall be shaken:

And then . . . they shall see the Son of Man coming in the clouds of heaven with glory and power (Matthew 24:29,30).

The sun there means the Lord as to love; the moon, the Lord as to faith; the stars, the Lord as to the cognitions of good and truth; the Son of Man, the Lord as to the Word; a cloud, the sense of the letter of the Word; glory, the spiritual sense and its transparence in the sense of the letter.

[113] It has been granted me to know from much experience that man has communication with heaven by means of the Word. When I was reading through the Word from the first chapter of Isaiah to the last of Malachi, and the Psalms of David, it was granted me to perceive clearly that every verse communicated with some society in heaven, and that in this way the entire Word communicated with the whole of heaven.

[114] XIV

Without the Word no one would have any knowledge of God, of heaven and hell, of a life after death, and still less of the Lord.

This follows as a general conclusion from all that has thus far been said and shown; as that the Word is Divine Truth itself, Nos. 1-4;

The Word is the medium of conjunction with the angels of heaven, Nos. 62-69; Everywhere in the Word there is a marriage of the Lord and the Church, and consequently the marriage of good and truth, Nos. 80-89;

The nature of the Church is according to its understanding of the Word, Nos. 76-79; The Word is also in the heavens, and from it the angels derive their wisdom, Nos. 70-75;

Through the Word also the nations and peoples outside the Church derive their spiritual light, Nos. 104-113; besides much more that might be mentioned.

From these considerations it may be concluded that without the Word no one has spiritual intelligence, which consists in the knowledge of God, of heaven and hell and a life after death; nor has he any knowledge at all of the Lord, of faith and love to Him, and consequently of redemption, although this is the means of salvation. The Lord also says to His disciples:

Without me ye can do nothing (John 15:5);

And John said:

A man can receive nothing, except it be given him from heaven (John 3:27).

[115] There are some men who maintain from firm conviction that without the Word a man can know of the existence of God, of heaven and hell, and also something of the other matters taught in the Word. They thereby weaken the authority and the holiness of the Word, if not with the mouth yet with the heart. Therefore, one may not argue with them from the Word, but from the light (lumen) of natural reason; for they do not believe in the Word but in themselves. Inquire then, by the light of reason, and you will find that there are two faculties of life in man, called the understanding and the will; and that the understanding is subject to the will, and not the will to the understanding; for the understanding merely teaches and points out the way. Inquire further and you will find that mans will is his proprium, and this when regarded in itself is entirely evil, and in consequence of this, that falsity arises in the understanding.

2. Having learned these things, you will perceive that a man of himself does not desire to understand anything but what comes from the proprium of his will; and that there is no possibility of doing this unless there were some other source of knowledge. Man from the proprium of his own will does not desire to understand anything but what relates to himself and the world; anything beyond this is in thick darkness to him. For instance, if, when looking at the sun, moon and stars, he should reflect on their origin, he could not but think that they are self-originated. He could not think any more profoundly that many of the learned men in the world who, although they know from the Word that God created all things, yet acknowledge nature as creator. Still more would they do so had they known nothing from the Word. It is credible that Aristotle, Cicero, Seneca and other ancient sages who have written about God and the immortality of the soul first derived their knowledge from their proprium? No; they obtained it by tradition from others who first learned it from the ancient Word. Nor do writers on natural religion derive their knowledge from themselves; they only

confirm by rational deduction what they learn from the Church, which has the Word; and it is possible that some of those who confirm truths do not believe them.

[116] It has been granted me to see people, born in remote islands, who were rational in civil matters, and yet knew nothing about God. In the spiritual world they appear like apes and live almost like them; but being men, and consequently born with the capacity to receive spiritual life, they are instructed by angels; and they are made alive by means of cognitions concerning the Lord as a man. What a man is of himself is very evident from those in hell, where there are also prelates and scholars, who do not wish even to hear of God, and therefore cannot utter His name. I have seen these and conversed with some of them. I have also spoken with some who burned with anger and fury when they heard anyone speaking of God.

2. Consider, therefore, what that man would be like who never heard of God, when this is the character of some who have heard of God, and who have written and preached about Him. There are many such from among the Jesuits. That they are of such a character is from the will, which is evil; and the will, as was said before, leads the understanding and deprives it of any truth it may have from the Word. If man of himself could have known that there is a God and a life after death, why has he not discovered that a man is a man after death? Why does he imagine that his soul or spirit is like wind or ether, which neither sees with eyes, nor hears with ears, nor speaks with a mouth, until it is reunited with its own dead body and skeleton?

3. Imagine therefore, doctrine for worship derived from the light of reason alone; would it not teach that self should be worshipped, as has been done for ages, and is still done today by some who know from the Word that God alone is to be worshipped? No other worship can be derived from mans proprium, not even that of the sun and moon.

[117] Religion has existed from the most ancient times, and the inhabitants of the world everywhere have had a knowledge of God, and some knowledge of a life after death. This has not originated from themselves or their own intelligence, but from the ancient Word mentioned above, Nos. 101-103; and in later times from the Israelitish Word. From these two Words forms of religion spread to the Indies and their islands, through Egypt and Ethiopia to the kingdoms of Africa, from the maritime parts of Asia to Greece, and thence to Italy. However, as the Word can only be written by representatives, that is, by such things in the world as correspond to and signify heavenly things, therefore religion with many nations was turned into idolatry, and in Greece into Mythology. Divine attributes and properties were turned into so many gods, and over these men

set one supreme deity whom they called Jove from Jehovah; while it is well known that they had some conception of paradise, some knowledge of the flood, the sacred fire, and the four ages from the first or golden age to the last or iron age, by which in the world are signified the four states of the Church as described in Daniel 2:31-35. It is also known that the Mohammedan religion, which succeeded and destroyed the former religious systems of many nations, was taken from the Word of both testaments.

[118] Finally, let me describe what those become after death who ascribe all things to their own intelligence, and little, if anything, to the Word. They first become like drunken men, then like fools, and finally as idiots they dwell in darkness. Let everyone, therefore, beware of such madness.

[THIS CONCLUDES THE DOCTRINE OF SACRED SCRIPTURE]
There are two doctrines to follow in my works to come.

CHAPTER 6

Words to the Wise!

I.   It is a true statement that death is not real.

II.   It is also true that life cannot be created, only death.

III.   God is in man and man is in God.

IV.   The story of Adam and Eve is a made up story of history that represents mans regeneration.

V.   There never was a worldwide flood of water, which destroyed all people on the face of the earth other than eight people. The flood is representative of the falsities that flood, or cover over the truths in the Church at its consummation.

VI.   The book of Revelation is a book of the life of the Lord, and how it will play a part in the regeneration of every human being. This book speaks of past, present, and future.

VII.   In John 21:25 it speaks of all the miracles Jesus did, and says to put them in a book would fill enough books that possibly the world could not hold them. Have you worked this out in your head? The only way this is possible is if the Lord did His miracles within, and through each and every human ever born. For this world can hold a huge amount of books; think about it.

VIII.   Every person healed by the Lord was healed according to their spirit, and the physical healings were only representative.

IX.   Mary Magdalene, Mary the mother of Jesus, and Mary the mother of James, Joses, and Salome were all the same women.

X.   Jesus never called Mary his mother, but instead called her woman.

XI.   Heaven and hell were both created and populated by human beings, and still are.

XII.   The sun is a ball of fire that never moves, the earth actually moves around it.

XIII.   The world as we know it will never be destroyed.

XIV.   There is no such thing as a Rapture, and the Lord is not a respecter of persons.

XV.   When the Lord does return to the world, you will not see him with your eyes.

XVI.   The Lord does return at the end of every Church, and every man is a Church eventually.

XVII.   If a tree falls in the woods does it make a sound if no one is there?

XVIII.   What is darkness but light in the shade?

XIX.   If you wish to be saved, you will become as a child, appearing as a simple or even ignorant man to the world. Do not attempt to stand out.

XX.   Jesus entered the world as an example to us in humility, but what world did he really enter?

XXI.   Do not believe that you are a Christian if you choose Paul's teachings over the Lords.

XXII.   When you come to know who you are, you will inherit the world, and all that is in it. For the meek shall inherit the earth.

XXIII.   Do not steal, but when you enter a rich mans house take possessions out with you.

XXIV.   To be a true Christian you must always answer yes or no, and never stop to think about your answer. If you can do this in all goodness and truth you have surely found yourself. When we hesitate, we begin to act from our own thoughts, when we answer swiftly, we answer from the Lord; if it is in faith.

XXV.   The Lords students asked Him, Do you want us to fast? And: How should we pray? Should we give to charity? What diet should we observe? The Lord answered plainly: If you fast you will bring sin upon yourselves; and if you pray you will be condemned, and if you give to charity you will harm your spirits. When you go into any region and walk through the countryside, and people receive you, eat what they serve you and heal the sick among them. What goes into your mouth will not defile you, but what comes out of your mouth, this will defile you.

XXVI.   What man sees as his end is only the beginning of life. For we are dead in this world.

XXVII.   For a woman to become saved she must first become man.

XXVIII.   You do not become a man until you leave this world, so what are you at this time?

XXIX.   To be a man we must first have conjunction with the Lord.

XXX.   Every part of the human body corresponds to something in the Lord, as well as the spiritual world.

XXXI.   If you believe in one God and you live a good life you will be saved, no matter what religion you are.

XXXII.   All children who die in youth go to heaven, and are raised by angels.

XXXIII.   Heaven and hell are everywhere, but angels and spirits live forever within human beings.

XXXIV.   If you shun the evils you do, and do not accept them as your own, then they are not your sins; if you take credit for any good you do, you are in sin and are robbing the Lord. What a human being does is not his own acts; he only accepts them as his own, and the Lord allows him to believe they are his own while he is in this world.

XXXV.   You reap what you sow, but this does not come from a single act, for to sow is to spread abroad, or in other words you sow evil when you commit sins more than one or two times, and they actually become habit. There are evil lives within you, and so you are bound to slip from time to time, therefore do not accept these evils as your own.

XXXVI.   The gate to the spiritual world is inside your brain, and connects your physical body to your spirit.

XXXVII.   The Old Testament God you read about is how babes in the Church actually understand God in the beginning of their Christian life, but this is by no means the true God we worship. God is love and can have nothing to do with evil; he doesn't even send people to hell, but they go there on their own.

XXXVIII.   Every man will live forever in happiness within their own heaven, and we will each live-forever in our own hell, only we go there when we are disobedient.

XXXIX.   If no one sin is greater than another, why do Christians believe some are condemned to eternal punishment?

XL.   If you are a preacher or minister looking to build a bigger Church you are lost, and do not know the meaning of salvation. You are attempting to do a work, which God has already taken care of when he said the human body is His temple. So the material building does not matter, people will still be saved, but you will have to make another round of it. YOU ARE NOT SAVED BY ANYTHING YOU CAN DO!

XLI.   This world is dead, and we are not from this world. When we leave this world we will return to life. No one has ever entered the kingdom of heaven but he who came from heaven.

XLII.   There is nothing new under the sun; what has been will be again. Yesterday must forever exist within today in order for there to be a tomorrow. When man reaches his peak, God will be there to rescue him.

XLIII.   Nothing in this world that is harmful to man was created by God, but by the affections of man. When certain affections from a certain harmful thing are no longer thought of in the world, that thing which is harmful to man will die off. For the thought from affection keeps a thing live or existing in this world. So man does have power from himself, but it is only evil.

XLIV.   Cave men as we know them have never existed in this world, for man has been in existence for Aeons, and has been even more advanced than we are today. We only think on an elementary level, and therefore believe man had to start from scratch. Man has always been taught by angels from the Lord, but the more evil he becomes the less he has a connection with the Lord and these angels.

XLV.   The answer to being saved is love. Love your neighbor before yourself and you will be saved. But in order to do this you must be lead by God, in which case you must love God above all things. If you put yourself before your neighbor you will not be saved; yet!

XLVI.   Preachers must learn to explain to people why little babes and children die young. They must be able to explain why good people live life poor sometimes, and die young; whereas evil people become rich, and livelong lives. Learn to explain these things, and you will know God. So I will get you started:

XLVII. Babies die young, as do young children, because this is their final lifetime in this material realm and God has a reason for letting them pass on early. They can complete their regeneration in the heavens because they are already in innocence, and will be raised by angels, so as to eventually become an angel. As far as why God does not stop their death, this is because man has free will and the child could have died from their parents being irresponsible, or even evil. They could have passed so as to teach someone something. Or they could have passed on because God knew they would be a future Hitler, and He wished to save many thousands of lives. For you must remember, you can begin life in this world as an evil, horrible person; and go on to later in life be a saint, wishing nothing more than to please God, but this would take much explanation. The point is we are not guaranteed the life of a saint if we begin life as a good loving child, or person. For all men are born into evil, everyone. So God always does what is best for mankind, but this does not mean He always stops evil actions to do so. We inherit evil and must therefore shun it so as to not become our own. And by the way, No! God does not permit the suffering of a child or baby, this is a dreamed up disastrous fantasy from man. It is disastrous because it causes men to believe God is cruel. What we see as suffering in this world is from the hells, and is not real. Yes we feel pain, but never more than we can handle; that is a promise from God. As far as good people dying young, and being poor, this is a fallacy. For no man is good, and we only fantasize that we are good in our own eyes. But God is not a respecter of persons, and anyone can be rich or poor. Anyone can die young, and we are permitted to die because of the laws of Divine Providence. Every man has a set time he is to leave this world; he can be young, or old; he can be tall or short; and he can be rich or poor. But we are all evil and must eventually learn this, and therefore it is Gods grace that we are even still alive to begin with. For every day a man walks out of his house God keeps him from being killed before his time; but when his time comes God cannot interfere, even if it is a baby. So God can only stop a death when the person's time is not yet, and so as to do what is best for all of mankind. But what is best will always coincide with that persons set time to die, for it has been preset by the laws of Divine Providence. For in order for every man to be saved they must be regenerated through their own free will, and this all happens according to the life every man or woman chooses to live. Do not put yourself above another man and say you, or your brother, sister, mom, dad, or uncle is a better person than someone else. And look around you, it is not always so great to be rich, or well off. I should know for I am happier now than I have ever been in life, and I live in a two bedroom apartment with my wife. My grandchildren live upstairs in the upper part of the house with my daughter and son in law. And we are not materially rich, but we are happy. So there are no set living standards as to what will make a person happy, this we must find by how we live our live, but we all must first find love. I hope this helps some to better understand God, for He is pure love, and wishes the death or harm of no one.

XLVIII. You will not always be living in this world, but you will always possess a human body, no matter who you are.

No one Sin is Greater than Another!

Now I know you have heard this saying before, and I have stated it in my works, therefore I should provide some explanation to this statement, as the Lord has seen fit to provide some light to this subject. According to mans senses in the world he believes that some sins man commits are worse than others. He believes that the more a sin is harmful to the comfortable lifestyle man wishes to lead the worse that sin is. Therefore if a man steals it is worse than a lie, and therefore he can do jail time for theft, but rarely for lying. Part of the reason for this is because man does not realize that every man, as far as being a child of God, is heir to the world and everything in it. Therefore no one man should own any one thing over any other man. But because of mans inherited greed he believes he should hurry and gat all he can for himself and his family. And at one time he was given what is called squatters rights as far as land goes. But this is not enough for man and he wishes to own it all, and rule the world if he could. Therefore people today try and get all they can, not intending on sharing with anyone. And sins are measured according to how much of a threat a persons actions are to our comfortable lifestyle. And so sins all have a man made set level as to their extremities of evil. But with God no man should own anything in this world over another man, and we all should have eventually learned to share among one another, so that no one had too much, nor anyone too little, as the bible teaches. If this were practiced more in the world today, men would learn to be more forgiving among one another, and would not be keeping a record of someone's wrong doings. And if you love, and forgive someone of their offenses enough times, they will eventually change for the better. This is why Jesus said to forgive your brother seventy seven times in a day; which means to forgive as many times as it takes for someone to come around. God never approved squatter's rights, and therefore never said that anyone can take possession of anything as their own unless he may receive it from another as a good will offering. Therefore all of this mess has been created by man, out of his own greed over the ages. For God has always provided man with the basic necessities in life, and those who do not have these things do not have them sometimes because of the abundance of sin in their life, or they may be poor so as to teach someone else compassion. For many men must learn that they are selfish, and would actually stand by and allow another person to go hungry, or homeless, or to do without the basic necessities in life. And what we see in the world is not poverty all the time, for we are spoiled today, and do not know what true poverty is. Yes there are those who go hungry, but they go hungry because we are not as much a Christian nation as we think we are. And governments are not as generous as they wish us to think they are. Every man in every public office has the ability, and the inherited evil to do his job in a dishonest manner, so as to lie to the public, and to steal from the public whenever they please. Anyone who is not aware of this is still a child. So do not trust man, but only trust those who you know to be of the uncorruptable generation; for these are of the New Church doctrine. If a man puts not his neighbor before himself he is not of the spoken of,"UNCORRUPTABLE GENERATION," AND IS NOT OF GOD. But no man who is in good, or attempts to live a good life will ever do without basic necessities from God. The people God allows to do without, so as to serve as examples to man, and to permit man to attempt to help them out of love for their neighbor, are those who choose to do without, or those who are not willing to work. Or they are the family members of those not willing to work. But God is merciful, and sees to the good of every human being. Therefore all the suffering you have been shown on your television screens are a falsified truth from many men today. The problem is largely blown out of proportion. I mean, really, you see on television the funds they collect to feed the poor, and to clothe and house the poor. Where is it all going, not to the poor, but to the greedy and dishonest? So do you really think more of the same will feed or clothe any more people? Give your blessings to another first hand, and then you will truly know they have been blessed, and leave the dishonest people to God. Why do you think our government seeks our help to feed the poor, when they waste enough funds to feed the poor in the world many times over? Because they get the money, or at least their cut. Do not worry about the poor a thousand miles away from you, for God has them covered, whether you wish to believe it or not; but concern your self with the poor God sends to you, and that are around you, and you will have done your part in life. Do not put your trust in every sad story you hear, when you as a man or woman can do nothing about it, for as I have said, God is in control of all situations. If I believed every news cast ever put on television I would be a fool, for a person who lives for self or the world would surely lie if it were to their benefit, and they knew they could get away with it. But as I said, we will all eventually be forgiven, for man is not at fault, because he was born into sin, and therefore God shows His mercy to every human being every day. But even though "He knows not what he does," we are not to put our trust in man, but only in God. I could go on and on with examples, but the point is, I have never seen the righteous forsaken. Neither have I neglected to see God show MAN MERCY time and time again. But as I was saying, God provides all men with their basic needs, even if the basic need is a bottle, or pack of cigarettes for some. Why? Because He would not begrudge a man his last cigarette, or drink; and for some this is how they see it. But when people in this world help someone they usually take the credit instead of giving it to God. But no man is good from himself, and all good comes directly from God, and God uses human bodies to carry out His acts of mercy, or good works. If more men realized this, this would be a much better world. So when you read the commandment, "Thou shalt not steal", Exodus 20:15; keep in mind that this pertains mainly to stealing from God by not giving glory to Him for the good you do. As far as stealing in this world, if you realized that all is already yours, you would realize that you can only steal in this world when you make yourself a part of this world, and live for self and the world. For by doing this you no longer are an heir to God, and all is not yours, but another's. For we are only heirs when we are in love to the Lord, and wish the good of a neighbor before our own. If you are one of these then by all means all things are yours. Therefore what you take in this world you take for another, and not yourself. For you are a child who owns everything, but are not yet mature enough to realize what things you should have. Therefore let God provide for you what He wishes you to have from the family fortune, and you keep busy in life by doing for others. When you do this, there is nothing you can take that is not already yours, but do not offend, do not harm, and do not take what is not needed. Now if you do not see that what I speak is true then you can go to your bible and read the New Testament. When you get to Paul's teachings you will see that he also became aware of these truths in life, and in his teachings, even though he abused these things at times. For Paul was a proud man who enjoyed boasting. Now you might ask, what has this subject to do with the statement that, "No one sin is greater than another?" First it shows how man is totally living in fantasy in this world, and is actually living in a reverse order compared to Gods order. Every thing that man believes today comes from the opinions of different men and women over the ages, and what we see and hear today is the outcome, or product of mans distortions of Gods ways and commandments for a civil, moral, and righteous man. For as I have said, God never intended for man to own land as his own, but that all of the land should be divided as one needs it, so that no one had too much, and no one had too little. And if a man did have excess land, he would be willing to give to another who was in need. This not only goes for land, but for all things in our world. And as you can see we have caused all things in our world to happen in a reverse order. Therefore, if you do the opposite of most things, you will be correct. And as far as sins are concerned, if you learn to have a forgiving heart as the Lord teaches, you will have no need to keep any record of mans sins. For as the Lord teaches, He does not keep a record of mans sins, nor does He remember them; but not because He cannot, but because He chooses out of love for mankind not to. This being the case, there is no one sin greater than another.

Notes of Wisdom!

1. Every human being is a spiritual form, and when he lives within the material world, he is the ruler of a spiritual world.
2. When we leave the material world, and go on to the spiritual world, we are servants to a human being in the material world, which is why we must, as physical human beings learn to serve others.
3. Man will always be a servant, for he was created to do so, and therefore will always serve mankind by the use he performs in the spiritual world.
4. To one day rule with the Lord is to learn to serve, and to love the good as well as the evil, which is what Jesus taught us all in his teachings, as well as his life.
5. When we leave this material world we will have chosen our love, and we will be the best we could have been in the material world.
6. With a good spirit, or Angel, the good is in the very inmost center, and the worst spirits are on the most outer perimeters of his spiritual body.
7. A mans best spirits are the ones that rule the life of that man, and at the same time teach him to be a servant in our world, as well as the one to come.
8. Are spirits ever trapped within a human being? No, because spirits do not exist within time or space. Spirits choose who they dwell with according to the agreeing affections. For if two different spirits do not agree as to a single affection, they cannot share the same human being, or the same spiritual society. The more two spirits agree as to their affections, the more chance they have of being a part of the life of the same human being, and the closer they live among one another in the same spiritual society.
9. Can two spirits who are very closely matched, so much so as to be almost identical, still live their life within two different human beings? Yes, because the spiritual world is seen in the Lords eyes as a single man, and therefore all spirits and angels share a connection, as the spiritual world overlaps itself at all times. In other words, a single spirit can be with two or more men at the same time, by sharing the same society within the spiritual world.
10. So if a single spirit can be found within two or more men at the same time, where will that spirits consciousness be when this is taking place? The spirit will

217

believe he is each man, sharing each mans consciousness separately, with each man having his own separate consciousness as well.

11. For each and every affection is a spirit, or man, and each would not be sufficient to provide the thoughts of every man ever born into the world, especially since there are many planets out there. Therefore, wherever an affection is called on by any human being, that affection is provided to him, by both human beings sharing the same spiritual society at the same time.

12. Now there are certain affections, or spirits that remain with a man at all times, because they make up his love, or society, and they also make up his heaven. So he is the god of his heaven, until the Lord teaches him differently. This happens when we become a New Church; or a new heaven and a new earth. When a man becomes a New Church, he then learns to be a servant, and not a ruler. He also learns not to judge people for who or what they are. He learns to accept everyone just the way they are, while at the same time being a good example to all. This is when we begin to bless those who persecute us, or learn to love our enemies. This can only be done through the Lord, with him working on the inside of us.

13. We are never free from any spirit, whether good or evil, and they can return to us a thousand years down the road, so as to live in our lives, or just to be used as a temptation to us, so as to teach us. For we never stop learning, and we never learn every detail to every situation, which is why we can be tried at any point in our lives.

14. Spirits do not dwell within our fleshly human body, but they dwell within our inner man, or our spiritual man. This spiritual man of ours is no bigger or smaller than the spirits and angels all combined together within us, for the spiritual world takes up no space, no matter what the number of spirits or angels.

15. A single spirit has one consciousness, but he forms the consciousness of many, many human beings at the same time. Such as my affection could represent strawberries as my ruling love, and every human being that thinks of strawberries at the same time, at any given point in time, would draw on that affection of mine, and therefore would be sharing my consciousness all at the same time. And yet, my consciousness still dwells within the same heavenly society the whole time.

16. Many spirits and angels make up a single thought of a single angel, or man. Such as the fact that from the accumulated evil, not so evil, not so good, good, and best thoughts from affections in a heavenly society, they all combine together to make up a single angel, or man. But is that man always as good as his best spirits or angels from within? No he is not, for we all go through different states, which are controlled by the Lord, and are basically put in place to keep all men from being bored to death. And these states cause us to draw our affections from all different spirits and angels within our heavenly society. Therefore no man can always be at his best behavior, or thoughts of affections. But when we

leave this material world for good, our spiritual society from within is made up of the best possible spirits and angels as the Lord saw fit, to match up with our own ruling love. For when we leave here for good, whatever our love is when we die is what it will remain forever.

17. If this is my final life in this world, because I have completed my regeneration as far as the material world is concerned, where will the location of my consciousness be once I wake up in the spiritual world? I know I will be in the spiritual world, but where will that location be? Well, where are my thoughts right now, while I am sitting here writing this book? They appear to be in my head, but they are not actually in my head. Each one of my affections cause a separate thought that has the appearance of being at the top of this fleshly body, in its head. At the same time, these affections are as to appearance, within many other people's bodies inside their head, as well. So if these thoughts are here in me, and there in them at the same time; where are my thoughts, really? They exist within the spiritual world, where me, and another person, and another person, and another person, and finally maybe a million other persons all share the same spiritual society, at this very moment in time. And this means we are all actually in the same place at that exact moment in time, even though it appears according to our fleshly bodies that we are all half way across the world, away from one another. For this material world is only the apparent truth, which means it only appears to be the real world, when all along the real world is the spiritual world.

18. So where am I at this moment in time? I am in the spiritual world living in fantasy, or dreaming. When I go to sleep tonight, and my spirit separates from my body, I will be waking up in the real world, which is the spiritual world.

19. If we are to render unto Caesar what is Caesars, and render unto God what is Gods, we must make a mental note as to what is Gods and what is Caesars. I came from God, and all that I truly am is God, so any part of me that is not God belongs to this material world. Although no part of me actually belongs to the material world, but only apparently. And anyone who understands their bible knows that the Word, when speaking of Caesar, is speaking of the material world we live in, and the ways of the world. Now because Gods ways are not like the worlds ways, we cannot live for God and the world at the same time, for it would be like serving two masters, of which Jesus spoke against. Therefore since I choose to live for and serve God, I will have no part of the world unless it is for the good of another. For it is a truth that I should do my best to provide for my family, since they do not truly understand that God is the actual provider. But I must let God lead me in all things, and attempt nothing that does not first come from him. The more we buy into the worldly system of things, the more we are a part of the world, and the flesh. I do not serve the flesh, and therefore I do not cater to the cravings of the flesh.

20. How do we know if our thoughts and ideas come from God, and not ourselves? If your thoughts are for the good of self, or the flesh, they are from you. If you

pray for God to bless someone financially, or with material things, beyond what they need for everyday life, you are praying from self. The things of this world are temporary, and should not be a part of our prayers, but we should pray for others, and not ourselves. For God already knows your needs, and you should know that he will provide for your needs. So we are to pray for those who do not know this, and who attempt to provide for their own needs, or fix a certain situation, and in turn make things worse. For if we seek mercy for our friend, neighbor, or enemy, God will give mercy to them because a child of his asked him to do so. Not that this is the only time God shows mercy. You see, many people are in sin, and do evil acts simply to lash out at someone, such as God, because they do not understand why bad things happen to them. But the truth is, bad things happen to everyone, and this is because we actually reap what we sow. Many do not think that statement is really true, but it is very true. So when we pray, we should pray for someone else, and we should be praying for their souls to be healed, we should be praying for God to put peace in their heart, and we should be praying for their spiritual good, and not the things that have to do with their flesh, or their cravings in this evil world.

21. Does this mean that if a friend, neighbor, or enemy has lost their job, their car, their family, and their home; all in a days time, that we should not pray for these things to be returned? No, we should not pray for these things to be returned. What we should pray for is that Gods will be done in their life, and that God would have mercy on them and their family. We should also pray that God would help them find some peace in it all, so they can accept the fate God has allowed in their life. This is what a good, loving Christian should ask the Lord for, when he prays for another. If you ever pray for yourself, you should always pray that Gods will be done in your life, and this will cover all things that have to do with you.

22. Should we fast when we want something bad enough? No, we should pray the prayer I mentioned to pray for self, and wait for Gods will to be done. Fasting is only permitted for those who are still babes, or the ignorant in the Church. For fasting is another form of works, and we are to do no works from self, in order to be saved. The works we do should come from God in us, and should be for the good of someone else, not ourselves. We cannot save ourselves, but we can be used by God to help save others. The way he uses us is to do for others as you would do for yourself, and to at all times lead by example.

23. Whoever has not yet accepted the Lord is still a Jew! For we are not Jews from our outer appearance, but from what we are on the inside (Romans 2:28).

24. There were three Mary's that walked with the Lord, His mother, His sister, and Mary of Magdala, his companion. His sister, and mother and companion were Mary. Let he who has eyes see what the spirit tells him.

25. Jesus tricked everyone; he did not appear as he was but in a way not to be seen. Yet he appeared to all of them. To the great he appeared as great, to the small

as small. To the angels he appeared as an angel, and to humans as a human. And he hid his word from everyone. Some looked at him and thought they saw themselves. When before his students he appeared gloriously on the mountain, he was not small. No, he became great, and he made his students grow so they would know his immensity.

26. The Lord said to the students, "From every house you are in, take out possessions, but take things into the Fathers house, and do not steal what is inside and run off.

27. The Lord would never say "My Father who is in heaven," unless he had another Father elsewhere. He would have simply said, "My Father."

28. Those who sow in winter reap in summer. Let us sow in the world to reap in summer. Winter is the world, summer the other realm. It is wrong to pray in the winter. From winter comes summer. If you reap in winter you will not reap. You will pull up young plants. At the wrong season no crop is yours. Even on the days of the Sabbath the field is barren.

29. A Gentile doesn't die, never having been alive to die. You who find truth are alive; another may die, being alive. Since Christ came the world was made, cities adorned, and the dead buried. When we were Jews we were orphans with only a mother. When we turned Christian we had a Father and a Mother.

30. What a Father has belongs to his child, but not while the child is still little. When the child is grown, however, then the Father turns over all he possesses.

31. The Lord said blessings on you who were before you came into being. Whoever is, was, and will be.

32. Truth didn't come into the world naked, but in types and images. Truth is received only that way. There is rebirth and its image. They must be reborn through image. What is the resurrection? Image must rise again through image. The bridegroom and image enter through image into truth, which is restoration. It is right that those who don't have it take on the name of the Father and Son and the Holy Spirit. But they have not done so on their own. If you do not take on the names for yourself, the name "Christian" will be taken from you. You receive them in the oil of the chrism, the aromatic unction of the power of the cross. The messengers called this power "the right and the left." YOU ARE NO LONGER A CHRISTIAN, BUT CHRIST. (Yeshua said, Whoever drinks from my mouth will become like me. I myself shall become that person, and the hidden things will be revealed to that one.)

33. Jeshua said, "It will not come because you are watching for it." No one will announce, "Look here it is," or "Look there it is." The Fathers Kingdom is spread out upon the earth and people do not see it.

34. Jesua's students said to him, when will the dead rest? When will the new world come? He said to them, What you look for has come, but you do not know it.

35. Yeshua said, "A prophet is not accepted in his hometown. A doctor does not heal those who know the doctor.

36. Yeshua said, "Have you discovered the beginning and now are seeking the end? Where the beginning is, the end will be. Blessings on you who stand at the beginning. You will know the end and not taste death.

37. Yeshua said, If you fast you will bring sin upon yourselves, and if you pray you will be condemned, and if you give to charity you will harm your spirits. When you go into any region and walk through the countryside, and people receive you, eat what they serve you and heal the sick among them. What goes into your mouth will not defile you, but what comes out of your mouth will defile you.

38. Yeshua said, this heaven will pass away, and the one above it will pass away. The dead are not alive, and the living will not die. During the days when you ate what is dead you made it alive. When you are in the light what will you do? On the day when you were one you became two. But when you become two, what will you do?

39. The Lord rose from the dead. He became as he was, but now his body was perfect. He possessed flesh, but this was true flesh. Our flesh is not true flesh, ours is only an image of the true.

40. Yeshua said, if your leaders tell you, "Look, the kingdom is in heaven," then the birds of heaven will precede you. If they say to you, "Its in the sea," then the fish will precede you. But the Kingdom of heaven is inside you and it is outside you. When you know yourselves, then you will be known, and you will understand that you are children of the living Father. But if you do not know yourselves, then you dwell in poverty, and you are poverty.

41. Jeshua said, how miserable is the body that depends on a body, and how miserable is the soul that depends on both.

42. Yeshua said, the kingdom is like a shepherd who had a hundred sheep. One of them, the largest, went astray. He left the ninety-nine and looked for the one until he found it. After so much trouble he said to the sheep, "I love you more than the ninety-nine. (This refers to the fact that the ninety-nine are now one with the Lord, and the Lord cannot Love himself as another, but must love the other more than himself. Once the one, which went astray becomes one with the Lord also, the Lord will love him less than one that later goes astray.)

43. When a human is born into this world, are they ever born into it again, exactly as they are the first time? No! Because a spirit is never the same, and changes with each moment in time, as well as separate from time. For we all add different affections, which are spirits, to our being as we grow and mature as spirits, or angels. And since the human body is an exact correspondence to the spiritual body, they always change, in accordance with the spirit. Therefore, no two human beings will ever be identical, no matter how far apart they are born in time. However, affections do return to a spirit, sometimes a thousand years down the road, so to speak. For as a mans tastes change, so too do his affections throughout the ages. But just because an affection may leave a certain spirit for

a time, does not mean it is not still connected to that spirit in some manner, for this is what allows an affection to return after a long period of time. But when an affection, or spirit returns to an angel, or spiritual society after a long period of time, that angel, or society no longer lives within the same human being, but has moved on to another. For as every human must be an improvement to the one prior, so too must be his spiritual society. But it takes much time before a spiritual society is totally replaced by another.

44. If you were to take one hundred million men in a single world, and none existed at the same time, but one of these hundred million were born, one after the other, every one of these men would experience the same exact experiences in their lifetime, so that each would have walked in the others shoes, or footsteps. But what we do not know is how this is caused to happen, and what the details are. But keep in mind that each of these men are the next level improvement to the one before them. If you were to look at men today in our material world, you could not see the evidence that this is so, but it is. You see, when we look at things in our world, we trust what our physical senses tell us, and this is where we come up with the details that we come to call truth in our world. But what we call truth in our world is only the apparent truth, whereas the real, or actual truth is in the spiritual realm. So when a man is born in the material world, this is only because birth cannot take place in the spiritual world.

45. When you go to sleep at night, and you dream, you are in the spiritual world. But no one ever dreams all night long, even though they are asleep for the whole duration. When they lose consciousness of where they are, as well as who they are, they can be replenished with a consciousness that belongs to just about anyone. For instance: I can go to sleep tonight as myself, remembering all the things I said and did today; but when I awaken tomorrow, I can awaken as someone else, having the consciousness and memory that belongs to that person alone; knowing their complete lifelong history. And because I awaken as this person, I am responsible for this persons decisions for that day, believing that I am really this person; when all along I am a spirit, or angel who lived long ago, as we all are, and will continue to live within other human beings till forever. We are all separate men because we are somewhere along the line born as a single human being, even though we are actually many. We are one in the flesh, but many in the Lord. As far as the present is concerned, we are who we believe we are, but tomorrow that will change. I mean, if you think about it, God is in control of every human mind, and can put our consciousness within any human being he wishes, tomorrow, once that person's consciousness is broken, by sleep. As I think of it, I say to myself, hey! I know almost every detail of my life since I was a child, so how can someone wake up tomorrow as me, knowing everything I know now, and them believing for sure, that they are me. Well, every spirit or angel has access to the memory of another spirit or angel because we are all connected in the Lord, which is exactly where we are right now. The only reason

I do not have the memory of every spirit or angel ever born, at this moment, is because only the Lord can store all the memory of everyone ever born. You could say he is the main computer, and we are just computer chips, who are loaded with different information, every day of our lives. But when we are loaded with this information, we believe that we have always had it, and that we have been this same person since this human body, which we possess, was born into the material world. Today I am Daniel Gross; tomorrow I could be Carol Gross, AND WALK IN HER SHOES; and the next day I could be a Chinese, African, Russian, or Spanish person, half way across the world, who doesn't even know who me or my wife are, so as to walk in their shoes as well. But as we continue in this life switch, as you may wish to call it, we do not retain our original memory, of yesterday, but we take on the memory of the person we are today. So whose life do we assume every day, and why? Every human being, spirit, or angel must continue to learn, and grow in wisdom until forever. Therefore we must trade lives with people every day in the material world, so as to experience, and eventually conquer every trial, or situation in life, or creation. In order to accomplish this we must enter the life of another, who is in that situation at any given time. We can go to sleep tonight, and wake up tomorrow on the planet Mars, and be a certain citizen of that world, or planet. We could sleep tonight, and wake up somewhere else in the world, where it is exactly the same time as when we went to sleep. For we all are aware of time differences in the world. Do you know why there are moods, or states in life? Because you can go to sleep as a happy woman, and wake up as an unhappy man. Or you can go to sleep as a scared man, and wake up as a very brave, and proud woman. If I go to sleep tonight, depressed, and thinking of suicide, someone else will wake up as me tomorrow, still thinking of suicide; and this is controlled by the company we keep in the spiritual world. For if you draw from suicidal spirits today, they will return to that human body tomorrow, but as someone else. So if someone else enters your body tomorrow, your suicidal thoughts, and affections will enter into another human being tomorrow, and will harm that person's life, possibly. So be careful what you think, say, and do in life, for we affect many other lives, which we are not aware of. Where a tree falls, therein will it lay. So, when you go to sleep at night, whatever your thoughts are set on is what decides whom you enter tomorrow, and what trials you will endure. It is a fact, that in the Word, death, or to die means to sleep, which leads me to this statement. It is appointed to man to die once, and then the Judgment. Have you heard this statement before? You should have for it is in the bible, and it is so true. For every man lives for the day, sleeps, or dies to his flesh that night, and is reborn in his spirit, but within another human being. Each man also goes through the four seasons in his life, in which it ends in the winter, where he will once again sow his crop, and will reap in summer, which is when he is reborn, within another. The four seasons he endures during his lifetime of a day is morning, noon, evening, and night; so as to begin life anew at the next morning, or spring. But he cannot reap in spring, for he is a child, and is in innocence from the Lord. Noon is summer, or young adulthood, and this is when we begin to reap that in which we sowed in the past life, or yesterday night, which is winter. And as there are four seasons in creation, so too are there four stages in mans life. Starting with childhood, then young adulthood, adulthood, and old age. Spring, summer, autumn, and winter. Morning, noon, evening, and night. These are the times of our lives. But lets now speak of the fact that God recreates the past, so as to feed the present and the future with beastlike affections until forever, and gradually advancing on up to all levels of wise affections. If the past were not recreated, men would all be wise, and loving, because we all advance, or grow in love, wisdom, and knowledge until forever. Yes we are born less wise, and more beastlike than when we are older, but as man has advanced throughout the ages, he is by no means as beastlike as those in the past. The Lord cannot recreate these beastlike affections in man during the present because man must advance throughout time, and never remain the same. So the beastlike affections must come from our past, but the past is always in the Lords present. For even the past, and the future are the present within the Lord. So what do we have so far?

1] Man is first created with a beastlike nature, but he is by no means a beast.

2] Every affection that man draws from the Lord throughout his lifetime, stays with him, and makes up his love in life, till forever.

3] Once any man becomes wiser or more mature, he cannot go back to living in the beastlike manner in which he once lived, and he must continue to grow in wisdom and learn many different affections of love.

4] Affections are men, or people, and they will remain the same till forever. Whatever affection a man represents, he will represent till forever, and will provide that affection to all of creation till forever.

5] Because a man must provide beastlike affections to mankind till forever, and because even he must grow in wisdom and love till forever, it is his opposite, or counterpart who will provide the beastlike affection to all of mankind, and not his heavenly affection, which is what we all eventually represent. And because we all represent heavenly affections eventually, we must all remain as beasts in the past, for the past is the opposite of the future. Therefore what we will all become is the exact opposite of what we all once were. And because of this, even our opposite life, image, or counterpart will forever continue to provide a use for all of mankind.

6] Does this mean that all men will forever continue to be reborn, or reincarnated? Yes it does, however it will not be in the future, but in the past. For it is a truth that man is created to provide a use for the past, present, and the future.

7] It is not however; the fleshly body of ours that is being reborn in the past, but our inferior half of our spirit is born into this human being, and becomes a part of his consciousness, or life. We will never be the controlling spirit of that person, but will mix with his spirit, so as to create another spirit. Kind of like conception, or having a child from one man and one woman. And we cannot enter this person's life unless he first draws from the spiritual society in which we as a spirit live. But because he is born of a beastlike nature, he will at first draw from our beastlike affections, which are our opposite affections in hell.

8] Do not think that all hells are evil, or that one is as bad as another. For there are levels of degrees in the hells, as far as good and bad, as there are in the heavens. For the opposite of the lowest heavens is the best of the hells. And the opposite of the best heavens is the worst hells. For the opposite of not so good, is not so bad; and the opposite of very good, is very bad.

9] So in the past they draw from beastlike affections in the future, and the beastlike affections that are in the future are replenished by those of the past. And all are the present within the Lord alone. If those men in the future were not replenished with beastlike affections from the past, they would eventually run out of beastlike affections, and mankind would cease to exist. For every human being, spirit, and Angel lives within their own equilibrium, which is midway between heaven and hell; and they must remain there till forever, choosing either good thoughts from heaven, or evil thoughts, or not so good thoughts from hell. For man must always remain in free will to choose good and evil for himself. However, if man does not continue to provide the evil from the past, so as to storehouse it in the future, man could not continue to exist anymore, for the design of Gods original creation of mankind would be disrupted, or destroyed.

10] So basically, man will always begin his life as evil, because of him wanting to feed, and please his flesh. The past must continue to be recreated, and the future remains as the storehouse for the past. Man will always go through moods or states in life, and he needs these negative affections, as well as the positive, to provide his thoughts within each and every state he enters in his life until forever.

Now I wish to continue to speak on this subject, for there are many things that need explaining, if we are going to be able to grasp the idea I am attempting to share with you. And I know there will be many, who cannot accept these sayings, and for those of you who fit this category, I can only say, it is not yet your time, and I suggest you keep praying for guidance and enlightenment.

Now you are probably wondering why there has to be a past, continuously recreated in time or the created realm, by the Lord, when there are already good and evil affections in the spiritual world now, that provide all of mankind with his good and evil affections for his thoughts every day. Well, the good affections for thoughts are continuously being provided by the Lord in heaven, through influx that is constantly passing down through the different heavens, until it eventually reaches every man. And when these affections reach each man, he either uses them for good thoughts and acts, or he can turn them into evil thoughts and acts, depending on whether he is in a good state or a bad, or evil state at that particular point in time. And you may say well, isn't there enough evil men in the world today to provide all the evil affections needed for mankind's continued existence? The answer is no, there is not, because man draws his affections from the spiritual world, and not the other way around. And because God replenishes the good affections in time constantly, man must provide the evil affections in time constantly. So because of this, man must also exist in the past, present, and the future just as God does. The difference is we are created, and he is not. We are finite, but he is infinite. We will forever owe our existence to the Lord continuously recreating us all, whereas the Lord will never owe his existence to anyone. So man does not provide, or supply evil affections in the present, but he draws on, or takes from the supply of evil affections that are constantly being supplied by those in the past; and by mans mixing his affections with those he draws from the storehouse, he creates new evil affections so that the hells can stay in stride with the heavens. For remember, for every affection that exists within the heavens, there must be an exact opposite affection of bad or evil to be found within the hells, at all times. And not only does every man have to be supplied with his own evil, as well as good affections, until he leaves this material world, but every spirit and angel must be supplied with his own good and bad affections as well. But these all can by no means be supplied with their affections of evil simply by those men who live in the material world today. And remember this, spirits and angels do not supply themselves with affections, but they provide affections to the material world. Spirits and angels receive their affections from their own society, and not outside that society. But if an affection is a man, no matter what world he exists in, and we all continue to advance in wisdom, love, and maturity, what happens to the evil affection, that those in hell use to represent, but have moved on to a better society in the spiritual world? And what happens when man no longer acts or lives as beasts do, and he is a little, or a lot more godlike? In other words, is it not a fact that if man is to continue to become better, or greater in heavenly wisdom, and the lowest of these in the world still above the beasts by far in wisdom, from where do the beastlike affections continue to be provided for the spiritual realm? For if man is offered the greatest affections of wisdom and love, he must also continuously be offered the most worst of the affections of wisdom and love, which are beastlike to the most extreme. Where do these affections come from; again, the past! And again; they cannot be offered by the present. So no matter how advanced mans wisdom becomes, he must always, according to Gods plan, be offered the lowest of affections until forever. If man did not exist within the thoughts of God this could never had been possible, but because of our Father and Gods love, he has made it possible.

You may say to yourself, well what is so loving about a God that provides evil to his children? But he is not providing evil to his children; he is allowing the evil to also become his children, eventually. For there is not a creature that has ever lived that can disregard Gods love till forever, without eventually becoming a loving being himself, no matter how long it may take for him to do so. For God did not directly create evil, but man did; and God will save all men in spite of themselves; good and evil. Evil was permitted to exist so as to create lives that were separate (at least apparently separate) from God. For God cannot be happy just loving himself, and wanted to create children to love, and to be loved by him, and others. We are not really separate from God, and we do not even have a separate consciousness from him, but he allows us to live as though it were this way. By doing it this way, we see our selves as separate beings from God; at least at first, until we have matured, and have been regenerated by God, so as to eventually know whom we are. For who we truly are is God, but we are God, who he has bound by flesh, until our school of love and life is complete. As we grow worthy of his trust to rule certain people, things, and governments with the Lord, he will allow us to do so. But only he knows when each of us is ready, and only he can choose when to cut us loose. Yes, we are God, but we only represent one single affection of God. But what is of God is most certainly God, is it not? Yes it is! The fact that he chose to separate single affections from himself, and to house them permanently in a bubble called an atmosphere, and to allow them to believe they are separate beings from himself, and the rest of mankind, was Gods own will, and he has all the right to do as he pleases, for he is God. So even though we are all God, we will forever be required to submit to Gods rule and authority, for he alone knows what is best for us all. But do not forget we are all heirs to his throne, and we are truly his children, and therefore he sets no limits as to what each and every one of his children can achieve in their lifetime, and this is why he allows us all to continue to live forever. So if man has been around for ages upon ages, which should be understood by the simple fact that the past began with God, and in God. So if it began with, and in God; and God is the same yesterday, today, and forever, then man has been around since eternity. And who does not know that eternity has no beginning or end. Yes, man is finite, simply because he owes his existence to God alone, but to prove that man had a beginning can only be done by God, since he was truly the only one there at the time of mans beginning. Man was there, but only in a made up world, which does not really exist. So I will state once again, man has been around for ages upon ages, or since eternity, and everything God has created, or permitted to be created by man, has been for mans benefit alone. We find the bones or fossils of creatures in this world that have been berried for a hundred thousand, a million, or even ten million years, and we assume they lived for themselves in these time periods, and apply no connection to the fact that man was there in this same time period, living right along side these creatures. We have made no conclusions to the fact that these creatures may have been put there for mans benefit, and to actually aid in mans daily efforts or chores, somewhere along the line. These creatures are known as Pre-Historic animals, or Dinosaurs. And they not only lived during the building of the Pyramids in Egypt, but they have lived during many different Ages, and will return just the same, for many Ages to come, until forever. For the past does repeat itself, but it repeats itself in the past, where the past still exists within the Lord. We as men have all seen Dinosaurs before in our lives, even though we do not remember, and we have seen many lives living within human beings since the beginning of time, even though we have no recollection of any beginning of time. For all men will live forever as Angels, eventually, within a single human being. But the human being will be different for many days to come, many years to come, and even many Ages to come. For as I have explained, we enter a different human being every morning in which we awaken from the spiritual world, or our sleep. If you sit and think about it, even though God gives me these amazing revelations even as I am sitting here typing, we should all see, to some degree, that God has drawn a perfect plan for creation. And once we hear of the whole plan, if it is his will that I announce it all in full, or at least most of it, I am sure you too will agree, it is amazing. But let me first ask you a question: Do any of you really think God would create any creature that would harm a man, or even kill him, if he were a good man? So what kept Dinosaurs from killing good men? For I am sure we are all aware that they did not possess any exceptional reasoning power, to cause them to rationalize that it is wrong to kill a man, good or evil. Answer: Dinosaurs were created to serve man, and nothing more. Yes, they were used later for food, but this was not Gods predestined design, it was only a foreseen thing, in which God knew would eventually come about because of mans free will. And even though we were all once guilty of this crime, because we lived in the past, long ago, we will no longer see actual, material Dinosaurs again in the future. For they no longer have a place in this world we live in, where machines are used instead. They will however continue to exist throughout the past Ages, so as to still serve their intended purpose for mankind. If God were to never allow Dinosaurs to exist in the world ever again, why would he put them here in the first place, seeing that God is the same yesterday, today, and forever. Not only that, but God is not a respecter of persons, and he provides all things to all generations, so that all men experience the same situations throughout their lifetime. But even though we will all live forever, this does not mean that Dinosaurs will one day show up again in our future. For we have no need to learn to build pyramids any longer, for they are temporary, and are of this material world, which will one day fade away with time, if it is Gods will. We need only know that the wisdom behind the pyramids is found in God, and those he intends to show. For even though a generation may be ignorant in worldly knowledge, this does not mean they cannot be given Godly knowledge, no matter what the state of knowledge, or technology in the world. It is a truth that God will send his chosen back to the world within all different technological eras, and that the Kingdom of Heaven is forever presented to the innocent of the world, no matter what their maturity level in the world may be. For it is a truth that the Most Ancient Church, which is the Celestial, or Heavenly Church has existed throughout the past, no matter how wise or ignorant man may have been found to be. This is why God said his Wisdom will appear as foolishness to those who see themselves as wise in the world, and he will teach only those who see themselves as foolish, or unlearned in their own eyes. The pyramids have withstood the test of time to show those that were obedient to God, and were able to build wonderfully designed pyramids, as well as those who were disobedient to God, and these later built pyramids show the outcome. For when man later began to rely on his own knowledge, he not only lost the knowledge to build pyramids, but he killed off his Gigantic helpers in the Dinosaurs, as the evil began to once again grow throughout the world, as the church also declined in good and truth, and its consummation was eminent. Even today these pyramids stand as a testimony to these truths, and man chooses to use his own worldly explanations to explain Dinosaurs and pyramids. And as the future takes form, the pyramids are being created anew in the past, as a continued testimony to those to come. Do you ever look at the foundations of mankind's buildings, and then look at the foundation of Gods buildings, and wonder if we can ever achieve the wisdom of God? Well, my dear brothers, we cannot ever reach that height, but he allows us to go as far as our mind can ever take us. Do you however, believe that foundations, and signs of the times, are all that the pyramids were meant to teach us? They are also teaching us that man is the base, or foundation for the spiritual world, and that it is bigger because man wants it all, or at least as much as he can get out of this material world. On the other hand, the smaller in size we grow, or reach, the closer we come to the spiritual world, until we eventually vanish out of mans sight. We also gather from the point of the pyramid that the higher we go in the spiritual world, the higher we travel in the heavens, and the less we wish things for ourselves, but wish the good of our neighbor first. The Pyramids are a perfect material example of the Kingdom of Heaven. He who is greatest in this world will become least in the heavens, and he who is least in this world will become greatest in the Heavens. For to be higher up in the spiritual world is to be closer to God, and greatest in the heavens, but least in the material realm, where the peak of the pyramids are seen as their smallest point. God cannot build pyramids in the material world without using creatures from the material world to build them, and we know what creatures he used, don't we. For God is not a worker of magician's tricks, but causes all things in this world to be created from this world. There are no pyramids being built now, because there are no Dinosaurs around now; and there are no Dinosaurs around now because man has come to a point where he relies mostly on his wisdom to create and build in this world, and God has stepped back so as to show him what will become of mans creations and devices. Man has always wanted more, and he has for generations come up with ways to make more, and to make life easier on himself. For an example: could you imagine a man today cutting down a tree with a two-man hand saw? And can you imagine him cutting it into pieces with a saw, as well? Man believes that if he devises a way to save time, that he can cut more wood, sell more wood, and make more money. But who sends the buying customers to him in the first place? God does! Who allows it to get cold enough to need wood to burn in the first place? God does! And who allows a man to live each day, and to get out of bed, and gives him the strength to cut the wood in the first place? God does! So if a man uses a chainsaw to cut down a tree, or even two trees in a day, who will guarantee whether or not he even sells one stick of wood when he is done? God does! This not only applies to wood, but to every job a man, or woman goes to every day. God chooses if we get a raise, forty hours, or even if the boss sends us home early for three days, and we only get paid for two. God decides if we work all week, or even if a self employed, or some other type employed person, has any work at all each week. He decides if the weather is good, or if we get three feet of snow, get snowed in, and don't get paid for two or three weeks. And all these things are decided by God, even though all men have free will. How? Because you are not a single man in this world, but your human life is controlled by many, many human beings from the past, who live within you, and God chooses which ones to let live within you, so as to effect his will in you every day. Yes we have free will, but we don't know where we are drawing our thoughts of affections from each moment, and God does; and so he can decide who is where, within each man. Still don't understand? Lets try one more time:

You are a human being, or man, and you have free will. But you are not one human being, or man wrapped up in that fleshly person you call yourself. You are also a spirit, or spiritual being, and your spirit lives within the spiritual realm at all times. Your spirit lives within what is called a society, and it lives there with an unlimited number of other spirits and Angels. And every society, or man has at least two evil spirits, and two Angels living within him, at all times, but this number grows as man grows and matures. So since each spirit or angel represents a single affection, and your thoughts in a single day are made up of millions of different affections, you have millions of spirits or angels, or both, living within you in the period of a single day. And these spirits and angels are people just like you. The only difference is that you think you are that fleshly person that you look in the mirror at every day, but you are not. That flesh is nothing more than the base of a pyramid, and supports the spiritual world within. And just as there is a spiritual world living within man, so too is there one living within the pyramids of old. You don't see them because they actually exist within another world; but we will cover that at another time. So as I was saying, this fleshly human body we carry around every day is only the form, or shell for our spiritual society to live in and act out our thoughts and life, till it takes on another human form. But it could take on another human form tomorrow. This is because God cannot control a person's free will, but he can control what spirit enters your fleshly body tomorrow morning before you wake up. And this spirit can be of any nature he chooses, because he chooses what state you will be in when you wake up. But this spirit must represent the affection, or state in which you were in when you entered sleep that night. And God has control of these issues. Therefore, God is in control of every human being, till forever. Even if God wishes a certain thought or act from you in the middle of the day, he can cause this by the spirits he allows into your society that day, with each spirit being in the exact state he wishes them to be when they are called on by you and your thoughts. The changes in affection and state are always done within the spiritual realm, within your society, so as to never cause confusion within this material world.

46. In the material world all things are given life either by a seed, larvae, or a womb. And all these are given their form from a thought of affection in the spiritual world. Every human body is created and formed according to the affection of the human subject. Which means we are as we think, and our bodies are formed according to our spirit, which resides within our minds. Yes we are created according to the affections of our parents, but we are innocent until we have eaten from the "Tree of knowledge of good and evil." This means we begin to think and live life from our own thinking, and no longer the Lords, which is our innocence in the beginning stages of our life in this material world. Therefore if you think, or will evil in your life, you become the corresponding evil affection in which you have given life to in the material world. The more evil you think, and therefore act on, the more ugly you become to others, even in appearance. The more good or loving your thoughts, and so actions are, the more beautiful you are seen in others eyes, even in physical appearance. Yes, you may appear ugly, to some degree in the mirror, as far as what you see, but the longer you draw on good and loving affections the more beautiful you will become. But you must remember, beauty is not seen as beauty to those who are evil, or bad people. Beauty is only seen by those who are also good and loving people, or spirits. For those in the hells, whether in the spiritual world or the material world see good as ugly, and evil as beautiful, for they live in a world of fantasy. But we are not here to love the evil in people; we are here to love the good and to shun the evil everywhere. But remember, all men, and women have a certain amount of good in them, and it is up to us to find it, and to love them because of it. So, whether you wish to believe it or not, you are what you think.

47. As we give life to the flesh as we think evil things, so too do we give life to all material things as we continuously think of them. And if we don't think of them, someone else does, and they are still given life, just sitting there waiting for you to be tempted, and to give in to its call, or drawing effect on you. For when a man quits smoking, the cigarettes do not go away, for other men in the world give them continued life by their constant thoughts of them. And because they stay around, you are often tempted, or tested by Satan, who is always trying to get you to go back to smoking. The same goes for alcohol, drugs, food, acts of violence, hatreds, revenge and many, many more things in this material world. For it is a fact that the Lord has permitted me to state to you; that if you were to remove the cravings of your flesh, by continuously shunning them all as evil,

and praying at the same time for the Lord to remove them from your life or desires, he would remove them, and replace each one with an affection from the heavens. He would also begin to give you much wisdom, as well as truths about his heavenly kingdom. For it is a fact that if we work with God, every evil deed we remove from our lives would be replaced with a good, and loving one. Every fantasy that we removed would be replaced by heavenly wisdom. But we must seek the Lord first, in order to achieve this, and we must always give the credit to him, because man can do nothing from himself.

48. If everything in this world is created from our thoughts of affections, why can't we create just about anything, including Dinosaurs again? Answer: Because we don't believe that we can create Dinosaurs again, and we cannot create anything we do not believe we can create. But this goes for all of mankind, and so those who believe, truly believe, could actually move a mountain. But what we don't understand is that God is truly the one who chooses what a man will or will not believe. For the things I now believe I could never have believed before in my lifetime, because my faith was weak, which all faith is given by God in the first place. To truly believe means to have no doubt whatsoever. Now who does not know that it is easy for a man to believe that he can blow a bubble with bubblegum? And because so many men have accomplished this in the past, all men now truly believe they can do it, every time they blow another bubble. The same goes for everything we do, or make in this world; and God still has complete control of these things, even though we do have free will. Of which I have already explained the details as to how it works. We are many, and we have people acting on our behalf that we never even knew existed before now. While I am awake, I only think of certain things, of which most of my thoughts are average every day thoughts, which are all of mine, and of which I believe them to hardly ever stray, or waiver, as far as my average affections go. As well, I know that all my thoughts lean toward my true love in life, whatever that love may be. For every human being represents a totally different love, as they always will till forever. There will never, ever be two identical loves found within the realms of creation; for that is Gods plan, and purpose. How many different loves are there? An infinite number, for God is infinite, and every love is taken from God.

49. I tell you the truth, whatever you bind on earth will be bound in heaven, and whatever you loose on earth will be loosed in heaven. Again, I tell you that if two of you on earth agree about anything you ask for, it will be done for you by my Father in heaven (Matthew 18:18). What do these verses truly mean? Answer: First of all, we think when we read the Word that everything that is spoken is in stone. We do not realize that things which are promised by God are only part of the truth, and many are not yet ready, or prepared for the rest of the truth yet. Yes we could move a mountain by our faith, but what would that accomplish for any man? Yes we could cause fire to come down out of the sky,

and destroy our enemies; but what would that do for a mans salvation? God gives us the faith to bind things, or to think and give things life, which are beneficial to our overall salvation. He is not interested in giving us power to please the fantasies of our flesh, and he will never do so. What you bind on earth is the same as saying what you give life to on earth. If you create something on earth you have created it in the spiritual world, but as its correspondence. For the spiritual world has all the things this world has, only they are the corresponding things, or the spiritual things that correspond to our material things. Therefore, whatever material things you loose, or let go of in this material world will be loosed, or let go of in the heavens. And when you loose, or let go of something of the world, or flesh, it will be replaced by something from heaven, because your heaven no longer contains these material, evil things; since you have now cut them loose.

50. Does all this mean that if I were to give up all the deeds, and wants of the flesh in this world that I would disappear into the spiritual world? Yes, in a way, only you will not disappear because God is not a God of confusion. You would simply enter a peaceful sleep, which man sees as death, and you would enter the spiritual world for good. When you sleep in the spiritual world you are actually in the material world; and when you sleep in the material world you are actually in the spiritual world. Therefore what they, or your spiritual society is thinking in the spiritual world while they are asleep, you are thinking in the material world while you are awake. And the same goes for those in the spiritual world. For when they are sleeping their fantasies take form in our material realm. Which means that when we sleep we are in our real realm, living life as a spirit. In the heavens if we are good, and in the hells if we are evil, or bad. So where are spirits and angels when they are not asleep? They are living out their lives in the spiritual world, which is what we would actually call the real world. For there, things are based on right and wrong, and not just to please our flesh. Things there represent doing for another, instead of ourselves. This is the heavens however, for the hells are the exact opposite of the heavens, where spirits who are disobedient are punished. But there is no actual death in the spiritual world; as well there is no actual death in our own. For death is nothing more than a fantasy, believed by only those who are living in hell at any given time. For if your spirit is in heaven, no matter what world you think you are in, you cannot believe in death, and you cannot be in fear. For there is no fear in love; that is when we truly learn what love is.

51. If I am going to go to sleep in this world, and wake up in another world, when I totally remove the deeds of the flesh; why would I want to totally remove the deeds of the flesh? For I have wonderful grandchildren in this world, and I do not wish to leave them. Answer: Because we know that we are not really leaving them, and are forever a continued part of their life. Only instead of being a part of their life in this world, we will do so in another. For remember, they are

spiritual beings as well, who will go on to the spiritual world for good, one day. But until they do, you will act as a member of their spiritual society, thinking you are actually them.

52. What happens when people of the world completely stop thinking about a certain person, place, or thing in this world? It degenerates, or rots, or deteriorates, or rusts; whatever the case may be. This is why when a person serves no use in this world, or has no love at all in this world, they die, or at least what appears as death takes place. For this is why we are each here in this world in the first place; so as to serve some use, or purpose to mankind. This is why when a spouse dies in old age; their partner follows shortly after, if they were truly in love. For their love has died in this world, and they can no longer be of any use to the world because they have given up the will to continue to live, and so must move on to eternal life. This happens to everything, which loses its purpose in our world. What remains, only remains because flesh continues to feed from it, or to draw a purpose from it.

53. WITH MUCH WISDOM COMES MUCH SORROW! This statement not only includes Godly wisdom, but worldly wisdom. For with much Godly wisdom, we come to learn that we cannot ever be good all the time if we are to help our fellow man. For we must be all things to all people, at any given point in time. Sometimes we must be merciful, sometimes we must be blunt, sometimes we must be gentle, or patient, and sometimes we must be firm, and even harsh you might say. And this hurts a man who wishes to love all men; and so we must sacrifice our selves, or our love for another sometimes, so as to teach them, or to rebuke them, and then set them on the right track. Worldly wisdom works the same way: For if we are wise, according to the worlds standards, and we are seeking God before we have been called, or even before we have been regenerated by God, we get very frustrated, and even sorrowful because we cant seem to understand Godly ways in an evil world, such as the one we live in. No matter how wise you appear to those of the world today, if you are seeking God, you must, and you will become as a child first, before you will ever find him. For to live for, or in God, you must give up your wisdom, and truths that are created from your worldly senses, and begin to completely live your life in faith, believing everything God teaches, or gives you from now on. For before we understood things as though they were partially true, but now we will see things as they truly are. Jesus said something to Peter that really made me begin to think, hey are we really suppose to be letting men teach us for the rest of our lives, or just long enough to wean us off the milk? For the Lord said to Peter: I tell you the truth, when you were younger you dressed yourself and went where you wanted; but when you are old you will stretch out your hands, and someone else will dress you and lead you where you do not want to go (John 21:18). The Lord told Peter this to show him what type of death he would glorify God by. In other words he would die to his flesh, and no longer be lead by his own

desires, but by the will of God. He would now begin to do things he never would have done before, because he wished to love all of his friends, neighbors, and brothers at all times. But what did Jesus do when he entered the Temple and found them exchanging goods for money and what not? He overturned the tables in anger, and rebuked them all. But he did this to teach them, by his rebuke; but it was done because of his love for all of mankind. He gained nothing for his flesh because of this, and he meant no ill will to his neighbor, he only wished to set things straight, and to teach what was right. And so with Jesus, as with all men who are saved, we will be called to do things we do not wish to do, simply out of love for our neighbor. Mostly all Christians today would not agree with this type of teaching, for the true way that is taught in the churches today is to always act in love, with a smiling face. But that is just what it is; an act, and we all have somewhere along the line done it well. For no one can act more loving than a Christian, and I should know, for I began my walk with the Lord in the same manner. I still to this day find myself acting out the role of a smiling, loving person, when at the same time, I am harboring bitter feelings for someone. No, I am not good all the time, for I am human, and I am not God. However, as often as I am permitted to love, be good, and show a true smiling face, I am more than happy to do it through God alone. For with mankind, to always be good, to always be loving, and to always wear a smile would be a lie, many times over. For man was created to enter into states throughout his lifetime, so as to not get bored with his lifetime of being the good guy all the time. Only God can be the good guy all the time, ant that is because he doesn't have to live among evil human beings all the time. For to be completely pure, perfect love, you cannot bear nor survive within the presence of evil. For God cannot ever be directly connected with evil, at any level. Therefore he dwells within a world that is within another world, and he created it to be that way. We are human beings only in appearance, but in reality, we are God. We reside within the heavens, and will do so till forever, even though we are finite beings. But we will share life till forever with human beings, who are bound midway between good and evil; or heaven and hell. Human beings are little gods, who were created in Gods image, and they rule their own little worlds, which are found to dwell within them; just like all of creation is found to dwell within the Lord, as his heavenly Kingdom, and he is the ruler of that Kingdom. We are little, or big (however you wish to look at it) atmospheres of affection, or love; and as we grow in life we learn more and more about love, and the evil human beings we share life with learn about love as well from us, and they go on to enter life when they put off the flesh, as another spirit, or angel. But do not ever accept the belief that you are a fleshly human being, for this material world, along with its different types of fleshly creatures; man included, is temporary, and fantasy. It does not truly exist, but it exists only within the accumulated affections of the Lord, and then only from the fantasies created from these affections. For the real beings live within these fleshly bodies we carry around, and the evil beings are those who act as a shell for us spiritual beings, you included. All evil beings and affections are derived from the fantasies of those who live for this material world. For because everything in creation must have an opposite, we live out our lives within the fleshly forms of our opposite images, or persons. For the inner or higher is good and it is real; as well the outer or lower is evil, and it is fantasy. To be good at all times, night and day would be to abandon our opposite image, or self, in which case they would be spirits who are doomed to eternal damnation forever; simply because we did not truly love our enemies, as the Lord plainly told us to do. I mean, why do you think he said to love your enemy? Because he knew that one day every man would learn that his true enemy is himself, or his opposite self. If you can live with your own evil thoughts, which we all have at some point in our lives, then you should have no trouble loving, and forgiving your enemies in the material realm. But even though it is true that "With much wisdom comes much sorrow," we will truly all be blessed in the long run, as long as we finish the race; and we will all finish the race, as God predestined it to be.

54. Why does a pyramid have four sides? Could anything stand without a base? The number four in the Word simply represents all goods in completion. And all through the Word numbers do not mean numbers, but something else is represented by each separate number. So the pyramid is also a hint to mankind that four represents the full state of mans lifetime. These four states are also four seasons such as spring, summer, autumn, and winter; or morning, noon, evening, and night; and also childhood, young adulthood, adulthood, and old age. And as man lives out these seasons in a single lifetime, they too are divided into states. So that each man, or woman can experience love and hate, good and evil, hot and cold, fast and slow, overweight and skinny, funny and serious, happy and sad, light and dark, long and short, poor and rich, smart and ignorant, ugly and pretty, good smells and bad smells, and on and on. And every human being will experience every one of these states or affections in their lifetime, with no exceptions. For how can we have compassion for a poor man, if we never walked in his shoes? And even though you may not remember experiencing many of these things in life, you have done so. The pyramid comes to a point because every human being goes back to the one being they came from, and then once again becomes one with God. The tip of the Celestial pyramid should be topped off with gold, for gold represents the ultimate, or Celestial heavens. If the tip is silver, it represents the spiritual heavens, and copper for the natural heavens. There are three heavens, which is why three pyramids were built alongside one another. There are many mysteries about the pyramids, of which I will divulge them as the Lord gives them to me.

55. When man was first created he was given free will from the beginning. Therefore once he went beyond childhood, into adolescence, he began choosing for himself,

in which case he no longer depended on the Lord to rule, or provide his decisions in life. This is when a man begins to eat from the Tree of Knowledge of Good and Evil, which is him relying on his own wisdom. Therefore when the first set of people died in the material world, they were evil, spiritually living in the hells, and therefore the heavens that were formed from this generation was only a representative heaven, not yet bringing in reformed, or regenerated souls. For a man must live out his full years in his lifetime before he can be regenerated, and become a New Church. So until man became hungry for the Lord, of his own free will, the Lord could not regenerate him. And so this is how it is with every human being who is born into the world. For we all must enter into and pass through a total of four stages, or seasons, before we can be prepared for heaven, and then be given the realization that we are truly an angel in the making. We must also enter into, and pass through four churches, before we become a New Church. These four churches being The Most Ancient Church, which existed in the world before the flood, and worshipped an invisible God, with whom no conjunction is possible; The Ancient Church, which existed right after the flood, also worshipped an invisible God; The Israelitish Church, which came immediately after the Ancient Church, and they worshipped Jehovah, who in Himself is an invisible God, but under a human form, which Jehovah Himself put on by means of an angel, in which He was seen by Moses, Abraham, Sarah, Hagar, Gideon, Joshua, and sometimes by the Prophets, This human form was a representative of the Lord who was to come, and because this was representative so too were each thing and all things in their Church were made representative ; and the Christian Church, which did indeed with the lips acknowledge one God, but in three persons, each one of whom was singly or by Himself God; thus they acknowledged a divided trinity, but not a trinity united in one person; and from this an idea of three Gods adhered to their minds, although the expression "One God" was on their lips. So none of the first four churches in the world have accomplished possessing the truth that joining God to himself and himself to God, which is actually done by God, is the ultimate goal God had from the beginning of creation. And by way of the final Church, which is to come into the world, which is called the New Church, this will be accomplished for all men.

56. So what is the duration of every mans life? ***

We are born into this material world as the Most Ancient Church. This Church was before the flood in the Word. We can communicate with the angels at this time in our life by correspondences. For everything a man does and says corresponds to an affection in the spiritual world. And since every child is in innocence, they are at all times in contact with the angels, and are actually at this period in their life being taught by God from within. They are also considered very wise at this time, though they have not learned to communicate with the people of this world yet, but still are wise as far as their spiritual society is concerned. At this time they worship an invisible God, for their spiritual society is still a child as far as knowing their God is concerned, or being ready to be entrusted with heavenly truths. This is because their wisdom comes totally from the heavens and the angels, or the Lord, and he cannot yet allow them to give truths to those of the material world. Plus everyone knows that the angels are very wise from the Lord alone, compared to man in this world, who is wise in his own eyes. So as long as man is in innocence, having childlike faith, he is wiser than all other men, for he seeks his wisdom from the Lord alone. And when we speak of the Most Ancient Church, we speak from the spiritual world in a man, not the material. For the Church does not actually exist in the material world, but is a representative Church at best. So we are born as "The Most Ancient Church," which is also childhood, morning, spring, and if you can accept it, at each of these stages we, or our spiritual society, is either in the Northern, Southern, Eastern, or Western quarter within the spiritual world. The reason we are in one of these or the other is because when these four quarters are spoken of in the Word they never pertain to the material world, but to the spiritual world alone, and represent the level of connection we each have at any given time to the Lord, who is the Sun in the spiritual world. Therefore East represents the Lord, and being in the good of love to the Lord in the spiritual world, from our interior man, or spirit; West represents being in love to the Lord as well, but in the exterior sense, or in an obscure sense; South represents being in truths from that love or good, in the interior sense; and North represents being in truths from that love or good, but in an exterior sense, or obscure sense. So while a man is still a child, he is in all of these states or seasons, you could say. But all of these examples form one person, or state, or spiritual society. Next we have the Ancient Church, which comes after the flood. It runs all during adolescence, and on into young adulthood. And these as well worship an invisible God, but more of the material world is now a part of their life, and they have begun to form images of God, using them to represent Godly, or heavenly things. And God does appear at times to them in the form of an angel, such as he did to Abraham. But no one calls God by the name Jehovah at this time. Still they are in good, but in an exterior sense alone. And they can no longer communicate with God and the angels through correspondences, at least very few can, at this time in their life. And so this church in their life is only representative. This state is also noon and summer, and this adolescent will go from north, south, east, and west in his daily life; but only as far as his spirit is concerned. This is the second state in a mans life, two more are to come. The third Church to come is the Israelitish or Jewish Church, whichever you wish to call it, for it is only representative in our life. This Church is the third Church in line and they are totally representative, and have no truths either at this time. This is the time during the Prophets, where God speaks to the Prophets as well as sometimes shows himself to them in the form of an angel. This group still worships idols and performs sacrifices to other gods, but those who worship the true God now call Him Jehovah, who is no longer an invisible God, but he is now worshipped in human form. This human form is representative of the Lord who was to come. And because the Lord was representative, so were all other things of this Church. This Church as well does not possess truths. Now they worship God as a man because of the Messiah to come, but still they live by their senses and not in faith, and therefore have no conjunction with God as of yet. When the Lord comes, which is at the end of the fourth church, all sacrifices as well as things pertaining to sacrifices are abolished. This state, or season is what is also known as evening and adulthood. Still going through the four quarters in the spiritual world throughout their day. The fourth, and last Church on the list is The Christian Church. This Church is the final stages in the Church, in a mans life, or his Day of Judgment. This is the day before the coming of the Lord. This Church did indeed acknowledge one God with the lips, but in three persons, each one singly, or by himself God. Therefore they say one God but think three. Still they teach of an invisible God, and therefore can have no conjunction with him yet. They do not yet realize that God came into the world, and assumed a human, so as to have conjunction with man. This state in life is also known as night, and old age. This is where man has matured to his fullest, and is ready to be regenerated by God. Therefore, the old Church, which consisted of a total of four representative Churches, is at its end, or consummation. The Lord now returns in His spiritual sense of the Word, and teaches the man what it is time for him to know. A Last Judgment now takes place and a vastation process before the New Church is brought in his life. Evil is totally separated within his Church, and they are sent to their corresponding hells. While those of the true Church, who are left, form to create a New Church, from a society in heaven called Michael. For all New Churches are formed by the Gentiles in the world, but also by the society called Michael. The Gentiles are those who have not been corrupted by falsities, and were not a part of the old Church, but outside it. These are the spirits who always felt that they never fit into that Church. So now the fourth Church, called the Christian Church, has reached its end. Judgment has been assessed, and all things are now back in order. The Lord brings in the New Church in the mans life, and He begins giving truths to the man, or Church. The man now begins living life in faith in the Lords teaching, and leading in his life. No longer is there fear of death, or of not finding truth. All truth is now provided, only according to the truths the man has. For the Lord does not add new truths, but teaches the man from the truths he already has in life. For we are taught according to our love, in our spiritual society. But believe me, you know much, much more than you think you know. As far as the number three being the number of completion, this is completion in the material realm, where man has conjunction with the Lord, and is now body, soul, and spirit. Or Father, Son, and Holy Spirit. Father is the soul, Son is the body, and Holy Spirit is the spirit. And together they make the Lord, of which we are images of the Lord. And as I have said before, it takes three to make all things, whatever it may be. For everything needs a body, a soul, and a spirit; including a rock, if you can believe it. Now the only reason we do not leave this world immediately after becoming a New Church, or new being is because our days in this material world have not been completely fulfilled yet, and there is still more to do. For God has designed it so that you leave this material world at the exact moment he wishes you to leave it, and you will not be taken a moment sooner. For you must remember, you never actually die, but everyone lives forever. You also do not enter, and pass through all four seasons, or churches in a single lifetime in the material world, but it takes several, each mans days being different of course. Therefore, even though you go from being a baby, to adolescence, to young adulthood, to adulthood, and on into old age in a single lifetime in this world, does not mean that you have entered into, and passed through four Churches in that course of time. This is why there are so many different levels of maturity, and ignorance in the world today, because each of us are at a different season, or Church, or state in our lives, in which we are not all in our final state of regeneration by God. And as a matter of fact, very few are in that state or season; which is why the Word says: Enter through the narrow gate. For wide is the gate and broad is the road that leads to destruction, and many enter through it. But small is the gate and narrow the road that leads to life, and only a few find it (Matthew 7:13). So you see when the Word speaks of the number of people who enter the heavens, it speaks of those whose spirits have been prepared, or regenerated each moment, or hour, or day, or week, or month, or year. But in reality, time is not even involved, and the Word is not speaking of the material realm at all. For at the consummation of the seasons, or the Church in any mans life, a Last Judgment then takes place, and few within that human beings spiritual society actually make it to the heavens, and the rest go to the World of Spirits, or the hells. As far as the material world is concerned, we will have no recollection of these things, but only those who actually make it into the heavens, in our spiritual society. For a mans spiritual society consists of the bad as well as the good, but all are still separated by atmospheres in the spiritual world, which also protects the good from the evil, as well as the evil from the evil. So is this all there is to Gods plan of creation and salvation? No, for we have only scratched the surface. Do you now wonder why the Lord allows the good and the evil to live together in the spiritual realm? Yes the evil do live outside, on the perimeters of a society in heaven, and the most evil live on the outside, or perimeter of a society in the hells. For the heavens and the hells are all arranged according to the level of good and truth found in each society, and then the least perfect are situated at the exterior, or the perimeter of each society. And as the good advance upward or inward in a society, so too do those below who are more evil, advance inward or upward in theirs, or another society. The

Lord is always willing for a spirit to change societies, and it is up to the spirit as to whether he remains in that society, for the others of that society cannot cause him to leave, and neither do they wish it. Spirits and angels advance in their levels of good and truth until forever, and continue to advance in societies for this reason. This means that all spirits and angels will reach the same destination in the spiritual world; at least eventually. For we all continue to grow in wisdom and maturity until eternity. So when you are talking or looking, and watching another persons actions, do not assume that you know what they are thinking or going through in their life, for we do not even come close to understanding all the different scenarios which can be applied to every affection or situation in a persons life. Just because you see a person crying or laughing does not mean they are necessarily sad or hurt if crying; and happy or just heard a funny joke if they are laughing. Just because a man robs a liquor store, with what could be a toy gun, and only takes food, does not mean he wishes to hurt, or steal from someone. His family may have not eaten in a week, in which case he has now become desperate, and only wishes to feed his family. If you are a concerned citizen, does this mean you should shoot this person down in cold blood, if you happen to have a gun at the time, should you mind your own business; jump the person, hoping they don't shoot you; or should you call the police and let them handle it? If you are a police officer, should you shoot this person; wait them out; try and physically retain them; attempt to arrest them; call for backup; or simply try and talk them out of it? All these scenarios play a part in a persons thoughts during a situation such as this, and man always has a choice as to how he actually deals with it. Things are not always as they seem, and this is usually the case, more often than not. Should a man die for trying to feed his family, even if he breaks certain laws? Should a man be willing to shoot a man over food, or because he has a gun in his hand, but is just trying to get out of the store? I think you know that with the given state of our world today, a police officer would more often than not shoot this man; even though I am not picking on police officers, or any certain man. But the truth is, mercy is not a qualification for making the police force. And because there are so many different kinds of people in the world, and because everyone thinks differently, and has free will to do so, most men as police officers would not risk their life to save another. Therefore they would shoot, and ask questions later. But just as we are all forgiven for our mistakes, bad decisions, and even our bad decisions that were made on purpose; men will continue to kill for the wrong reasons. People will harm others, lash out at them at the wrong time, judge them in all different circumstances, and usually be wrong in their judgment of them. We will always continue to be cruel at times, laugh at others mistakes, put others down, or talk behind their back, not even knowing their true situation. The whole point I am making is that you should learn to live and let live, judging no one for his or her actions or mistakes. For if you have not read what I have said about this before, listen now; "All men eventually walk in all other men's shoes, and will experience everything another man experiences, so as to one day have the ability to have compassion for all other men." We must learn mercy before we will ever see the gates of heaven. Remember that that guy you were just talking to is either not matured as far as you, or he has matured beyond where you are at this time; but either way, we continue to come back to this world until we get it right, and are completely prepared for our life in the heavens. No man is where every other man will not end up eventually, once his regeneration by the Lord is complete. Where my children and grand children are in their state in life, at this moment, is where I was also at one point in time; and where I am at this moment is where they will one day be as well; if not in this lifetime in the material world, then in the next, or the one to follow. But one thing is sure, they will live out their days as physical human beings, will enter into and pass through four complete seasons in their life, become a New Church or being, and will go on to enter the heavens as an angel, and as all men before and after them will, or did do. This happens because every single human being ever born is an extension of the life, and representative life of every affection, or life the Lord has ever lived, or will live. We are all one in the Lord, as He is one in us, and so we are an extension of our brothers, neighbors, friends, sisters, mothers, fathers, enemies, or children. We are all the next stage, or life of another man, and so we are one. My grandson is me, my daughter is me, my father is me, my grandfather is me, my great, my great—great, and my great—great—great grandfathers are me; on down the line until we reach the first man ever created, who is by the way, the Lord. You may think two people were created at the same time in the beginning, but this is not the case. One was created after the other, and they were just as we will once again all be. The Father provided the Soul, and the mother provided the form, or body. And this was the case with the first male and the first female. Both share the same soul in the Lord, but different bodies in the mother, or nature. Therefore, every man or woman ever born, or ever to be born have the same soul, just at a different state in the Lord, or in creation. We appear to have our own existence, and consciousness in our life, but we all share a single existence, or consciousness in the Lord. So in creation the Lord is divided up into different heavens, different societies, different affections, and different thoughts. Outside the Lords body, in darkness, in fantasy, or in sleep we have the hells, and as they come to awaken in life they are permitted to be included in life and in the Lord. All these different hells are where man resides while he lives in, and lives for the material world. As he lets go of certain things of the material world, he is raised higher, or more inward in the spiritual world, so as to eventually totally give up the material world, and its pleasures, and is then permitted into the heavens, but in the natural heavens. He is not allowed into the upper heavens until he actually passes on from this material world, and has completed his regeneration. A man, or woman can know they have completed this regeneration, and are now being prepared for eternal life in the spiritual world, within the heavens, when he or she has begun to give up the things of the flesh, and are continuously giving up more as each day, week, month, and year continues to pass by. So that by the time they leave this world this last time, they will have been separated from all desires of the flesh, things such as jealousy, revenge, lust for the naked body, ruling over others including your mate or spouse, material gain, the love of money or riches, the need to win all the time, the need for recognition over others, and many, many more things of the flesh. Holding on to these things is what keeps us in this material world. When we no longer require them in our life, we can then enter a better, more loving world, and so go on to live forever in love. Yes we will be one in the Lord, but we will all get to share in the overall consciousness of his thoughts, as we are mature enough to receive, and live them. If you are still a child, you will only be trusted with childish things in his everyday thoughts. The more mature you have become, the more of the overall thoughts and decisions you are permitted to make, as though they were your own. But whatever your love is, or whatever affection you represent in the Lord, these are the thoughts you will always be a part of living, and these are the areas you will be helping to make decisions on. You may say well, how can that keep me busy? Because you will be providing these affections to every human being of which your spiritual society resides within, at any given time. And so you will at all times be sufficiently busy, and will have no slack time that you do not wish to have. For out of all the people living in the world right now, as well as those on all the other planets, as well as those in the past, you are them, and provide the affection you represent, or love you represent, to every human being alive, or that ever was alive. For remember, the past is alive and well, in the Lord. Now, listen to this, the human being you are residing in right now is you, or an extension of you, and you are providing only the affection of thought that your spirit represents in that human being. Lets say you represent the love for spitting spitballs, and yes I know that is a weird love, but bear with me. Only when that human being is spitting spitballs will you be providing his thoughts of affections, and at all other times you will be in the perimeters of his spiritual society, waiting to be called on once again. But as far as how much your love and his love truly have in common, this will decide how often this human being calls on your thoughts of affections. Now, because we all have consciousness as long as we are awake, we are used in societies of other human beings, because the spiritual world overlaps in the Lord, and is in all men who call on each and every affection or man, ever created. So if your affection is to help others, so that this is all you can think of most of the time, your affection will be a part of the life and everyday thoughts of every human being who is in the love of helping others, at any given point in time, or in a day. And because the Lord is always with every man, and because you are with more men than any other is, you would be closest to the

Lord, and would be an angel who is highest in the heavens over all. But this is considering the fact that you are the most called on angel. The more our affection of good is called on by humans, the closer we are to the Lord; because we actually make up more of the Lords body. The more your evil affections are called on by human beings, the more you make up the hells, and the farther you are away from the Lord. Now if it is hard for you to make sense of all this, I ask that you back, and slowly read all this again, for it is very important that you get it. Our level of connection, or conjunction with the Lord all depends on how much our affection of good is used for mankind's thoughts in his everyday life. For because every man ever created is different than any man ever created, or ever to be created, this means we each represent an affection, or love, and that love stays with us for the rest of our days, unto eternity; for we are that affection in the Lords life. And so we are the Lord because we are of the Lord; and what is of the Lord is the Lord. This is very hard for man to accept if he has not read my earlier books, for all that I have written up to this point serves as proof to these statements I am here providing. So do not attempt to confirm any of this by itself, but get all the details I have given first, and then things will make much more sense to you all. I realize there are those who wont even consider what I am saying, but that is okay, for these words are for the chosen generation, or uncorruptable generation. So as I was saying, each of us is an affection of the overall man, who is actually the Lord. We become more of the Lord and our love expands in size, as we grow and mature, and as we receive more Godly wisdom. And in turn we provide, or become more and more a part of the good thoughts of affections within mankind. And this means our heavenly society grows larger and larger every moment, every hour, every day, year, and so on. Do we ever completely become the Lord? No! Because He is infinite, and we will always remain finite, and dependent on Him for our life. We do remain an angel to eternity, and grow continuously in wisdom and knowledge, but we will never match the Lord in these areas, or any others. The fact that you become an angel simply means you have reached a certain point in your life where you no longer require the things of a material world, and now choose wisdom and knowledge, or good and truth as your loves. As well you no longer require a body all the time, or form in order to live, but are happy just providing the thoughts of affections for mankind till forever. But what you are really doing is loving mankind, and allowing mankind to love you back, in the Lord, whenever they choose to do so, and according to their given free will. For if you truly love your neighbor, you wish to share all that you are, or possess with them, as well as become one with them. And how do you become one with your neighbor? By becoming one in the Lord, and making all that you are or have available to all others. Making your wisdom their wisdom, as well as your knowledge theirs. And this is the same as sharing all good and truth with your neighbor, so that they can one day learn to do the same.

57. How should a good Christian act in the world, whatever generation he lives in? Now we read many things that give us many different opinions as to how a good Christian should present himself to the world, and even how he should act when he is alone or at home with his family. One of the most believed fallacies in the church today is that a man is the head of the household, and that his wife is to only submit to him, and not the other way around. But this is not the case, and I will expound on this subject very shortly. We are also miss-led into thinking that a good Christian is to always be very gentle and loving, never showing a touch of anger, or rebuke toward another man. And that we are not to judge, or have harsh words with anyone. Now I know there are those who do not agree on all these points, but this is the basic accepted way of the Christian world. For we are supposed to obey the Ten Commandments, right? And if this is the case we must first love the Lord our God with all our heart and soul and mind and strength, and to love our neighbor as ourself. We must do unto others as we would that they do unto us. And although this is not one of the Ten Commandments, it is commanded by the Lord (Luke 6:31). We are to give to another expecting nothing in return. We are to give a man our coat if he asks for it, and not only our coat but our cloak as well. If he asks us to walk a mile, we should be willing to walk two. Basically what the Lord, as well as the rest of the Word teaches us is that we are to sacrifice our lives for our God and our neighbor. But who has the strength to do this in the present world we live in? Nobody, that's who! For it is told throughout the Word that man can do no good thing of himself. When we leave that church building on Sunday, or Wednesday night, we usually have a smile on our faces, pretending to be good, when the truth is, it is all an act. Why do I say this? Because I have been there, I am one of you, and God has shown me what we all really look like from within, in our spirits. Yes we smile, and sometimes we actually feel good, and do feel like smiling, but it is usually out of habit. For it is easy for a thief to love another thief, and a liar to love another liar, because they have something in common. But let another man look at your wife in church; let someone's son beat your son up after Sunday school; or let the same friend that you have sat next to in Church on Sunday cut you off on the road, and you not know who it really was. You see, it is easy to pretend to be a loving, forgiving, Christian in church on Sunday, but when you leave church it is a whole other story. When you get on the road you scream, or think mean thoughts about some other driver. When you get home you yell at your spouse for you having to do something they wanted you to do, when you just wanted to relax after church. Or you scream at your children because no one is watching now. Or you scream at your spouse because this is normal around your house. Whatever the case may be, we are a different person when we return home from Church, and this should not be. And I know preachers who will agree with me, and simply state that they are not perfect. But God does not expect us to be perfect,

he only wants us to attempt to do our best every day, and not keep coming up with excuses as to why we keep messing up. If you keep looking at other women in a lustful manner, and you tell your wife that you will continue to do so until God changes you, he will never change you. For we are to shun all sins as evil, and continuously ask God to remove the urge to do these things from you. But you are not to accept them in your life and wait on God to zap them out of your life, this is not his way. Now many of us would think that the only good Christian is an honest Christian, and one who does everything in life the hard way. You may say that you are meant to be poor for the rest of your life because you cannot wheel and deal like your car salesman friend down the street can. Or you cannot get a job that pays good money because you only have a high school education. And you may say that you would not ever steal a thing because you are a good Christian. And that if any man ever told you it was okay to steal, you would keep as far away from him as possible, right? Well, don't worry, I am not going to tell you it is okay to steal; only that one day you will, and you will be forgiven for it. There is not a totally honest, all out good loving, rich Christian in the world, and there never has been. You would not give your life for another man, or woman, or child because you would fear that you would lose your life. And this is not a trade any human being would make. If you say you would, you are wrong. Now I know there are many people who believe they would give their life for their own child, but this is not so either. You believe that out of your love for your child, but that love comes from God and not you. When the time came for you to give your life for your child God takes over as pure love and he is the one who saves your Childs life by using you to do so. And you may take the credit, as many men or women do, but you are not responsible. No human being is loving, and none will truly sacrifice their life for any other. The love anyone feels for someone else, whether it be a brother, a sister, mother, father, daughter, son, or anyone else we may love; is a love from God, and it only appears to be from us. Not only that but no man can be faithful to his wife without the help of God, and his Divine Providence of Conjugal Love for a spouse. So whether you believe yourself to be a faithful husband, an honest Christian, a loving father who would give his life for his child, or any other Christian, or just a man who can do no wrong in Gods eyes, you are mistaken. All of these qualities are affections provided directly from God, and can be taken away any time we become so self righteous as to need a wake up call. But God is always patient, and gives us ample time to learn these lessons on our own. So you say you would not steal do you? If your child were hungry enough you would easily steal. And do not ever think you have too much family, or resources in which you would never have to stoop as low as to steal to feed your children. There are times God allows us to lose all we have in order to teach us this lesson, just because nothing else worked to allow you to learn it in any other way. For God never just gives us one way out, but several. However, man is impatient, and he usually will not wait long enough for God to bring him out of a tough situation. Now what about lying, would you say that you would never lie? Hopefully not, because you will surely lie many times in your lifetime. The biggest problem however is that a man will steal, lie, or stand on a street corner simply to provide for himself and his selfish needs first. Many do this in place of working a job of some sorts. They of course will be forgiven these things because what we do in this world will not ever erase our eventual salvation. But man today suffers much, simply because he puts his needs before his loved ones or his neighbor. He will steal for himself, but not for a neighbor. He will lie for himself but not for someone else. He will fight with, and yell at his wife and children, but he will pretend to be a loving human being when he sees his church companions on Sunday. Well, I am going to quote a parable of the Lord Jesus, and I will return to comment: Jesus told his disciples: There was a rich man whose manager was accused of wasting his possessions. So he called him in and asked him, "What is this I hear about you? Give an account of your management, because you cannot be manager any longer" The manager said to himself, "What shall I do now? My master is taking away my job. I'm not strong enough to dig, and I'm ashamed to beg. I know what ill do, so that when I lose my job here, people will welcome me into their houses." So he called in each one of his master's debtors. He asked the first, "How much do you owe my master?" "Eight hundred gallons of olive oil," he replied. The manager told him, "Take your bill, sit down quickly, and make it four hundred." Then he asked the second, "And how much do you owe?" "A thousand bushels of wheat," he replied. He told him, "Take your bill and make it eight hundred." The master commended the dishonest manager because he had acted shrewdly. For the people of this world are more shrewd in dealing with their own kind than are the people of the light. I tell you, use worldly wealth to gain friends for yourself, so that when it is gone, you will be welcomed into eternal dwellings. "Whosoever can be trusted with very little can also be trusted with much. So if you have not been trustworthy in handling worldly wealth, who will trust you with true riches? And if you have not been trustworthy with someone else's property, who will give you property of your own? "No servant can serve two masters. Either he will hate the one and love the other, or he will be devoted to the one and despise the other. You cannot serve both God and money." The Pharisees, who loved money, heard all this and were sneering at Jesus. He said to them, "You are the ones who justify yourselves in the eyes of men, but God knows your hearts. WHAT IS HIGHLY VALUED AMONG MEN IS DETESTABLE IN GODS SIGHT (Luke 16:1-15). Now few men have ever explained this parable, for the explanation is given only when the Lord returns to the world. And so I will give the explanation just as the Lord provides it to me. Explanation will be found in my fourth book entitled "Wisdom of the Dead-Churches beware!"

58. Man does not even come close to realizing that he is heir to all things of the Father, and that according to the Lords words, "The meek shall inherit the earth." The meek are the Children of God, or the Uncorruptable generation. What this all means is that all that is in this world, which is not harmful to man is ours. We can do with it all as we please, because what we please is the Lords will in us.

59. To be a child of God while in this world you must separate yourself from the ways of the world, while at the same time remaining in the world, so as to do for others.

60. There are no marriage ceremonies in heaven, but there are husband and wives. There are also ceremonies to celebrate the joining of a man and woman, but the joining is of their soul, so as to become one; and this is done by God. So there is a female angel and there is a male angel, but the come together as one, and so are only known as a single angel.

61. Man will continue to become more wise until forever, and he will do so as an angel; but how he does this is by continuing offspring through human beings, and through his offspring he becomes more wise, by learning as they learn. Angels learn from man and through man, for there is a man, or a woman in this material world who represent every angel ever born out there, and this is where their homes are.

62. Angels do not learn directly from what we see, hear, do, say, taste, touch, or smell. They learn from the correspondences to these things, and can only talk to or through human beings when God allows it. They can see the lower heavens, but not the material realm, for our atmospheres are different.

63. Faith receives, love gives. No one receives without faith. No one gives without love. To receive, believe; to love, give. If you give without love, no one derives a thing from what is given. Whoever has not accepted the Lord is still a Jew.

64. What a father has belongs to his child, but not while the child is still little. When the child is grown however, then the father turns over all he possesses.

65. Jesus tricked everyone, he did not appear as He was but in a way not to be seen. Yet He appeared to all of them. To the great he appeared as great, to the small as small. To angels he appeared as an angel, and to humans as a human. And he hid his Word from everyone. Some looked at him and thought they saw themselves. When before his students he appeared gloriously on the mountain, he was not small. No, he became great and he made his students grow so they would know his immensity.

66. Some say the Lord died first and then ascended. They are wrong. He rose first and then he died. Unless you are first resurrected, you will not die

67. The Lord said to his students, "From every house you are in, take out possessions, but take things into the Fathers house and do not steal what is inside and run off.

68. His students said to him, when will the dead rest? When will the new world come? He said to them, "What you look for has come, but you do not know it.

69. From these last few verses I hope you can see that we are all asleep, living in dreams created by our evil lusts in this world; past, present, and future. Man has caused the world to be like it is today because God allowed us free will to create this world as our own representative paradise, and this is what we made it. But every man as he matures will slowly wake up and see himself for who he really is. I have been given that pleasure, and my one main goal in life is to share with the world these things before I go home for good.

Wisdom of the Dead!

Now who does not know that the dead tell no tales? Who does not believe that when we die we no longer exist as we once were, such as possessing fleshly bodies? Therefore we are at least different to some extent, are we not? But what if you had proof that we are already dead? And if you are already dead, how can you die, moving from death to death? Well, I intend to show you that we are indeed already dead, and therefore the end of this state in every human's life is to become alive. And when we become alive we remain alive forever. And of course we will all have no other knowledge, other than that we are alive; thinking still that we will die when we leave the human body for good. But those who have been regenerated will know for sure that they are alive, and will know that they will go on to live forever. While at the same time, those who have left their human bodies behind, but are still evil will enter the hells after this lifetime, and will have to endure another lifetime in the material realm. They will still be dead in the sense that they do not know who they are, and they still believe that the human body they possess is who they are. But as I have said before, the human body is dead, and always will be. So if you live for the flesh, or the world you are dead. Not that God does not wish for us to enjoy our life while we are in this world, but He expects us to eventually come to put Him and our neighbor first in our lives, in which case we will live much happier lives until we leave this world. For you can still enjoy material things and put God first in your life. This however, is not possible until a man, or woman becomes regenerated by God. So you as a human being will live in this world with free will for as long as you live, doing what ever your heart tells you to do. But while you are living as you please, God is actually leading you in all things. You do not know this because you are wrapped up in worldly things. But God allows each human being the belief that they control their life, and that everything they do is of their own wisdom, and will. This is because even though we begin life as a child we all grow up into the adult state, and we actually believe we are now adults; when the truth is we are still children who possess a body, which gives us the appearance of being adults in the world. But as it is, every human being goes through a long regeneration process, and does not reach the full end to this process until they become a New Church in the world;

some after they leave this world. But there is still regeneration going on in their lives, as we will truly continue our regeneration unto eternity. But while we are human beings in the world we must reach a certain state in our regeneration before we can be permitted to enter the heavens. Because of this each man is regenerated at his own pace, according to his own free will. In other words a person cannot receive any good in their life unless they wish it, or will it. And so each man, or woman take less time, or more time than another in being prepared for the heavens. So until they are completely ready, they choose after life in this world to enter the hells, and be a part of the material realm once again. And this means they will awaken one day, soon after death in this world (although death does not exist), and they will share the consciousness of another human being, and will be a part of the hells in the life of this human being. But they do not have to remain within this one human being because they are in hell and they are not always called on by a single human being. And so they will awaken each day within whatever human being the Lord decides to provide the affection they represent to, for the Lord even decides what state each of us is in at any given time. And the human we think we are is not a man, as we know it, but a little world or microcosm. Which means we have many, many lives living within our minds, as well as being a part of this whole human body we possess. For every action or thought is the accumulated actions or thoughts of those who live within our spiritual society, within our spirit, within our mind, and within our fleshly bodies. You are not who you think you are, and you do not think the thoughts you think you think. Your thoughts are single thoughts made up from many, many thoughts in the spiritual world. And that spiritual world is your spiritual world. And when a spirit apparently wakes up in this world every day, if he is a good spirit he wakes up in heaven; but if an evil spirit he wakes up in hell. And that heaven and hell can be within any human being God chooses it to be within. And still no matter what human you are in you will always have their memory, believing you have always been that person ever since you were born. If God wishes you to change human bodies, He can cause this to happen any time He wishes, without you knowing anything of it. For we are already asleep in this world, in which case we just move from one dream world to another, all at the hands of God. This may seem very unbelievable to many, but it is all true. For because our lives have been created within a type of dream world, God can make the impossible, possible with all men, whenever He chooses. Now you may think things are a lot more simple than this, because within this world things seem much more simple than this, but this is because our world is the ultimate of all things. We are the effect that is created from the cause, which is created from the end. What this all means is that life begins in the spiritual world, and it all ends in our world as the effect. Another way of putting it is that the spiritual world is actually where all thoughts are given life, and they enter the material world through mans mind as understanding, in which case each man wills that which is according to his free will, and is then put into action from his or her will. And so this world acts as a covering for the life, which actually goes on in the spiritual realm. And of course it also acts as a machine for spirits, so that they can put their thoughts into action. For we are the forms created for the spiritual world, so that love can be carried out. For you cannot love without all the different senses that are provided to man. And when a man becomes an angel he still retains all his senses because he is still living within a human form, and simply has changed worlds. This is of course all regulated by the different atmospheres man and angel live within. For man lives within an aqueous atmosphere and angels an ethereal atmosphere; and the difference causes the different worlds, as well as the sight to be different. So what all this amounts to is that what man sees as death, and many times the end of their life is just the beginning of another life to come. We not only go to sleep at the end of our life in this material world, but we go to sleep for the most part, each and every night in this world. And sleep in this world is a type of resurrection for all. Even spirits and angels must have a night, or a time to sleep so as to change human beings or states. And this is what is meant by the saying, "To everything there is a season." For all must sleep and all must wake up. And sleep represents death, whereas to awaken represents life. When they sleep in the spiritual realm they are awake in the material realm. When they sleep in the material realm they are awake in the spiritual realm. So where do we receive wisdom if we are dead in the material realm? Wisdom comes from God and life. As each human being is born into the world they provide another vessel for spirits and angels to live life within until forever, so as to continue gaining wisdom and knowledge until forever; becoming more and more perfect. And as the angels become more and more perfect, so too do the heavens. The wisdom you are gaining throughout your life in this world is being shared with every angel and spirit ever created from day one. You cannot ever keep it to yourself because you are not a single person, and you are never actually alone. In this apparent world we are all little worlds, or little gods, or little angels, or little heavens, or little hells. We are many and eventually we learn to do for the many, and to pray for the many. And eventually we even learn that our prayers are only to ourself, and that to please God we can only do this by our actions. For God is the supreme, He is the all in all. We are the little all, and He is the big all, does that make sense to you? We are in Him and He is in us, and together we make up the Lord God. And because together we make up the Lord, we can eventually rule with Him as his children, or heirs. But the ruling we will do will be for the good of mankind and not simply just to rule. For we will no longer be seeking our own good or pleasure, and still our own good and pleasure will be provided by our loving God, and then our neighbors. We are all potential angels who will eventually all become angels. We are all little gods because we are his children, and He is allowing each of us to grow up at our own pace; allowing us all to experience being children, and giving us truths for our gradual maturity, so as to eventually become mature enough to be trusted with all things. And so because we will eventually inherit all things, when we know this we have begun the process of inheriting all things. And as He gives us truths He will give many heavenly things to us with these truths. It doesn't matter what things we share with mankind because they are not yet mature enough to understand how these things can be, and therefore they will not yet believe them. And so these things that I write under the guidance of the heavenly Father as the Lord God are only meant for a select few, and these few know who they are. You know that you are living within a dead world where we are all the life in this world. The fact that we know this and they do not doesn't really matter, for their time will come. And until their time comes we are here to love all of mankind, providing our daily lives; that is those that remain, as an example to all. Right now I feel myself ascending into the heavens, and I am completely at peace. I have not left my physical body, as heaven is everywhere. As long as I remain in this present state the angels who are from this one society in heaven will remain with me. But as soon as I leave this state of heavenly bliss they will move on to another, providing the affections they provide all the time, to another human being. These angels can even be my angels, but they are free to go where the Lord sends them, which they will see as their own free will, and still return to me when the time arises. When they sleep they will be awake in this world with some human being. When however they are awake they are with me, if they are my angels, or a part of my angelic society in the spiritual world. Spirits are different however, for they do not have the freedom that the angels have. They remain in the material realm within the same human being, so that they do not share their bad habits with other societies, making those societies worse off. They are from time to time permitted to visit other societies, but if they are not similar in affections, they leave of their own free will. The Lord of course regulates these things so that no one spirit can do harm to another spiritual society. So what I am saying is that spirits know no better than that they are the person they possess, whereas an angel, no matter where they are knows they are not the person they possess, and that they lived long ago in the material realm. So even though a spirit moves from human to human, they have no knowledge of it, ever. Therefore an angel is much wiser than a spirit, and much older. Man shares all that he knows with all in the spiritual world, but all spirits and angels receive truth according to the level of love they are in to the Lord. So because the spiritual angels and angelic spirits are in love to the neighbor, they are less wise than the celestial angels who are mostly in love to the Lord. These angels do not need to think before they speak the truth for they speak at all times according to Love, and so they will only answer yes or no, never having to reflect on the subject. And if a celestial angel were to reflect, they would be in falsities and removed from the Lords presence. For when we reflect on a subject we are adding mans wisdom to the answer. If however you do not reflect, and your answer is simply yes or no, you are answering in faith, and are then in the Lords will and presence. This however is only if your intentions are good and not evil, for if you are evil, and you do not reflect, then you are in the hells, and your answer does not matter. So what is the wisdom of the dead? That would be the wisdom of the world. If you wish to live according to the Lords good pleasure, do not allow yourself to draw your thoughts from spirits of the world. Intend good or love in all things of your life, and let you answers either be yes or no, and add nothing more. There comes a time in every man or woman's life where they have to think about their actions around others, and what example they are representing to them. Then they have to learn to take their good examples and apply them to their everyday life, so that people will know they are sincere in their actions. This is rarely done today by those in the Church, and this is what drove me away from the organized Church. If you intend on truly being a Christian, or any other faith that believes in one God, and in living a good life then live life by your actions around everyone, and not just when you are in the publics eye. Do as you say and say what you intend on doing, and not as the Pharisees do in the New Testament of the Word. Do not seek salvation by your works or good deeds, but do all of these things simply because you are Gods children, and you wish to do as your Father. We are all already, saved in due time, and so we must live our lives by faith grounded in our works of charity. We must continue to do the things that we already know are proper in order to live a good clean, Christian life. We know where we are from and now we must do what it takes to get back there.